THE
RANDOM HOUSE
WORKBOOK

fourth edition

Ann Jessie Van Sant

COLUMBIA UNIVERSITY

RANDOM HOUSE • NEW YORK

THE RANDOM HOUSE WORKBOOK

fourth edition

Fourth Edition
987654321
Copyright © 1984 by Random House, Inc.

ISBN: 0-394-33249-0

Design: Meryl Levavi

Manufactured in the United States of America

Acknowledgments

Pp. 4, 57, 61, 125, 163, 171, 233–234, 286–288: © 1982/83 by The New York Times Company. Reprinted by permission.

P. 8: Excerpted from "The Specter of Conventional War," *Harper's*, July 1983. Copyright © 1983 by John Keegan.

Pp. 9, 25, 84, 90, 91, 117, 127, 143, 149, 151, 159, 179, 184, 190, 191–192, 221, 297, 331, 333: Certain material excerpted or adapted with permission from *Consumer Reports*, Copyright 1978, 1979, 1983 by Consumers Union of United States, Inc., Mount Vernon, New York 10550.

Pp. 17, 41, 341: Reprinted from *Smithsonian* by permission of Donald D. Jackson.

P. 21: Reprinted from Peter T. White, "Nature's Dwindling Treasures: Rain Forests," *National Geographic*, January 1983, by permission of National Geographic.

P. 35: Reprinted from Rick Gore, "A Bad Time to Be a Crocodile," *National Geographic*, January 1978, by permission of National Geographic.

Pp. 39, 105, 189, 253–254, 338: Reprinted from *Science Digest.* © 1983 by the Hearst Corporation.

Pp. 47, 49: Reprinted by permission of Smithsonian Magazine.

Pp. 92, 133, 327: Reprinted from *Smithsonian* by permission of Adele Conover.

P. 93: Reprinted from John W. Young and Robert L. Crippen, "Columbia's Astronauts' Own Story: Our Phenomenal First Flight," *National Geographic*, October 1981, by permission of National Geographic.

Pp. 93–94: Copyright © 1983 by Harper's Magazine. All rights reserved. Reprinted from the August 1983 issue by special permission.

P. 104: Reprinted from Allan C. Fisher, Jr., "Mysteries of Bird Migration," *National Geographic*, August 1979, by permission of National Geographic.

Pp. 131–132, 155: *The Sciences*, May/June, 1983. © by The New York Academy of Sciences.

P. 137: Copyright © 1983 by Harper's Magazine. All rights reserved. Reprinted from the March 1983 issue by special permission.

P. 160: From "The Chemical Defenses of Termites," Glenn D. Prestwich. Copyright © 1983 by Scientific American, Inc. All rights reserved.

P. 165: Reprinted from *Smithsonian* by permission of Carrol B. Fleming.

P. 172: Reprinted from Jane Vessels, "Delaware: Who Needs to Be Big?" *National Geographic*, August 1983, by permission of National Geographic.

Pp. 192–193, 253, 328, 332: Excerpted by permission of SCIENCE 83 Magazine, copyright the American Association for the Advancement of Science.

P. 225: Reprinted from Mary D. Leakey, "Tanzania's Stone Age Art," *National Geographic*, July 1983, by permission of National Geographic.

P. 250: Reprinted from Noel Grove, "Swing Low, Sweet Chariot!" *National Geographic*, July 1983, by permission of National Geographic.

P. 254: Reprinted from Martha A. Whitson, "The Road Runner: Clown of the Desert," *National Geographic*, May 1983, by permission of National Geographic.

Pp. 271–272, 301: Reprinted from Allen A. Boraiko, "The Indomitable Cockroach," *National Geographic*, January 1981, by permission of National Geographic.

Pp. 279–280, 283, 298, 301, 354: Reprinted by permission of Natural History Magazine.

Pp. 281–282, 342: Reprinted from *Smithsonian* by permission of Richard L. Williams.

P. 305: Reprinted from Geoffrey B. Sharman, "They're a Marvelous Mob: Those Kangaroos!" *National Geographic*, February 1979, by permission of National Geographic.

PREFACE

The Random House Workbook is designed to accompany *The Random House Handbook* by Frederick Crews. It follows the terminology and, to a large extent, the organization of the *Handbook.* However, since the *Workbook*'s discussions of grammar and rhetoric are complete and self-contained, it can also be used on its own.

Many of the examples and exercises are based on the work of my students (marked with an asterisk) or on that of published writers (documented in notes). I have often adapted the published material, some pieces lightly, others extensively, for the purpose of the explanation or exercise. The use of work by many different writers offers two advantages: variety of content—there are pieces on small claims courts from *Consumer Reports,* on Tanzania's Stone Age art from *National Geographic,* and on damming the Amazon from *Natural History,* for example—and variety of style. Even when adapted, most pieces retain the original writer's "voice."

The *Workbook* begins with a streamlined review of grammar that focuses on sentence function (Chapter 1); it provides the concepts and terms necessary for the exercises in editing and revision in later chapters. Chapters 2 and 3 concentrate on the most common and troublesome problems of usage, punctuation, and capitalization. Chapter 4 shows students how to get the most out of their college dictionary and provides a comprehensive review of spelling rules. Teachers may assign these chapters in whatever order best meets the needs of their students.

While the first four chapters are thus largely concerned with matters of convention, Chapters 5 and 6 offer students opportunities and methods for revision. These last chapters—on sentences and paragraphs—focus not on technical correctness but on effective writing. Many of the exercises allow students to experiment with various elements of style and to revise their own work.

Each section of explanatory material in the *Workbook* is followed by a summary. The exercises, which can be used either for group work in class or for individual assignment, are distributed throughout each chapter so that students can practice immediately the points they have just read. Printed on separate tear-out sheets, the exercises can be removed for convenient correction, leaving the explanatory sections intact for future reference. In addition to the exercises, there are comprehensive review tests at the end of each of the first four chapters, a pretest at the beginning of Chapter 3, and review and revision exercises at the end of both Chapters 5 and 6. An instructor's manual, containing an answer key for the exercises and tests, is available on request from Random House.

I owe special gratitude to Frederick Crews for his careful reading of the manuscript and to my students for what they have taught me and for allowing me to use their writing here. I also want to thank Steve Pensinger, Elisa Turner, and Jennifer Sutherland at Random House, who have been patient and helpful throughout the stages of this project; Santi Buscemi (Middlesex County College), Michael Hennessy (Southwest Texas State University), Craig Snow (University of Arizona), Ron Sudol (Oakland University), and Nancy Zuercher (University of South Dakota), who criticized the manuscript chapter by chapter, giving me invaluable suggestions for revision; and Sue Van Sant Palmer (Austin Peay State University), who gave me practical advice and many supporting examples from her students' writing. Thanks are also due Batya Harlow, friend and former student as well as typist, for her patience through several drafts of the manuscript. And I owe special thanks to Josie Loos for her kindness and encouragement while I was working on the project.

TO STUDENTS

This workbook is intended to help you write more effectively. It begins with an overview of sentence function, because an awareness of how the parts of a sentence work is useful for analyzing a sentence's effectiveness. The first four chapters concern matters of convention (grammar, spelling, and so on) while the last two (on sentences and paragraphs) focus on revision skills. The workbook will have "worked" if it helps you to review and revise your own writing.

Many of the examples and exercises are derived from the essays of my students (marked with an asterisk) or from articles in magazines (documented in notes). If you are interested in the topic of an exercise or example that originally appeared in a magazine, you can check the note at the end of the chapter in order to find the source. For example, the article on black bears used for Exercise 3–4 appeared in the April 1983 issue of *Smithsonian* (Adele Conover, "Getting to Know Black Bears—Right on Their Own Home Ground"). Or the paragraph about the death of the lightweight boxer Duk Koo Kim (Exercise 3–2) was in its original form part of an article in the May/June 1983 issue of *The Sciences* (Louis Lasagna, "Death in the Ring"). Since I have adapted a number of these pieces for the purpose of the exercise or explanation, their form in the workbook may vary from their form as originally published.

When I refer to writers in the explanatory text, I use *he* if the writer is a man, *she* if the writer is a woman. When I mean writers in general, I use the plural (*writers*) in order to avoid using masculine pronouns to refer to both men and women.

CONTENTS

1 RECOGNIZING SENTENCE ELEMENTS AND THEIR FUNCTION: AN OVERVIEW — 1

Complete or Incomplete? — 1
- Exercises 3

Phrases and Clauses — 5
- Exercises 7

Sentence Parts: Subject and Predicate — 11
- Exercises 13

Sentence Elements: Subject and Verb — 15
- Exercise 17

Verbs Made of More Than One Word 19
- Exercises 21

Sentence Elements: Objects and Complements — 23
- Exercise 25

Verbs With and Without Objects and Complements: Transitive, Intransitive, and Linking Verbs 27
- Exercises 31

Sentence Elements: Modifiers — 33

Adjectives and Adverbs 33

Prepositional Phrases 34
- Exercises 35

-Ing and -Ed Forms: What Are They When They Are Not Verbs? — 37
- Exercises 39

Subordinate Clauses as Sentence Elements — 41

Noun Clauses 41

Modifying Clauses as Adverbs 41

Modifying Clauses as Adjectives 42

A Further Note on Clauses 42
- Exercises 43

Review Test I — 47

Review Test II — 49

2 SOLVING PROBLEMS OF USAGE   53

Sentence Fragments   53
  Independent Fragments   53
  Unacceptable Fragments   54
  • Exercises   57
Predication   63
  • Exercises   65
Nouns   67
  Number   67
  Possessive Case   67
    Double Possessive   68
    Subject of Gerund   68
  • Exercises   69
Pronouns   73
  Pronoun Chart   73
  Choice of Case   73
    Subjective Case for Subjects/Objective Case for Objects   73
    Pronoun Case before -Self and -Selves   74
    Possessive Case   74
    Interrogative Pronoun Case: Who versus Whom   75
    Relative Pronoun Case: Who versus Whom   75
    Confusingly Similar Forms   75
  • Exercise   77
  Pronoun Reference   79
  Agreement—Pronoun Shifts   79
  They: Not Equal to *Someone* or *Anyone*   80
  • Exercises   83
Verbs   85
  Verb Chart   85
  Tense   85
    Sequence of Tenses   87
  • Exercises   89
  Voice: Active and Passive   91
  • Exercises   93
  Mood   95
    Sequence of Tenses in Impossible Conditions and Wishes   96
  • Exercises   97
  Subject-Verb Agreement   99
  • Exercises   103
Modifiers   107
  Comparison   107
  • Exercise   109
  Misrelated and Dangling Modifiers   111
  • Exercise   113

Parallelism   **115**
- Exercises   117

Review Test   **119**

---

3   PUNCTUATION AND CAPITALIZATION   125

Pretest   **125**

End Punctuation and Beginning Capitalization   **127**

End Punctuation   127

Period   127

Question Mark   128

Exclamation Point   129

Beginning Capitalization   129
- Exercises   131

Punctuation Within a Sentence   **135**

Independent Clauses   135
- Exercises   137

Commas in a Series   141

Commas Between Coordinate Modifiers   141
- Exercises   143

Modifying Clauses and Phrases   145

Restrictive and Nonrestrictive Elements   146
- Exercises   149

Superfluous Commas   153
- Exercises   155

Semicolon   157
- Exercises   159

Colon   161
- Exercises   163

Dashes, Parentheses, and Brackets   167

Dash   167

Parentheses   168

Brackets   169
- Exercises   171

The Apostrophe   175
- Exercise   177

Quotation Marks   179
- Exercises   183

Various Uses of Capitalization   **187**

Titles and Subtitles   187

Names   187

Units of Time   187

Ranks and Degrees   188
- Exercise   189

Review Test   **191**

4 WORDS   197

Using Your Dictionary   198
    • Exercises   201
Spelling   205
    Adding Prefixes   205
    Adding Endings (Suffixes)   205
      Single and Double Consonants   205
      Final -e   206
      Final -y   207
      Final -ie   207
    Ie versus *Ei*   207
    Frequently Misspelled Words   207
      • Exercises   211
    Spelling Plural and Possessive Forms   217
      • Exercises   219
    Hyphenation   223
      • Exercises   225
Meaning   227
    Confusing Words   227
    Roots and Prefixes   227
    Context   228
      • Exercises   229
Appropriateness   237
    Connotation   237
    Diction   237
      • Exercises   239
Holding Your Reader's Attention   243
    Conciseness   243
      • Exercises   245
    Figurative Language   247
      • Exercises   249
Review Test   253

5 SENTENCE REVISION   259

Main Assertions   259
    Recognizing Main Assertions   259
      • Exercise   261
    Align Meaning with Grammatically Important Words   263
      • Exercises   265
Subordination   269
    Coordination versus Subordination   269

Subordinate to Clarify Assertions   270
Subordinate to Establish Relationships   270
  • Exercises   271
Bound and Free Subordinate Elements   275
  Clarifying Sentences by Reducing Bound Elements   276
  Placement of Free Subordinate Elements   276
  • Exercises   279
Subordination in a Paragraph   289
  • Exercise   291

Matching   **293**
  • Exercises   295
Variety   **297**
Significant Pauses   297
Vary Your Sentence Patterns   298
  • Exercises   301
Revision Exercises   **307**

---

6   PARAGRAPH REVISION   313

What Is a Paragraph?   **313**
  • Exercises   317
Paragraph Development   **321**
Adding and Subtracting Sentences   321
  • Exercises   323
Direct, Pivoting, and Suspended Patterns of Development   327
  • Exercises   331
Paragraph Unity   **337**
  • Exercises   341
Paragraph Continuity   **345**
  • Exercises   349
Paragraph Revision   **357**
Review and Revision Exercises   **359**

THE
RANDOM HOUSE
WORKBOOK
fourth edition

RECOGNIZING SENTENCE ELEMENTS AND THEIR FUNCTIONS: AN OVERVIEW

1

COMPLETE OR INCOMPLETE?

1. More than 600,000 people videotaped the last episode of M*A*S*H.
2. Sponsored by Geritol.
3. A book on famous movie stars of the thirties.
4. Your overdue fine is $35.00.

A **sentence** expresses a complete thought. Without knowing the terms for any grammatical elements, you can usually tell whether a group of words is a sentence by asking whether it seems complete. Of the examples above, only the first and last are sentences. Items 2 and 3 are incomplete.

Exercise 1—1

NAME _____

After each complete sentence, write C in the space provided. Use each incomplete item to make a complete sentence of your own. Write it in the space provided.

Examples: a) Benjamin Franklin wrote *Poor Richard's Almanac.*

C
_____

b) If I had a hammer.

If I had a hammer, I could hang this picture.
_____

c) Hitting the umpire.

Hitting the umpire will get you tossed out
of the game.
_____

1. Time is money.

_____

2. The 1984 World Series.

_____

3. In spite of anything you say.

_____

4. Don't rock the boat.

_____

5. When baseball and football players go on strike.

_____

6. That tomorrow is a holiday.

_____

7. If I were you.

_____

8. Bluejays are obnoxious.

_____

9. What you do not know.

10. The most popular main dish in the United States is fried chicken.

Exercise 1–2[1]

In the spaces at the right, indicate whether each of the following word groups is complete (C) or incomplete (I).

Examples: a) Speed skiing is a dangerous sport.   *C*

             b) Both the mental and physical demands.   *I*

1. Europeans were the first to keep records of speed-skiing times. _____

2. In 1960, Luigi di Marco, an Italian, became the first skier to break 100 miles an hour. _____

3. An annual event and a national sport. _____

4. They must be in peak condition physically. _____

5. To hold position against the force of the air. _____

6. No doubt because of its rigors. _____

7. There are only about 200 speed skiers in the world. _____

8. Thirty can make it into world class competition. _____

9. Danger is ever present. _____

10. Five fatalities in four decades. _____

PHRASES AND CLAUSES

1. At the zoo.
2. The zookeeper hates living at the zoo.
3. When the zookeeper's daughter applied for a job.

The first example—*at the zoo*—is a **phrase**. The words of a phrase make sense together but do not complete a thought and do not include a subject and a verb (p. 15). As you can see from example 2, *at the zoo* fits as a unit into the sentence and tells us *where* the zookeeper hates living. Other phrases are *last night, going home, in the refrigerator, beyond my expectations.*

The second and third examples above are both clauses. A **clause** is a group of words that contains a subject and a verb. Some clauses, for example, *The zookeeper hates living at the zoo,* express a complete thought and are said to be **independent**. An independent clause can stand by itself as a complete sentence.

Other clauses—those that do not express a complete thought—are said to be **subordinate** (or dependent). *When the zookeeper's daughter applied for a job* leaves us waiting for the rest of its meaning; even though it has a subject and a verb (*daughter applied*), it is not complete and cannot appear alone.

Subordinate clauses are introduced by subordinating words like *when, because, that,* and *who*:

when the zookeeper retired
because the ticket-taker quit
that the zoo was in an uproar
who was pleased

Other subordinating words are *if, since, although, for, after,* and *which.* Simply dropping the subordinating words will convert certain subordinate clauses to independent clauses and thus to complete sentences:

- The zookeeper's daughter applied for a job.
- The zookeeper retired.
- The ticket-taker quit.
- The zoo was in an uproar.

A second way to make a complete sentence is to combine a subordinate clause with an independent one. Such combining may require simply *adding* the subordinate clause to an independent clause, or it may require *embedding* the subordinate clause in the independent one:

ADDING:
- *When the zookeeper's daughter applied for a job,* her father would not give her a letter of recommendation.

- Everyone got in free *because the ticket-taker quit.*

- The newspaper reported *that the zoo was in an uproar.*
- The only person *who was pleased* was the newspaper reporter.

SUMMARY

Groups of words that make sense together are either phrases or clauses. A group of words without a subject and verb, which fits as a unit into a sentence, is a phrase. A clause is a group of words with a subject and a verb. There are two kinds of clauses: independent and subordinate. An independent clause expresses a complete thought and can therefore be a complete sentence. A subordinate clause is introduced by a subordinating word and does not express a complete thought.

Exercise 1–3

NAME _____

Make complete sentences using the following phrases and subordinate clauses.

Example: in the next century (phrase)

It may be common to travel in space in the next century.

1. when travel agencies book flights to Mars (subordinate clause)

_____

2. eating space snacks (phrase)

_____

3. making hotel reservations on Saturn (phrase)

_____

4. if lengthy hibernation is required (subordinate clause)

_____

5. on a six-month flight (phrase)

_____

Exercise 1—4²

NAME _____

Indicate whether each of the italicized clauses is *independent* (ind) or *subordinate* (sub).

> *Example:* The two weapons *which have dominated the battlefield since World War II* are armored vehicles and strike air-craft. *sub*

1. The tank, which began as a simple trench-crossing machine impervious to machine-gun bullets, *has evolved into an aggressive gun platform.* _____

2. *It is destructible only by high-energy projectiles of great accuracy.* _____

3. *Although the tank has proved highly "survivable,"* it is now threatened by many new weapons, in particular precision-guided missiles. _____

4. Since tanks are predators more often than victims, *such an improvement in antitank weaponry may not seem deplorable.* _____

5. *But submunitions also threaten frightful mutilation to human beings caught in the open.* _____

6. *One such weapon ejects seven hundred bomblets capable of discriminating between "hard" and "soft" targets.* _____

7. When the bomblets strike armor, *they detonate with armor-piercing effect.* _____

8. *When they strike earth,* they jump to waist height before exploding. _____

9. *Some bomblets fail to detonate but remain primed.* _____

10. *Such military jetsam creates an unmarked and unintended minefield.* _____

Exercise 1—5[3]

NAME _____

Underline the subordinate clauses in the following sentences and circle the subordinating words.

Example: (Although) nearly half the packaged foods sold in the U.S. carry a

nutrition label, few people take the time to read those labels carefully.

1. Although some people may not want all the information, many people ignore the labels for other reasons.

2. It is possible that they cannot make sense of all the numbers.

3. Because people have this problem, the Food and Drug Administration and the Department of Agriculture recently began a drive to create simpler, more useful labels.

4. Since the format of existing labels is confusing, the new labels will present information in simpler forms.

5. The new labels will begin to appear on the market after they have been tested for about a year.

SENTENCE PARTS: SUBJECT AND PREDICATE

- 1. The police officer gave me a ticket.
- 2. An apple a day keeps the doctor away.
- 3. Subway tokens are no longer cheap.

The two parts of a complete sentence are a subject and a predicate. The **subject** is what the sentence is about. The sentences above are about *the police officer, an apple a day,* and *subway tokens.* The **predicate** tells us something about the subject. It characterizes the subject or tells what the subject does or did. In the sentences above, *gave me a ticket* tells what the police officer did; *keeps the doctor away* tells what an apple a day does; and *are no longer cheap* tells what subway tokens are.

Fill in the blanks of the examples below to make complete sentences:

1. _____ fought in the Civil War.
2. _____ hit the jackpot.
3. _____ is a major river in the United States.
4. _____ is impolite.

Whatever you put in the blank functions as the subject of that sentence. Possible subjects are

- 1. *Robert E. Lee and Ulysses S. Grant* fought in the Civil War.
- 2. *Only very lucky people* hit the jackpot.
- 3. *The Mississippi* is a major river in the United States.
- 4. *Whispering during a movie* is impolite.

Make complete sentences of the following examples by adding predicates:

1. The Miami Dolphins _____.
2. The Gold Rush _____.
3. All the students in my writing class _____.

Even if you do not know who the Miami Dolphins are, you can make a sentence about them; and whatever you say about them is the predicate if they are the subject. Possible predicates for the examples above are:

- 1. The Miami Dolphins are famous for their defense.
- 2. The Gold Rush occurred in 1848.
- 3. All the students in my writing class were late on Monday.

Exercise 1—6

NAME _____

Make complete sentences by adding subjects and predicates as appropriate.

1. _____ is harmful to your health.

2. The movie *Gandhi* _____.

3. One hour of exercise every day _____.

4. _____ bring May flowers.

5. The Florida coastline _____.

6. _____ comes from the Appalachian mountains.

7. _____ hires student workers in the summer.

8. The April snowstorm _____.

9. _____ succeeded his wife as superintendent.

10. Buying a personal robot _____.

Exercise 1—7

NAME _____

Underline the subjects of the following sentences once. Underline the predicates twice.

Example: <u>The college bookstore</u> <u><u>opens at 8:30 a.m.</u></u>

1. Pure olive oil becomes cloudy in temperatures below 45°.

2. The most useful firescreens have three panels.

3. First-class stamps cost three cents about twenty-five years ago.

4. Most Americans know very little about the metric system.

5. A little learning is a dangerous thing.

6. A rolling stone gathers no moss.

7. Littering is nasty and selfish.

8. Misery loves company.

9. Ireland, Italy, Germany, and Brazil are famous lace-making areas.

10. The word for wine in Italian is *vino*.

14

SENTENCE ELEMENTS: SUBJECT AND VERB

- 1. The highway <u>patrolman</u> <u>gave</u> me a ticket.

- 2. The ugly but lovable <u>creature</u> <u>followed</u> a trail of Reese's chocolate.

The main word of a subject is called the **simple subject**. It is the word that names the person, idea, or thing that the sentence is about. Sometimes the simple subject is two words; for example, in the sentence *Jack and Jill went up the hill*, both *Jack* and *Jill* are part of the simple subject. You can locate the simple subject by asking "What is the main thing that this sentence is about?" The sentences above are about a *patrolman* and a *creature*.

A word that names a person, an idea, or a thing is called a **noun** (p. 67). The simple subject is a noun or pronoun (for example, *he, she, it*, words that substitute for nouns, p. 73).

The main word of a predicate is called the **simple predicate**. In the sentences above, *gave* and *followed* are the main words that tell what the patrolman and the creature did.

A word that expresses action or a state of being is called a **verb**. The simple predicate is a verb. Since verbs are easier to recognize than to define, consider the following statements from which they have been omitted:

1. The grocery clerk _____ the money.
     (stole, lost, miscounted)
2. The student _____ every day.
     (studied, played, argued)
3. The man in the Houston Astros T-shirt _____ happy.
     (is, looks, feels)

Without a verb we are at a loss: we do not know what the grocery clerk did with the money or what the student does every day. We can more easily guess the meaning of the sentence about the man in the Houston Astros T-shirt, but even in this case (when the verb leads only to a description), we depend on it in order to gain an essential piece of information.

As the subject may contain two or more nouns (Jack and Jill), so may the predicate contain two or more verbs joined by connecting words such as *and* and *or*:

- Jack and Jill <u>went</u> up the hill and <u>fetched</u> a pail of water.

SUMMARY

A sentence must have a subject and a predicate. The subject may contain two or more nouns, and the predicate may contain two or more verbs.

Exercise 1—8[4]

NAME _____

Write the simple subject and simple predicate (verb) in the spaces provided after each sentence.

    Examples: a) Bats are blind but navigate very well.

          Bats   *are / navigate*

           b) Some bats migrate to warm climates in the winter.

          bats   *migrate*

1. Others cling to the limestone walls of their cave or retreat into its crevices for the winter.

    _____   ================

2. They lapse into a trance.

    _____   ================

3. Hibernating bats are very much like dead ones.

    _____   ================

4. Their body temperature drops to that of the air around them.

    _____   ================

5. Heart rate, respiration, and blood circulation slow down proportionately.

    _____   ================

6. Stored fat lasts the hibernating bat until the following spring.

    _____   ================

7. Any movement during the hibernation period threatens the bat's survival.

    _____   ================

8. Even waking up is dangerous.

    _____   ================

9. In the spring the bat's heartbeat increases more than a hundredfold.

    _____   ================

10. Its body temperature climbs at a rate of about two degrees per minute.

    _____   ================

Verbs Made of More Than One Word

- The grocery clerk is counting the money.

- The students are studying for final exams.

- The bats have lapsed into a trance.

The verb may be one word—*count, study,* or *lapse*—or more than one—*is counting, are studying, have lapsed.* Various forms of *be* (*is, are, was, were, been*), *do* (*do, does, did*), and *have* (*have, has, had*) allow us to express variations in meaning:

- The grocery clerk is counting the money.

- The grocery clerk has counted the money.

verb phrases

- You should study.

- The biology teacher may give a take-home midterm.

Words such as *may* and *should* (and in some uses *do*) are called auxiliary verbs, and we use them to express such variations in meaning as

EMPHASIS:
- I do like baseball.

OBLIGATION:
- I should write to my parents.

LIKELIHOOD:
- I may go home this weekend.

Other auxiliary verbs are *can, will, may, might,* and *must.*

The main verb (*study, give, like, write, go*) together with the auxiliary verb (*should, may, do*) is often called a *verb phrase*; the whole phrase—*should study, may give, do like, should write, may go*—is the verb of the sentence. Further examples:

- He should feel confident about the exam.

- Can you please whisper?

SUMMARY

The verb may be one word or more than one. Various forms of *be, do,* and *have* allow us to change the time sense of a verb. Auxiliary verbs allow us to express obligation, degree of likelihood, and changes in emphasis.

Exercise 1—9[5]

NAME _____

Write the verb (whether one word or more than one) in the space provided after each sentence.

Example: a) South America's rain forest contains an enormous variety of
plants and animals.   *contains*
b) The destruction of even a small
area can cause the extinction of a
number of species.   *can cause*

1. At least a third of all the earth's species live
within the rain forest.   _____
2. People have given scientific names to only a
fraction of them.   _____
3. The number of plant species in Amazonia
may be more than 40,000.   _____
4. The creatures of the rain forest have adapted,
over the ages, to special circumstances.   _____
5. The three-toed sloth has adjusted extremely
well to life in the trees.   _____

6. It can barely walk on the ground.   _____
7. It hangs upside down by its strong claws
most of its life.   _____
8. The female sloths even give birth among the
leafy branches.   _____
9. One kind of rain forest bee has developed a
special vibrating frequency.   _____
10. It can trigger a burst of pollen from a flowering plant.   _____

Exercise 1—10

Write a paragraph or several sentences of your own and underline the verbs.

_____

_____

_____

_____

_____

SENTENCE ELEMENTS: OBJECTS AND COMPLEMENTS

The two essential parts of a sentence are, as we have seen, a simple subject and a simple predicate (verb). (Even commands such as *Hurry!* and *Stop!* have an implied subject—*you*.) Other elements can be added.

                              S   V
SUBJECT AND VERB: • Sally plays.

                              S   V   D OBJ
DIRECT OBJECT: • Sally plays bagpipes.

A **direct object** receives the action of the verb directly. What does Sally play? Bagpipes. *Bagpipes* is the direct object of *plays*.

                              S   V   IND OBJ
INDIRECT OBJECT: • Sally gives her neighbors midnight recitals.

An **indirect object** is the person or thing to or for whom the action is done. To whom does Sally give midnight recitals? Her neighbors. *Neighbors* is the indirect object of *gives*.

                              S   V   C
COMPLEMENT: • Sally is a pest.

                              S   V   C
              • Sally is unpopular.

A **complement** completes the predicate by telling us something about the subject: what the subject is or seems or how the subject seems or feels. What is Sally? A pest. *Pest* completes the predicate by explaining what Sally is. How can Sally be described? As unpopular. *Unpopular* completes the predicate by describing Sally. Although the complement appears in the predicate, it identifies, explains, or describes the subject.

SUMMARY

A simple subject and a verb are the two necessary elements in a sentence. Sentences may also have direct objects, indirect objects, and complements.
The simple predicate, or verb, may be one word or more than one.

Exercise 1–11[6]

NAME _____

Write the simple subjects, verbs, direct objects, and complements of each of the following sentences in the space provided. If a sentence has a double subject, verb, object, or complement, write both. (The sample sentence has a double complement.)

Example: Cheese making is both an art and a science.

S (Cheese) making V _____is_____ O_____ C _art/science_

1. The names of cheese varieties are the names of cheese-making areas.

   S_____ V_____ O_____ C_____

2. The English settlers of the U.S. were soon making their own cheddars and similar cheeses.

   S_____ V_____ O_____ C_____

3. By the mid-1800's, the first cheese factories in the U.S. were appearing in upper New York State.

   S_____ V_____ O_____ C_____

4. Vermont and Wisconsin are the other famous cheese-making states.

   S_____ V_____ O_____ C_____

5. Cheese lovers have endless arguments about the natural superiority of one state's cheddar over another.

   S_____ V_____ O_____ C_____

6. The texture of a good cheddar is firm and somewhat dry and crumbly.

   S_____ V_____ O_____ C_____

7. Mr. Kraft patented the process for "process cheese" in 1916.

   S_____ V_____ O_____ C_____

8. Processed cheese is not a cheap protein source.

   S_____ V_____ O_____ C_____

9. The protein in processed American cheese costs about 70 cent per ounce.

   S_____ V_____ O_____ C_____

10. Tuna and peanut butter are much cheaper.

    S_____ V_____ O_____ C_____

Verbs With and Without Objects and Complements: Transitive, Intransitive, and Linking Verbs

- 1. The owl is blinking his eyes. [D OBJ]
- The owl is screeching.

- 2. The cat overturned the bowl of milk. [D OBJ]
- The cat purred.

- 3. Sally plays bagpipes. [D OBJ]
- Sally is unpopular.

Verbs may be transitive, intransitive, or linking. In both the owl sentences above, the owl is acting—*blinking* and *screeching.* In the first case, he is blinking something—*his eyes.* In the second case, however, the action stops with the verb. It does not go on to an object. Similarly, in the second examples, the cat overturned an object (the bowl of milk) in the first case, while in the second case the cat's action is limited to itself; *purring* does not go on to an object.

A **transitive verb** transmits an action to a direct object:

- The Greeks defeated the Trojans. [D OBJ]

- My neighbor paces the floor all night. [D OBJ]

Look back at the sentences in Exercise 1–11. All the verbs that have direct objects are transitive.

An **intransitive verb**, on the other hand, expresses an action that is complete without an object. The action does not take effect on any person or thing:

- The Greeks sailed away.

- My neighbor sleeps during the day.

Some verbs can be used transitively at one time and intransitively at another. Compare the following:

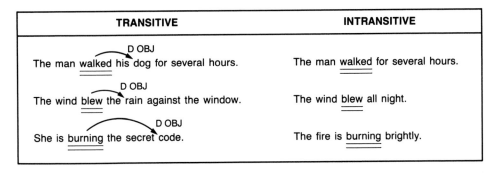

TRANSITIVE	INTRANSITIVE
The man walked his dog for several hours. [D OBJ]	The man walked for several hours.
The wind blew the rain against the window. [D OBJ]	The wind blew all night.
She is burning the secret code. [D OBJ]	The fire is burning brightly.

Some verbs have confusingly similar transitive and intransitive forms: *sit/set;*
rise/raise; lie/lay, etc.

TRANSITIVE	INTRANSITIVE
D OBJ Set the lamp on the gate-leg table.	Sit anywhere you like.
D OBJ Raise the window.	This bread rises for two hours.
D OBJ Did you lay your glasses on the stove?	The older child lies on the couch for her nap.

If you are not sure whether a verb is transitive or intransitive, look it up in the
dictionary. Verbs marked *v.t.* (verb transitive) must have an object, while verbs
marked *v.i.* (verb intransitive) cannot take an object. Verbs marked *v.t./v.i.* can
be used both ways.

Linking verbs, as you might guess, link or connect the subject to a complement. In *Sally is unpopular, is* links Sally to the word that characterizes her, *unpopular.* The most common linking verb is *be* (*is, are, was, were,* etc.). Others are
seem, appear, become, continue, grow, remain, look, sound, taste, feel, and *smell.*

           LV   COMPL   LV   COMPL
- 1. She remained silent but appeared pleased.

         LV   COMPL   LV   COMPL
- 2. He is a husband but remains a son.

In the first sentence the verbs—*remained* and *appeared*—link the subject to the
complements—*silent* and *pleased.* In the second sentence the verbs—*is* and
remains—link the subject to the complements—*husband* and *son.*

    Some linking verbs, such as *feel, taste,* and *smell,* are in other senses tran-
sitive. Compare the following:

LINKING:

                                   LV   COMPL
- The room with the catbox smells foul.

TRANSITIVE:

        TRANS V   D OBJ
- She smelled the perfume.

SUMMARY

Verbs may be transitive, intransitive, or linking. A transitive verb transmits action to a direct object. An intransitive verb expresses an action that is complete without an object. And a linking verb connects the subject to a complement.

Exercise 1—12

NAME _____

Write the verb of each of the following sentences in the blank provided at the right and indicate whether each is transitive (VT), intransitive (VI), or linking (L).

Example: Did you hear the alarm?   *did hear*   VT

1. Time flies. _____ _____

2. Coffee destroys vitamins. _____ _____

3. Last winter, it snowed in April. _____ _____

4. That suit flatters you. _____ _____

5. They live above the train station. _____ _____

6. Prices get higher every day. _____ _____

7. He is going to undertaker's school. _____ _____

8. Do you prefer a plain or a sugar cone? _____ _____

9. Will you set the table? _____ _____

10. Have you written a will? _____ _____

Exercise 1—13

Write three sentences, one with a transitive, another with an intransitive, and another with a linking verb. Underline the verbs and label them VT, VI, and L.

1. _____

_____

2. _____

_____

3. _____

_____

SENTENCE ELEMENTS: MODIFIERS

Adjectives and Adverbs

adjectives

- 1. Tossing a non-swimmer into the water is not a *harmless* prank.
- 2. The *cozy* room upstairs belongs to the supervisor.

In the examples above the italicized words are modifiers. **Modifiers** describe elements in the sentence; for example, *harmless* describes *prank*, and *cozy* describes *room*. Words that modify subjects, objects, and some complements are **adjectives**. In the following example fill in the blanks with modifiers:

S   IND OBJ

The _____ policeman gave the _____ driver a _____

D OBJ
warning.

S   D OBJ

The _____ student turned in a/an _____ lab report.

Whatever you put in the blank functions as an adjective. Possible sentences might be:

The ___large___ policeman gave the ___drunk___ driver a ___severe___ warning.

The ___new___ student turned in a/an _outstanding_ lab report.

adverbs

- 1. *Gradually* add sugar.
- 2. She dresses *very elegantly.*
- 3. Yesterday was an *unbearably* hot day.

Words that modify the verb are called **adverbs**. They give such information as how, when, or where the action takes place. For example, *gradually* tells how the sugar is to be added. Adverbs also modify adjectives and other adverbs. In *She dresses very elegantly, elegantly* is an adverb characterizing how she dresses, and *very* is an adverb characterizing *elegantly*. In *Yesterday was an unbearably hot day, hot* is an adjective modifying the complement *day*, while *unbearably* is an adverb modifying the adjective *hot*. Adverbs usually end in *-ly*, but there are exceptions (*well, very*, etc.).

33

Prepositional Phrases

1. *on* the table

               —PREP PH
* The book *on the table* is overdue at the library.

2. *from* San Francisco

* The snowstorm in Chicago delayed the plane *from San*
PREP PH
Francisco.

3. *by* hand

               —PREP PH
* Most coffee beans are picked *by hand.*

The phrases above act as modifiers by giving us further information about various sentence elements. The first word of each phrase is a preposition (*on, from,* and *by*). **Prepositions** suggest time, place, direction, manner, and the like. Following the preposition is its object (*table, San Francisco* and *hand*). The preposition and its object are called a **prepositional phrase**, and together they act as modifiers. In sentence 3, for example, *by hand* tells us how coffee beans are picked, while in sentence 2 *from San Francisco* tells us the direction from which the plane came.

SUMMARY

Modifiers describe various elements in the sentence. Adjectives modify subjects, objects, and some complements. Adverbs modify verbs, adjectives, and other adverbs. Prepositional phrases, composed of prepositions and their objects, are modifiers.

Exercise 1—14[7]

NAME _____

Underline 15 modifiers in the following passage. One is done for you as an example.

Crocodiles survived while their <u>close</u> kin the dinosaurs died out. Croc brains are far more complex than those of other reptiles. They learn readily. Crocodile hearts are almost as advanced as those of birds and mammals. In fact, their closest living relatives are the warm-blooded birds. Many crocodilians even gather brush to build nests, as birds do.

Full-grown crocodilians range in size from three feet to more than 25, from a few pounds to more than a ton. We can only guess how long they live—some for perhaps a hundred years or more.

A few species prefer solitary lives, but most, we now know, have sophisticated social orders. Their grunts, hisses, chirps, and growls each carry specific messages. They also use a "body language" of back arching, bubble blowing, and other physical displays. Crocs may communicate underwater, too, through low-frequency warblings inaudible to us.

A big Nile croc is cunning enough to stalk a human, strong enough to bring down and dismember a water buffalo, yet gentle enough to crack open its own eggs to release its young.

Exercise 1—15[8]

NAME _____

Underline five prepositional phrases in the following paragraph. One is done for you as an example.

As hordes <u>of mosquitoes</u> once again descend upon Americans, their numbers swollen in the Northeast and the West by heavy spring rains, reports of ingenious new methods to control this pest promise relief to the evening stroller and porch sitter, the early morning jogger, and the sleeper tortured by the insistent hum of a female mosquito in search of a meal.

Write sentences with five of the following prepositions and circle each prepositional phrase.

Example: Let's sit (in the front row.)

of	for	under	among
with	in	between	above
by	at	from	below

1. _____

2. _____

3. _____

4. _____

5. _____

-ING AND -ED FORMS:
WHAT ARE THEY WHEN THEY ARE NOT VERBS?

- 1. Someone *was smoking* in the elevator.
- 2. Please extinguish all *smoking* materials.
- 3. *Smoking* can be harmful to your health.
- 4. My desk *faced* the window.
- 5. *Faced* with two unacceptable choices, I became indecisive.

In the first example—*Someone was smoking in the elevator*—*smoking* is part of the verb *was smoking*. Not all -*ing* forms, however, act as verbs. Some are modifiers. In the second example, smoking modifies *materials*. In still other sentences, -*ing* forms act as nouns, filling such sentence functions as subjects, objects, and complements. In the third example—*Smoking can be harmful to your health*—*smoking* is the subject. Distinguishing -*ing* verb forms from -*ing* modifiers and nouns is not difficult. An -*ing* form preceded by a form of *be* (*am* runn*ing*, *was* rush*ing*, have *been* study*ing*) is part of the verb. An -*ing* form appearing without a form of *be* is either a modifier or a noun.

As the fourth and fifth examples show, -*ed* forms too have more than one function. In *My desk faced the window, faced* is a verb. In *Faced with two unacceptable choices, I became indecisive*, however, *Faced* is a modifier describing the subject *I*.

Further examples:

-ING AND -ED FORMS AS MODIFIERS:
- 1. I saw the girl *running* up the stairs.
  (*Running* modifies *girl.*)
- 2. Do you hear the sound of *rushing* water?
  (*Rushing* modifies *water.*)
- 3. The bus *carrying* the girls' basketball team skidded and struck the embankment.
  (*Carrying* modifies *bus.*)
- 4. *Abandoned* by their owners, many pets wander the highways.
  (*Abandoned* modifies *pets.*)
- 5. Finally *persuaded* by the arguments of his advisors, the President decided not to veto the tax bill.
  (*Persuaded* modifies *President.*)

-ING FORMS AS SUBJECTS, OBJECTS, AND COMPLEMENTS:
- 1. *Running* on hard pavement may give you shin splints.
  (*Running* is the subject.)
- 2. The zookeeper hates *feeding* the animals.
  (*Feeding* is the object.)
- 3. His worst habit is *snoring*.
  (*Snoring* is a complement.)

When an *-ing* or an *-ed* form acts as a modifier, it is called a **participle**. When an *-ing* form acts as a noun (filling such functions as subject, object, or complement), it is called a **gerund**.

SUMMARY

-Ing and *-ed* forms may act as modifiers. As modifiers, they are called participles. *-Ing* forms may also act as nouns. As nouns, they are called gerunds.

Exercise 1–16[9]

NAME _____

Indicate below whether each of the italicized forms in the following passages acts as part of a *verb* (V), as a *modifier* (M), or as some *other* sentence element (O). The first is done for you as an example.

A half-century ago, Dutch elm disease (1) *crossed* the Atlantic and (2) *scourged* America's elms, (3) *leaving* dead gray hulks (4) *standing* leafless in hundreds of parks and by countless roadsides.

(5) *Carried* from tree to tree by bark beetles, the fungal infection (6) *hopscotched* throughout the elm's range, (7) *reaching* the West Coast in 1975. Little could be done to curb the outbreak except to cut down and cart away (8) *afflicted* trees.

But several new approaches are (9) *showing* promise in the battle to save these stately shade trees.

The first step in (10) *creating* your own miniature garden is to select a container; it will determine what size plants you will need. Then take a walk through a wood, a meadow, or even a nearby vacant lot, (11) *keeping* your eyes open for a few small plants whose form or character arouses your curiosity. Useful tools are a flexible spatula for (12) *lifting* moss, a stout knife for (13) *digging,* and a wide, flat basket or box in which to carry home your finds. (If you wish to collect in a park or forest, check local regulations first.)

(14) *Caring* for a dish garden: (15) *Watering* is the most critical task. With a bulb-type sprayer you can cover every part of the garden without (16) *putting* an excess of water anywhere. Keep the little garden well (17) *groomed,* and refresh it occasionally by (18) *putting* it outdoors when the weather is mild.

The number of leatherback turtles, the largest marine reptile, has been (19) *dwindling,* and some scientists now believe they have (20) *uncovered* one cause: the killer plastic bag.

(21) *Mistaking* (22) *floating* plastic bags for jellyfish, their favorite food, the turtles swallow them, only to wind up with (23) *clogged* digestive systems.

Autopsies of the leatherbacks have (24) *revealed* stomachs and intestines completely (25) *blocked* by sandwich bags, potato chip bags, trash bags, and other plastic items.

1. __V__   2. _____   3. _____   4. _____   5. _____

6. _____   7. _____   8. _____   9. _____   10. _____

11. _____   12. _____   13. _____   14. _____   15. _____

16. _____   17. _____   18. _____   19. _____   20. _____

21. _____   22. _____   23. _____   24. _____   25. _____

Exercise 1—17

NAME _____

Write four sentences, one using an *-ing* modifier; one using an *-ing* form as a subject, object, or complement; one using an *-ed* modifier; and one using an *-ed* form as a verb.

1. _____

2. _____

3. _____

4. _____

SUBORDINATE CLAUSES AS SENTENCE ELEMENTS

Noun Clauses

SUBJECT:
- 1. *What you don't know* may indeed hurt you.
- 2. *How my monkey escaped* puzzles me.
- 3. *That my monkey escaped* is a problem.

DIRECT OBJECT:
- 4. I didn't know *that my monkey escaped.*
- 5. I can't imagine *how my monkey escaped.*
- 6. Do you know *when my monkey escaped?*

OBJECT OF PREPOSITION:
- 7. How can I tell you anything about *what I don't know?*

COMPLEMENT:
- 8. The truth is *that the parrot helped the monkey escape.*

Like single words and phrases, subordinate clauses function as ordinary sentence elements. In the sentences above, the first three subordinate clauses are subjects, the second three are direct objects, 7 is the object of a preposition, and 8 is a complement. Notice that the clauses are introduced by subordinating words: *what, how, that,* and *when.* Other subordinating words include *whether, where, who,* and *which.*

Modifying Clauses as Adverbs

- 1. Start *as soon as you hear the signal.*
- 2. Run *as if your life depended on it.*
- 3. *If you win the marathon,* I'll take you out to dinner.

Adverbial clauses are subordinate clauses that function as adverbs, modifying verbs. They are introduced by such subordinating words as *as soon as, as if, if, since, when, although, unless, while,* and *because.* Each of the italicized clauses above modifies the verb. The first indicates *when* the runner should start, the second *how* the runner should run, and the last the *condition* under which the runner will be taken to dinner.

Modifying Clauses as Adjectives

- 1. The woman *who adopted fifteen cats from the ASPCA* overestimated her family's love for animals.
- 2. Is this the picture *that you took while standing on your head*?
- 3. The saliva of vampire bats contains a chemical *which prevents the blood from clotting.*[10]

Adjectival clauses (also called **relative clauses**) are subordinate clauses that act as adjectives; they modify such sentence elements as subjects, objects, and complements (if they are nouns). Adjectival clauses are introduced by the subordinating words, *who, whom, which,* and *that. Who* and *whom* refer to people, *which* to things, and *that* to both people and things. In the sentences above, *who adopted fifteen cats from the ASPCA* describes *woman* (the subject); *that you took while standing on your head* describes *picture* (noun complement); and *which prevents the blood from clotting* describes *chemical* (a direct object). The word described by the relative clause is called the **antecedent**.

A Further Note on Clauses

You should think of a subordinate clause *as a unit of the whole sentence* and *as a unit in itself.* As units in the sentence, subordinate clauses have, as you have seen, various sentence functions:

SUB CLAUSE AS ADV
- Start *as soon as you hear the signal.*

SUB CLAUSE AS D OBJ
- The teacher knew *that you would not cheat.*

As units in themselves, they have an internal structure in which each word or phrase has a function:

subordinating words   S   V   D OBJ
   (as soon as) you hear the signal

subordinating word   S   V   ADV   V
       (that) you would not cheat.

42

Exercise 1—18

NAME _____

Use each of the following clauses in two sentence functions (subject, direct object, indirect object, or complement). In the space provided at the right, indicate the function of each.

Example: That you won a color T.V.

> *That you won a color TV will
> make you popular in the dorm.* _____subject_____
> *I heard that you won a color TV.* ___Dir. object___

1. what you want for your birthday

_____   _____

_____   _____

2. when I will study

_____   _____

_____   _____

3. whom we can trust

_____   _____

_____   _____

4. how we can improve our writing

_____   _____

_____   _____

5. that the guarantee had run out

_____   _____

_____   _____

Exercise 1—19

NAME _____

Write five sentences with adverbial clauses, using five of the following subordinating words: *although, since, after, when, if,* and *because.*

Example: *If you go to Florida during the hottest part of the summer, you can stay in an elegant hotel for about half the price.*

1. _____

_____

2. _____

_____

3. _____

_____

4. _____

_____

5. _____

_____

Exercise 1—20

NAME _____

Underline the relative clause in each of the following sentences and circle the antecedent.

> *Example:*   The health food (store), which is just down the street, is open from noon to midnight.

1. A word that names a person, place, idea, or thing is a noun.

2. An *-ing* form that acts as a modifier is called a participle.

3. The zookeeper who hated feeding the animals retired early.

4. His daughter, who got a job at a natural history museum, now stuffs animals.

5. The woman to whom I gave the ticket was wearing an Oakland A's cap.

Write five sentences with relative clauses. Underline the clauses and circle the antecedents. Use *who, which,* and *that.*

1. _____

_____

2. _____

_____

3. _____

_____

4. _____

_____

5. _____

_____

NAME _____

Identify each underlined word, phrase, or clause as a subject (S), verb (V), direct object (D. Obj.), indirect object (I. Obj.), complement (C), or modifier (M). (Some complements are modifiers. Label them either C or M.) Write your answers in the space provided below. The first is done for you as an example.

There is a terrific cowboy-and-Indian show (1) <u>playing around the country these days</u>. The (2) <u>star</u>, a husky, goateed fellow (3) <u>on horseback</u>, (4) <u>wears</u> a fancy buckskin (5) <u>jacket</u>, shiny thigh-high (6) <u>boots</u>, and a white (7) <u>Stetson</u>. (8) <u>When he is not shooting glass balls out of the air or rescuing pioneer women from Indians</u>, he is busy attending to urgent matters backstage. He turns up (9) <u>in posters and playbills</u>, in photographs and oil paintings, and even in a brief film where the public can see him (10) <u>announcing the show's other acts</u>. "Ladies and gentlemen," he (11) <u>proclaims</u>, doffing his hat with a courtly flourish, "permit me to introduce you to a Congress of Rough Riders of the World!"

If that (12) <u>sounds</u> a tad old-fashioned, there is good reason. The stalwart (13) <u>showman</u> is none other than that celebrated ex-Pony Express rider, buffalo hunter, and Indian fighter without peer, Col. William Frederick Cody himself. It is (14) <u>Buffalo Bill</u>!

(15) <u>For more than three decades around the turn of the century</u>, "Buffalo Bill" Cody (16) <u>toured</u> the (17) <u>country</u> with his fabulous Wild West show, (18) <u>dramatizing the legendary American frontier</u> even as the real one faded into history. Today "the last of the great scouts," as he liked to bill himself, is back in the saddle again. And once again, he is surrounded (19) <u>by some of his favorite troupers</u> from the good old days: (20) <u>sharp-shooting</u> Annie Oakley, cowboy star Buck Taylor, Indian chiefs Red Shirt and Iron Tail, and of course the great Sioux leader, Sitting Bull. This time around, though, the "show" is a bit more subdued than the original. It is a (21) <u>traveling</u>, multimedia (22) <u>exhibition</u>. Along with the films and artwork are costumes, a small arsenal of guns, and such things as a lock of his hair and a stuffed bison, all from the Buffalo Bill Historical Center in Cody, Wyoming, the town (23) <u>that William Cody helped to found in 1895</u>.

1. _M_   2. _____   3. _____   4. _____   5. _____

6. _____   7. _____   8. _____   9. _____   10. _____

11. _____   12. _____   13. _____   14. _____   15. _____

16. _____   17. _____   18. _____   19. _____   20. _____

21. _____   22. _____   23. _____

NAME _____

Identify each underlined word, phrase, or clause as a subject (S), verb (V), direct object (D. Obj.), indirect object (I. Obj.), complement (C), or modifier (M). (Some complements are modifiers. Label them either C or M.) Write your answers in the space provided below. The first is done for you as an example.

It was 38 below in Hibbing, Minnesota, when the sun kindled a purple fire (1) behind the snowy ore dumps (2) that rise up like foothills on the east side of town. Out at the fairgrounds, pickup (3) trucks (4) were already (4) rolling past a (5) striped carnival tent and into a fenced-off enclosure where, soon, a great clamor arose. (6) Huffing and puffing in the ferocious cold, (7) dozens of men and women (8) removed from their trucks (9) hundreds of excited dogs (10) which commenced to yelp, whine, clank their chains, and lap steaming water out of clattering metal pans. While bundled-up on-lookers waddled about in the confusion, (11) taking care to watch where they stepped, the dogs were hustled into harnesses, attached to sleds, and lined up. (12) "Are you ready, team?" the frosty lead (13) driver (14) bellowed at her (15) lunging chargers. "Go!" shouted the starter and, with that, the Hibbing International Sled Dog (16) Races were under way.

Many people think (17) that ever since the snowmobile revolutionized travel in the North Country two decades ago, the dog sled and the legendary huskies that pulled it have been teetering on the brink of extinction. As it happens, however, many people are (18) wrong. (19) Eskimos and Indians no longer rely on dog sleds as their principal means of transportation in the winter. The Royal Canadian Mounted Police (20) have not (20) sent out an official dog patrol since 1969. But as events in Hibbing and elsewhere make abundantly clear, dog (21) sledding seems to be in the midst of a revival these days. The main reason is the booming popularity of a heretofore unheralded sport: sled-dog racing.

1. _*M*_   2. _____   3. _____   4. _____   5. _____

6. _____   7. _____   8. _____   9. _____   10. _____

11. _____   12. _____   13. _____   14. _____   15. _____

16. _____   17. _____   18. _____   19. _____   20. _____

21. _____

NOTES

[1] Peter Miller, "Speed Skiing," *New York Times Magazine,* 20 Feb. 1983, p. 32.

[2] John Keegan, "The Specter of Conventional War," *Harper's,* July 1983, pp. 8, 10–11.

[3] "Government to Consider Simpler Nutrition Labels," *Consumer Reports,* 48 (1983), 108.

[4] Donald Dale Jackson, "Close Encounters with the Creatures of Another World," *Smithsonian,* Nov. 1982, pp. 77–78.

[5] Peter T. White, "Nature's Dwindling Treasures: Rain Forests," *National Geographic,* 163 (1983), 19.

[6] "American Cheeses," *Consumer Reports,* 48 (1983), 62, 65–66.

[7] Rick Gore, "A Bad Time to Be a Crocodile," *National Geographic,* 153 (1978), 91–92.

[8] Jane E. Brody, "Mosquito: The Enemy Reveals Its Ways," *New York Times,* 12 July 1983, Section C, p. 1.

[9] "Update," *Science Digest,* July 1983, p. 23; "Update," *Science Digest,* Aug. 1983, p. 29; and "How to Create a Miniature Garden," *How to Grow House Plants* (Menlo Park, Calif.: Lane Books, 1972), p. 37.

[10] Jackson, p. 78.

[11] Jim Doherty, "Was He Half Hype or Sheer Hero? Buffalo Bill Takes a New Bow," *Smithsonian,* Jan. 1983, p. 59.

[12] Jim Doherty, "A Legend Still Lives as Sled Dogs Race Across the Snows," *Smithsonian,* Mar. 1983, p. 89.

SOLVING PROBLEMS OF USAGE

SENTENCE FRAGMENTS

Independent Fragments

- 1. What then are our alternatives to an unacceptable dependence on foreign oil? *To find a renewable energy resource or to cut back drastically on our consumption.*
- 2. Participation in contact sports can be dangerous for young children. *But what about marathon running? Can that, too, be risky?*
- 3. *Seaweed.* It's been called nature's oldest beauty product.[1]

In order to be a complete sentence, a group of words must contain a subject and a verb and must express a complete thought. A part of a sentence that is punctuated as if it were complete is a **sentence fragment**. Each of the italicized segments above is a sentence fragment of a special kind: an **independent fragment**. Such fragments are a natural part of our speech and can be used in writing to create effects ranging from the urgent tone of an expert speaking to concerned listeners about a problem to the informal tone of conversation. The writers of the first two examples each assume the role of speaker, the first somewhat more formal than the second. The writer of the first example poses and answers an important question. Although the answer—*To find a renewable energy resource or to cut back drastically on our consumption*—is a fragment, it conveys a complete meaning in this context.

In the second example, the question—*But what about marathon running?*—is incomplete, but it, too, conveys a complete meaning in its context. In addition, this fragment suggests the development of thought natural to conversation.

As the third example shows, a one-word fragment, too, can be useful, causing readers to concentrate on one thing or idea. In this case, *Seaweed* provides a dramatic opening for a paragraph.

A fragment that conveys completeness of meaning in its context can be a useful tool for a writer.

Unacceptable Fragments

   x 1. I cannot go to the track meet tomorrow. *Because I have to study.*

   x 2. My roommate has decided to rearrange the room. *Which I like just as it is.*

   x 3. He finds it hard to live with some of his little sister's possessions. *Such as her cats, her dog, her goldfish, and her parrot.*

   x 4. *The worst part being over after my biology exam.*

   x 5. *The coach being the tyrant that she is.*

Each of the items above is a sentence fragment. Like independent fragments, these are partial sentences punctuated as if they were complete. Unlike independent fragments, these do not convey complete meanings. Clauses beginning with *because* or *which* are frequent sources of difficulty. To revise such fragments, join the *because* or *which* clause to the preceding sentence.

   • 1. I cannot go to the track meet tomorrow, because I have to study.

   • 2. My roommate has decided to rearrange the room, which I like just as it is.

A list of examples (following such words and phrases as *for example, for instance,* or *such as*) is a fragment when it stands by itself. To revise, join the list to the previous sentence:

   • 3. He finds it hard to live with some of his little sister's pets, such as her cats, her dog, her goldfish, and her parrot.

Examples 4 and 5 illustrate a different sort of fragment: the use of *being* as if it were a full verb. To revise you can change *being* to a full verb:

   • 4. The worst part *was* over after my biology exam.

Or you can make the participial phrase (*being* is a participle) a modifier in a complete sentence:

   • 5. The coach, *being the tyrant that she is,* will probably make us work out at 5:30 a.m. even on Saturday.

A third possibility is to use the participial phrase as an *absolute phrase,* which, instead of modifying a particular word, acts like an adverb to the rest of the sentence in which it appears:

   • *The coach being the tyrant that she is,* the workouts will probably begin early.

SUMMARY

Partial sentences punctuated as if they were complete are sentence fragments. Independent fragments convey complete meaning in their contexts and are often useful. Fragments that do not convey complete meaning should be revised.

Exercise 2–1[2]

NAME _____

In the space provided below, indicate which of the numbered sentences is a fragment. Circle any independent fragments.

(1) You expect a lot of sodium in salty foods, and one bite tells you that bacon is salty. (2) But how about a sweet pudding? (3) One half-cup of some instant puddings contains 404 milligrams of sodium, 102 milligrams more than a three-slice serving of bacon. (4) In fact, there is sodium in almost everything you eat. (5) From the briniest pickles to the sweetest chocolate syrups and candy bars.

_____   _____   _____   _____   _____

Exercise 2–2[3]

In the spaces provided at the right, indicate whether each of the following word groups is a sentence (S) or a fragment (F). Circle the fragments that could be used independently if they were answers to questions.

Examples: a) Speed skiing is a dangerous sport.   *S*

  b) Both the mental and physical demands.   *F*

1. Europeans were the first to keep records of speed-skiing times.   _____

2. In 1960, Luigi di Marco became the first skier to break 100 miles an hour.   _____

3. An annual event and a national sport.   _____

4. They must be in peak condition physically.   _____

5. To hold position against the force of the air.   _____

6. No doubt because of its rigors.   _____

7. There are only about 200 speed skiers in the world.   _____

8. Thirty of whom can make it into world class competition.   _____

9. Danger is ever present.   _____

10. Five fatalities in four decades.   _____

Exercise 2–3

NAME _____

Revise each of the fragments in the previous exercise by rewriting it as an independent clause (complete sentence), by joining it to the sentence before or after it, or by supplying a question to which it could serve as an answer.

Example: Both the mental and physical demands of
the sport are immense.

_____

_____

_____

_____

_____

_____

_____

_____

_____

Exercise 2—4

NAME _____

Each of the following passages has at least one sentence fragment. Join the fragments to preceding or following sentences or convert them to independent clauses. Write the revised version in the space provided below.

Example: College is more interesting than high school. Not only in class but outside class too.

College is more interesting than high school, not only in class but outside class too.

1. On Saturday I stay up late going to parties or just talking with my friends. Which I did not do very often when I was in high school.

_____

_____

_____

2. A three-day hiking trip requires stamina, good humor, and the proper equipment. Such as a well-designed backpack, sturdy hiking boots, and a good flashlight. And, of course, nourishing, probably freeze-dried food.

_____

_____

_____

3. In Florida we saw an enormous sea turtle. A dead one. It had been washed up on the beach.

_____

_____

4. No one knows who invented glasses, but many thousands of people have benefited from the invention. One that we cannot now imagine being without.

_____

_____

_____

5. Finals week is the worst and the best week of the semester. The worst part being the finals, the best part being free of them. At the beginning everyone stays up all night in fear. At the end everyone stays up all night, too. But in relief and excitement.

_____

_____

_____

Exercise 2—5[4]

NAME _____

The following paragraph has eight unacceptable fragments. In the spaces provided below, indicate the number of each fragment. The first is done for you as an example.

(1) Archeology and baseball have a lot in common. (2) Some scholars prefer to call baseball a science. (3) It is not. (4) Since events can scarcely ever be duplicated by experiment. (5) Or predicted beforehand. (6) It is not mathematics. (7) Though it has a high degree of mathematical beauty. (8) It is not engineering. (9) In spite of its sturdy and enduring forms. (10) For the stresses are never quite under control. (11) It is not art, where the creator can organize his shapes and colors. (12) To express his purposes and change them if he wants. (13) "He wishes he had that pitch back"; but he never will. (14) He may be picture perfect, an artist on the mound, yet he is a workman. (15) Subject to fortune's wind. (16) But an archeologist, never certain what he will find under the earth, never able to dig the same dirt twice with the same results, is in a profession similar to baseball. (17) Where unpredictable and unrepeatable events are life's blood.

<u> 4 </u>   _____   _____   _____   _____   _____   _____

Exercise 2—6

Revise the fragments from the previous paragraph and write your revisions in the space provided below.

_____

_____

_____

_____

_____

_____

_____

_____

_____

Exercise 2—7

NAME _____

Write two independent sentence fragments, supplying the context that makes them independent. In addition, if there is an unacceptable fragment in your writing, revise it and write it below.

1. _____

_____

2. _____

_____

3. _____

_____

PREDICATION

- 1. The volcano erupted.

- 2. More than 600,000 people taped the last episode of M*A*S*H.

- 3. Hitting the umpire is self-defeating.

To make a predication is to put a predicate together with a subject in order to say something. *The volcano* is a subject matched with the predicate *erupted*. *More than 600,000 people* is a subject matched with the predicate *taped the last episode of M*A*S*H*. And *Hitting the umpire* is a subject matched with the predicate *is self-defeating*.

A predication error occurs when the subject and some part of the predicate do not go together, when they are mismatched:

   x One *reason* sports are so popular *is because* many people were athletic when they were young.

The simple subject, verb, and complement of this sentence are *reason is because*. But *reason* cannot be *because*. A complement must function as a noun (identifying or explaining the subject) or as an adjective (describing or characterizing the subject). *Reason* cannot be identified, explained, or described by *because*. To revise this sentence, we can say *The reason is that*:

- The *reason* sports are so popular *is that* many people were athletic when they were young.

A similar kind of mismatching occurs in the following sentence:

   x Real *friendship is when* my roommate typed my paper for me.

This sentence says *friendship is when*. But *when*, which is neither noun nor adjective, cannot characterize or explain *friendship*.

Of course not just any noun will work, as the following example shows:

   x Real *friendship is* my *roommate* when she typed my paper for me.

Although both the subject and the complement are nouns, *friendship*, an abstract noun, cannot *be* a person. Possible ways to rewrite this sentence are

- By typing my paper for me, my *roommate showed that* she was a real friend.
- My *roommate gave* new *meaning* to the word *friendship* when she typed my paper for me.

63

In the following example the mismatching occurs because a prepositional phrase is made to occupy the position of subject:

x *For* students working their way through college always *have problems* with money.

To locate a workable subject, we can ask *who has problems.* Since students have problems, *students* should be the subject.

• *Students* working their way through college always *have problems* with money.

Some predication errors are structural problems involving relative pronouns:

x 1. The man from India told us about many *things which* we had not heard of *them* before.
x 2. But if you have a *roommate that neither of you* has any hobbies in common, you will not get along.

In the first sentence, *which* refers to *things* and functions in its own clause as the object of the preposition *of.* The problem arises because an unnecessary *them* has been inserted as object of the preposition. *Them* is unnecessary because its function is already filled by the relative pronoun *which.* Revising requires omitting *them*:

• The man from India told us about many *things which* we had not heard of before.

The second sentence seems to be a combination of two structures that cannot work together: *If neither of you (has anything in common with the other)* and *If you have a roommate who (has no hobbies in common with you).* The word *that* in *If you have a roommate that neither of you* refers to roommate but has no function in the clause it introduces. Possible ways to revise the sentence are:

• It is not easy to get along with a roommate with whom you have no hobbies in common.
• If you have a roommate with whom you have no hobbies in common, getting along will not be easy.

SUMMARY

To predicate something is to choose a predicate to go with a subject. Faulty predication occurs when the subject and some part of the predicate do not logically or grammatically go together. Locate the important grammatical words (subject, verb, objects, and complement) and make sure that they work together.

Exercise 2—8

NAME _____

Each of the following sentences has an error in predication. In the space provided, rewrite enough of the sentence to revise appropriately. In some cases you may need to rewrite the whole sentence.

Example: Faulty predication is when the subject and predicate are mismatched. *Faulty predication occurs when . . .*

1. The situation in the Middle East is an equally dangerous area.

_____

2. The best dessert is my mother when she makes apple pie.

_____

3. The writing teacher will have office hours until 4:00 p.m. tomorrow, which she usually does not stay until then.

_____

4. One of the jokes I really liked was the day we hid the Bunsen burners.

_____

5. Just because you got a C+ on the first paper is no reason you cannot get an A in the course.

_____

6. Robert Burns wrote many songs that people do not know that he wrote them.

_____

7. Taking a swimming class is one place you have to learn to depend on yourself.

_____

8. Why Eve offered Adam the apple is because she did not want to be selfish with it.

_____

9. Elm Street which was blocked to traffic was because of the trees that fell during the storm.

_____

10. My roommate and I have agreed that the one which has company, the other one will leave.

_____

Exercise 2—9

NAME _____

If your teacher has indicated that a sentence in your writing has a predication error (or if you have located such a sentence yourself), revise it and write both the original and revised versions in the space provided below.

_____

_____

_____

_____

NOUNS

Number

SINGULAR	PLURAL
town	many towns
pancake	18 pancakes
flavor	31 flavors
fox	two foxes
child	a dozen children
ox	several oxen
leaf	fall leaves
mouse	many mice
body	several bodies
monkey	too many monkeys

Nouns are the names of people, places, things, and ideas. As you have seen, they function in sentences in various ways—as subjects, objects, etc. Nouns that can be counted are either *singular* (one) or *plural* (more than one). Most nouns are made plural by the addition of -*s* or -*es* (one pancake, 18 pancakes; one fox, two foxes). Nouns ending in *y* are a special case. They are made plural by the addition of -*s* if the *y* is preceded by a vowel: monkeys. But if the *y* is preceded by a consonant, the *y* changes to *i* before the addition of -*es*: body—bodies. Some nouns are irregular and require an irregular spelling change for the plural form: one child, a dozen *children*; one mouse, many *mice*.

Possessive Case

SINGULAR POSSESSIVE	PLURAL POSSESSIVE
child's reaction	children's reaction
boy's room	boys' room
fox's hole	foxes' hole
hero's reward	heroes' reward

The other change in a noun's form indicates possession. The identifying mark of the possessive case is the apostrophe. Add -*'s* to the singular form to make the singular possessive (hero's reward). If the plural form is made by adding -*s* or -*es* (*boys, heroes*), the plural possessive is made by adding an apostrophe after the *s* (*boys'* room, *heroes'* reward). If a plural form is irregular (*child, children*), the plural possessive is made by adding -*'s* to the plural form (*children's*).

double possessive

- the death of Lincoln
- the dreams *of young men*
- the drawings *of my sister*
- **x** that cousin *of Ellen*

- Lincoln's death
- *young men's dreams*
- the drawings *of my sister's*, my *sister's* drawings
- that cousin *of Ellen's*, *Ellen's* cousin

The possessive case can often be expressed by a prepositional phrase (*the dreams of young men*) as well as by -'s. It is usually a mistake to use both forms at once: **x** *the dreams of young men's*. Sometimes, however, the meaning can be clarified by using a double possessive: *the drawings of my sister* may mean the drawings she drew or the drawings drawn of her; to make the possessive meaning entirely clear, we can say *the drawings of my sister's*. The double possessive is regularly used with the name of a person—*that cousin of Ellen's*—except when the relationship of possession is unique or very well known: *the mother of John, the plays of Shakespeare*.

subject of gerund

- **x** We can hardly object to the tobacco company president smoking a cigar.
- We can hardly object to the tobacco company president's smoking a cigar.

The subject of a gerund is usually in the possessive case. In the example above, president is the subject of the gerund *smoking*. This form should be distinguished from a participle modifying a preceding noun:

- 1. I heard the *child playing* the toy xylophone all night.
- 2. The *child's playing* the toy xylophone all night kept me awake.

In the first sentence *playing* is a modifier; in the second *playing* is a noun and functions as the subject of the sentence.

SUMMARY

Nouns are the names of people, places, things, and ideas. Nouns that can be counted are either singular or plural. They are made plural by the addition of -*s* or -*es* or by an irregular spelling change. The other change in a noun's form indicates possession. The identifying mark of the possessive is the apostrophe. The possessive can also be expressed with a prepositional phrase (*the child's* or *of the child*). A double possessive is to be avoided except in special cases when it clarifies meaning. The subject of a gerund is usually in the possessive case.

Exercise 2—10

NAME _____

Give the plural form of each of the following words. Check your dictionary as necessary.

Example: porch __*porches*__

1. cottage _____   6. story _____

2. key _____   7. louse _____

3. vehicle _____   8. campus _____

4. life _____   9. company _____

5. box _____   10. friend _____

Give the singular and plural possessive forms of the following words. The first one is done for you as an example.

	SINGULAR	PLURAL
1. cottage	*cottage's*	*cottages'*
2. life	_____	_____
3. box	_____	_____
4. story	_____	_____
5. fish	_____	_____
6. family	_____	_____

Exercise 2—11

NAME _____

Change the following phrases to the corresponding possessive forms.

Example: *The treason of Benedict Arnold:* _Benedict Arnold's treason_

1. The mysteries of Edmund Crispin: _____

2. The exercises of the workbook: _____

3. The beauty of women: _____

4. The life of an immigrant: _____

5. The highlight of the evening: _____

6. The aches and pains of childhood _____

7. The equipment of the divers: _____

8. The experience of the student: _____

9. The form of the noun: _____

10. The end of the day: _____

Exercise 2—12

NAME _____

If there are one or more errors in the formation or use of the possessive in the following sentences, circle them and supply the correct form(s) in the space provided. If a sentence needs no correction, write C.

Example: Benjamin Franklin was trained
in his (brothers) printing shop. _____*brother's*_____

1. Benjamin Franklin flying a kite to test the electricity of a thunderstorm is well known. _____

2. Also well known is one of Franklins books, *Poor Richards Almanac.* _____

3. The Franklin stove, a cast-iron heating stove which looks like an open fireplace, is an invention of Franklin's. _____

4. Franklin signing the Declaration of Independence followed a long period of diplomatic service in England and preceded an appointment to negotiate a treaty with France. _____

5. The autobiography of this famous statesman's reveals his practicality and his faith in people. _____

PRONOUNS

PERSONAL PRONOUNS			
singular	subjective	objective	possessive
First Person	I	me	my, mine
Second Person	you	you	your, yours
Third Person	he	him	his
	she	her	her, hers
	it	it	its
plural			
First Person	we	us	our, ours
Second Person	you	you	your, yours
Third Person	they	them	their, theirs
RELATIVE PRONOUNS			
	who	whom	whose
	which	which	of which
	that	that	
INTERROGATIVE PRONOUNS			
	who?	whom?	whose?

Personal pronouns substitute for nouns. As the chart indicates, they are *singular* or *plural* and undergo extensive changes in form to show changes in function. The **subjective case** (for example, *I, we*) is used for subjects and complements; the **objective case** (for example, *me, him, her, them*) is used for direct and indirect objects and objects of prepositions; the **possessive case** is used to show possession and for subjects of gerunds. Unlike nouns, pronouns change form to show changes in *person*. As the chart indicates, *I, we, me, us,* etc. are called first person; *you, your,* and *yours* are called second person; and *he, she, it, they,* etc. are called third person.

Choice of Case

subjective case for subjects/objective case for objects

- **x** *Her and me went* together.
- • *She* and *I* went together.

- **x** *Us* fellows hid the Bunsen burners.
- • *We* fellows hid the Bunsen burners.

Use the subjective form for pronouns that function as subjects (*she and I,* not *her and me*). As you would not say *Me went by myself,* you should not say *Her and me went together.* When a pronoun is followed by the noun for which it stands (*us fellows, we fellows*), you can determine the case of the pronoun by temporarily dropping the noun. As you would not say **x** *Us hid the Bunsen burners,* you should not say **x** *Us fellows hid them.*

x The dean put *we fellows* on probation.
• The dean put *us fellows* on probation.

Do not overcorrect. When pronouns are used as objects, use the objective form. Again, when you use a pronoun followed by a noun, omit the noun to see how the sentence sounds. Since you would say *The dean put us on probation,* you should say *The dean put us fellows on probation.*

pronoun case before -self and -selves

x He hurt *hisself* while skiing.
• He hurt *himself* while skiing.

x The Lord helps those who help *theirselves.*
• The Lord helps those who help *themselves.*

Except in the third-person masculine singular (*himself*) and in the third-person plural (*themselves*), -*self* and -*selves* are added to the possessive form of the personal pronoun: myself, ourselves; yourself, yourselves; herself, *him*self, itself, *them*selves.

possessive case

DISTANT OBJECT:
x I typed *she and her brother's reports.*
• I typed *her and her brother's reports.*

Use the possessive case even when the pronoun is far away from the object possessed. As you would not say, **x** *I typed she reports,* you should not say **x** *I typed she and her brother's reports.*

SUBJECT OF GERUND:
x I objected to *him using my desk* without asking me.
• I objected to *his using my desk* without asking me.

As is true for nouns, the possessive case of pronouns is usually used for the subject of a gerund: • I objected to *his using my desk.* (Do not confuse the subject of a gerund with a pronoun modified by a participle. The latter is common after verbs such as *hear* and *see:* • *I saw him using my desk;* • *I heard them running*

74

up the stairs. In these sentences *him* and *them* are objects of *saw* and *heard* and are modified by the *-ing* forms.) Further examples of subject of gerund in possessive case:

- The teacher was surprised at *their* offering to clean the lab.
- She was less surprised when she learned of *their* hiding the Bunsen burners.

interrogative pronoun case: who versus whom

x *Who* did you ask?	• *Whom* did you ask?
x *Whom* do you think you are?	• *Who* do you think you are?
x *Who* does this belong to?	• *To whom* does this belong?
x *Whom* is without faults?	• *Who* is without faults?

The distinction between *who* and *whom,* although often ignored in conversation, is still retained in standard written English. People who might easily say *Who did you ask?* prefer *whom* when such a sentence is written. To determine which to use, answer the question with a sentence containing a personal pronoun: *I asked him.* If the pronoun answer is objective, the question word (*who/whom*) should be objective too.

relative pronoun case: who versus whom

- x The man *who* I gave the message to said he was the sales manager.
- • The man *to whom* I gave the message said he was the sales manager.

The problem of choosing between *who* (subjective) and *whom* (objective) occurs in using relative as well as interrogative pronouns. The case of a relative pronoun is determined by its function in its own clause. In the example above, the relative pronoun is the object of the preposition *to* and must therefore be in the objective case: • the man *to whom* I gave the message.

Do not overcorrect. Avoid training your ear to prefer *whom* in all instances.

confusingly similar forms

its/it's   whose/who's   there/their/they're

Its is a possessive form and means *belonging to it. It's,* on the other hand, is a contraction; the apostrophe indicates that a letter has been left out (*it is* contracts to *it's*). Like *its, whose* is a possessive form and does not have an apostrophe, while *who's* like *it's* is a contraction (*who is* contracts to *who's*). These words sound alike but have different meanings.

Their, like *its* and *whose,* is a possessive form. *They're* is a contraction (*they are* contracts to *they're*). *There* sounds similar to both but is different in meaning.

SUMMARY

Pronouns change form to show changes in function. Use the subjective case for subjects and the objective case for objects. Use the possessive case to show possession; generally use the possessive case for the subject of a gerund. Distinguish between confusingly similar forms (for example, *its/it's*).

Exercise 2—13

NAME _____

Choose the correct pronoun and write it in the corresponding space at the right. The first one is done for you as an example.

Samuel Langhorne Clemens was a steamboat pilot, miner, newspaperman, and printer. He was also a famous novelist, (1. who/whom) many of his readers would not recognize except by his pen name —Mark Twain. Even after we know of (2. him/his) adopting it, we are so used to *Mark Twain* as a name that we are likely not to think of (3. its/it's) original meaning—*two fathoms deep.* Creating (4. himself/ hisself) as a character is related to (5. him/his) using his personal experience for stories. The writer Mark Twain is, in part, a made-up character and, in part, S. L. Clemens, (6. whose/who's) experience is the basis for the adventures of his made-up characters.

Perhaps his most famous characters are Tom Sawyer and Huckleberry Finn, each of (7. who/whom) appears in the other's story. The former is romantic, enterprising, and self-reliant, but the latter is the one (8. whose/who's) story is the more remarkable of the two.

Huck is imprisoned in different ways by his tramplike father, on the one hand, and by the very proper Widow Douglas and her sister, Miss Watson, on the other, all three of (9. who/whom) try to make Huck into something he isn't. Although living with a drunken father has its disadvantages, (10. him/his) staying with the widow and her sister is equally intolerable. Huck is far happier when he escapes them all and floats down the Mississippi with Jim, Miss Watson's runaway slave (11. who/whom) he helps in the journey to freedom and from (12. who/whom) he learns practical wisdom. On the raft, (13. he/him) and Jim are not only two runaways, but man and boy. As we watch (14. them/their) surviving and enjoying (15. there/their/they're) adventures, we see that Mark Twain is demonstrating admirable ethical standards through (16. there/their/they're) conduct and not through the legal and moral systems of those living in towns along the river.

1. _whom_

2. _____

3. _____

4. _____

5. _____

6. _____

7. _____

8. _____

9. _____

10. _____

11. _____

12. _____

13. _____

14. _____

15. _____

16. _____

Pronoun Reference

1. **x** The *St. Patrick's* Day parade was held yesterday. *He* was an Irish saint.
   - The parade in honor of *St. Patrick* was held yesterday. *He* was an Irish saint.

2. **x** The governor pardoned the condemned criminal. *It* angered many people.
   - The governor pardoned the condemned criminal. *His doing so* angered many people.

3. **x** After my uncle visited my father in Hawaii, *he* decided to write a story about it.
   - After visiting my father in Hawaii, my uncle decided to write a story about his experiences.

Personal pronouns allow us to avoid repeating nouns, but the pronouns have no meaning of their own. They get their meaning from the nouns for which they substitute. The noun for which a pronoun substitutes or to which it refers is called an **antecedent**. Problems arise when the antecedent is *not specific* or *not clear*. In the third example—*After my uncle visited my father in Hawaii, he decided to write a story about it*—*he* may refer to *father* or *uncle* and *it* may refer to *Hawaii* or to an unspecified antecedent such as *his trip* or *his experience*. Implied rather than specified antecedents occur in the other examples as well. Because *It* in *It angered many people* does not refer specifically to a preceding word or idea, the reader must work to clarify the writer's meaning. The first example may seem less offensive, but it, too, is imprecise. *He* of *He was an Irish saint* refers to a possessive form *St. Patrick's*.

Agreement—Pronoun Shifts

1. Writing is difficult. Right now I'd rather be sitting in the sun on the library steps.
   x When *a person* is there, *you* feel very relaxed.
   - When *I'm* there *I* feel very relaxed.
   - When *people* are there *they* feel very relaxed.
   - When *you're* there *you* feel very relaxed.

2. **x** *Anyone* who knows *their* material well and can present it in an interesting way is a good lecturer.
   - *People* who know *their* material well . . .

3. *Everyone* must decide for *himself* how to vote.
   - *All* people must decide for *themselves* how to vote.

Pronouns should generally be consistent in person and always be consistent in number with the nouns or pronouns to which they refer. You should not shift in the same sentence from one person to another (**x** *When a person is there,* *you feel very relaxed* should be revised in one of the ways suggested above), and you should not shift from singular to plural. Words like *anyone, each, anything, everyone, no one, neither, either, someone, something* and *nothing* are singular and should not be matched with *they, them,* and *their.* Sentences matching these singular forms with plural pronouns (for example, **x** *Anyone who knows their material can be an interesting lecturer*) are often heard in conversation but are not acceptable in writing.

In the past, the masculine forms—*he, him,* and *his*—were used to refer to both men and women. For example, in the sentence *Everyone must decide for himself how to vote, himself* was taken to include both sexes, not just men. This use of masculine forms has, however, become increasingly unacceptable. *Everyone must decide for themselves* would allow writers to avoid the masculine form, but such a shift from singular to plural (*everyone—themselves*) is still unacceptable in standard written English. Using both the masculine and feminine forms (*decide for himself or herself*) will sometimes work, but a whole passage written that way would be tiresome. The best solution is to use plural forms whenever possible: • *All people must decide for themselves how to vote.*

They: Not Equal to *Someone* or *Anyone*

1. **x** *They* said on the radio that it is going to rain.
   • The radio announcer predicted rain.

2. **x** *They* say in the financial aid office that the new budget cuts will cause about half of us to lose our loans.
   • The people in the financial office say . . .
   • The financial aid director says . . .

3. • If you want to learn to ski, you will first have to learn to fall down.

4. • Any student knows that *you* can't get away with a four-page term paper.
   • Anyone knows that a student can't get away . . .
   • Students know that they can't get away . . .

You should avoid using *they* to mean *someone, everyone,* or *people.* Revise in order to express your meaning more precisely. *The financial aid director says* or even *someone in the financial aid office said* is more precise than **x** *They say in the financial aid office.* If you want to address your reader directly, you should of course use the pronoun *you.* In the third example above the writer is addressing the reader, and there are, of course, numerous examples of the writer's addressing the reader in this workbook. Further, if you should want to create an informal tone, you can use *you* to mean *one* or *everyone.* In the fourth set of sentences above, any of the choices would work, depending on the tone of the rest of the piece.

80

SUMMARY

Personal pronouns should be clearly related to the nouns to which they refer. Unspecified or unclear antecedents create confusion. Do not shift between singular and plural pronouns, and do not shift from one person to another in the same sentence. Avoid using *they* to mean someone, everyone, or people in general.

Exercise 2—14

NAME _____

Choose the correct pronoun and write it in the corresponding space provided at the right. In some cases more than one choice may be correct. The first is done for you as an example.

The most famous Scotsman may be Robert Burns, (1. who, whom) wrote or rewrote songs that everyone has heard since (2. their, his, her, no pronoun) childhood. He wrote many songs that (3. you, people) probably recognize whether or not (4. you, they) know of Robert Burns. How many people, for example, know (5. who, whom) wrote "Auld Lang Syne"? Although along with other English speakers (6. we, us) Americans sing it every New Year's just at midnight, how many of us realized it was in Scots dialect? Burns was also famous for being in love with many women, to one or all of (7. who, whom) he might have written "My Love Is Like a Red, Red Rose," another song in Scots dialect. Although he never came to America (8. hisself, himself), Scottish immigrants brought Burns with them, because it was (9. they, them) (10. who, whom) brought his songs. It is, therefore, to (11. they, them) as well as to Burns that we owe our thanks for

1. ___who___

2. _____

3. _____

4. _____

5. _____

6. _____

7. _____

8. _____

9. _____

10. _____

11. _____

> Should auld acquaintance be forgot
>   And never brought to mind?
> Should auld acquaintance be forgot
>   and auld lang syne!
>
> *Chorus:*
>
> For auld lang syne my jo,
>   For auld lang syne,
> We'll take a cup o' kindness yet
>   For auld lang syne.

Exercise 2–15[5]

NAME   _____

Several of the sentences in the following passage have pronoun problems. In the space provided after the passage, revise each problem sentence. If a sentence needs no revision, write NR in the space provided. The first one is done for you as an example.

1. They made the first practical fountain pen in the 1880s. 2. Although it was an improvement over previous pens, they had many disadvantages. 3. Unlike a pencil, it had to be held right-side up and at a certain angle. 4. They were apt to splotch and leak and unless you used a blotter, you had to wait for the ink to dry.

5. In 1938, they invented the ballpoint pen, and they promised to solve all the shortcomings of the fountain pen. 6. The ballpoint was in demand by the military during World War II, since they were better suited to the battlefield than the fountain pen was. 7. There was great demand for the first ballpoints, which were sold to the public in 1945. 8. Eager customers formed long lines; everyone wanted to buy the new pen because they heard that it could even write under water. 9. But the first ballpoints did not write well: their ink clogged and corroded the balls, and they tended to leak. 10. The ballpoint was rescued from disrepute by the development of a better ink. 11. By 1952, it was outselling the fountain pen two to one.

1. The first practical fountain pen was made in the 1880s.

_____

_____

_____

_____

_____

_____

_____

_____

_____

_____

_____

_____

VERBS

PRINCIPAL PARTS			
	infinitive (base)	past tense	past participle
Regular	walk ignore promise	walked ignored promised	walked ignored promised
Irregular	sing sit cost buy	sang sat cost bought	sung sat cost bought

Tense

Present: • I *buy* an ice cream cone at Baskin Robbins every day.

Past: • I *bought* one yesterday.

Future: • I *will buy* one tomorrow.

Present {

Present: • I *hear* the doorbell.

Present Progressive: is + [base]-ing
• My roommate's dog *is barking*.

Present Perfect: has + [base]-ed / have + [base]-ed
• My roommate *has helped* me with geometry for six months.

Past {

Past: [base]-ed
• I *watched* the 1983 World Series on T.V.

Past Progressive: was + [base]-ing
• I *was planning* to go to the games.

Past Perfect: had + [base]-ed
• I *had counted* on buying my tickets at the gate.

Future {

Future: will + [base]
• He *will turn in* his paper tomorrow.

Future Progressive: will be + [base]-ing
• He *will be writing* it all night.

Future Perfect: will have + [base]-ed
• He *will have typed* it by the time you get up.

Every verb has three principal parts. The first part is the **infinitive** or **base form** (*ask*). The other two parts are the **past** (*asked*) and the **past participle** (*asked*). In regular verbs (those that follow the usual pattern), the latter two parts are made by adding *-ed* to the base form. Other verbs are irregular, which means that their principal parts are formed by changes in spelling rather than by the addition of *-ed*. See the inside back cover of this workbook for a list of principal parts of irregular verbs. When you are unsure about principal parts, check your dictionary.

The three major tenses are past (*I bought an ice cream cone*), present (*I buy an ice cream cone every day*), and future (*I will buy an ice cream cone tomorrow*). All tenses are formed from (1) the three principal parts, (2) the present participle (*-ing* form), various parts of the verbs *be, do,* and *have,* and the auxiliary verb *will.* **Tense** allows us to express occurrences in time (*She studied hard yesterday*) and to express the relation of one time with another (*I will call you before I leave* or *I will sign the Pass/Not Pass form after you finish the last paper*).

In general, the **present tense** expresses action that is occurring now:

- I *hear* the doorbell.
- I *want* Swiss almond vanilla on a plain cone.

or action that occurs frequently or customarily:

- Italians *drink* a lot of espresso.
- She *teaches* aerobics four nights a week.

The **past tense** expresses action completed in the past:

- Air fares from New York to the west coast *went* up last week.

And the **future tense** indicates action that will occur after another action or at a later time:

- I *will ask* her to call after she wakes up.
- They *will arrive* between 9:00 and 10:00 in the morning.

The **progressive tenses** indicate action that is in progress in the present:

- No one *is studying* now.

action that was in progress in the past:

- I *was studying* when the fire alarm went off.

and action that will be in progress in the future:

- *Will* anyone *be studying* tomorrow during the football game?

Perfect tenses indicate action that was completed before another action began or before a certain time:

- Most of the freshmen *have taken* advantage of the orientation tour offered by the library.
- He *had studied* Spanish only one year before he went to Mexico.
- She *will have typed* the paper before you get up.

In addition, the **present perfect** indicates action which began in the past but continues in the present:

- My grandmother *has lived* in St. Louis for many years.

sequence of tenses

- **x** 1. Yesterday after finishing the exam, Eve *thought* she *makes* a C.
- **x** 2. But this morning she *had discovered* that she *is making* an A.
- **x** 3. She *hopes* that she *had gotten* another A.

In a sentence or longer passage, the first verb establishes a point of reference for the verbs that follow. This relationship between verbs we call **sequence of tenses**, and this sequence expresses a precise sense of perspective. If one of the tenses does not belong to the orderly sequence, a reader or listener will be disturbed or confused. Compare the sentences above with the revised versions that follow.

LOOKING AT THE FUTURE FROM THE PAST:
- Yesterday, after finishing the exam, Eve *thought* she *would make* a C in chemistry.

LOOKING AT THE PAST FROM THE PAST:
- But this morning she *discovered* that she *had made* an A.

LOOKING AT THE FUTURE FROM THE PRESENT:
- She *hopes* that she *will get* an A on tomorrow's physics exam.

ACTION TO BE COMPLETED AFTER OR BY A CERTAIN TIME IN THE FUTURE:
- After she *takes* that exam, she *will have finished* for the year.

CAN/COULD; WILL/WOULD

I *could* not *help* him yesterday. I *can help* him today.

She *hoped* she *would get* a B. Now she *hopes* she *will get* an A.

Could and *would* may be thought of as the past tenses of *can* and *will*. When a main verb such as *hope, think, say, ask,* or *insist* is in the present tense, it may be followed by *can* or *will*. If the same verbs are in the past, they will be followed by *could* or *would*.

- I *hope* I *can go*. He *thinks* he *can finish* by tomorrow.
- I *hoped* I *could go*. He *thought* he *could finish* by tomorrow.
- Every week I *say* I *will do* my homework on Friday night.
- Every week I *said* I *would do* my homework on Friday night.
- Yesterday after finishing the exam, Eve *thought* she *would make* a C in chemistry.

SUMMARY

A verb has three principal parts, regularly formed by adding *-ed* to the base form of the verb and irregularly formed by changes in spelling. Verbs have three major tenses: present, past, and future. These plus the other tenses are formed from one of the three principal parts (often in combination with forms of *be, do,* and *have* or with the auxiliary verb *will*) or from the present participle (always in combination with a form of *be*). Tenses are used to express occurrences in time and the relationship of one time with another. In a sentence or longer passage, each of the verbs has a precise time relationship with the other verbs, which we call sequence of tenses. A disrupted sequence of tenses creates confusion for a reader or listener.

Exercise 2—16

NAME _____

In some of the following sentences -ed forms have been omitted. If the sentence is correct, write C in the space provided at the right. If not, circle the incorrect forms and write the correct ones in the spaces provided at the right.

Example: My freshman roommate fast one day a week and gave her food money to UNICEF.   ___*fasted*___

1. The plane that crash in New Orleans was carrying 250 people.   _____

2. Everything was suppose to be lock up by 5:00 p.m.   _____

3. The coach undoubtedly influenced the board's decision.   _____

4. The people who organize this party were not very organized.   _____

5. Because air fares have increased, many students can go home for a visit only once a year.   _____

6. The man from Indonesia asked me if I had ever taste monkey brains.   _____

7. What I am suppose to do and what I will do can be very different.   _____

8. The Rent-a-Wreck clerk said he fill the tank before he gave me the car, but the gauge is sitting on empty after twenty miles. I am fairly sure Rent-a-Wreck is a trustworthy used-car place.   _____

9. That Columbus discovered America in 1492 is just about the first fact that everyone learns.   _____

10. Tobacco companies use to be able to advertise cigarettes on T.V.   _____

Exercise 2–17[6]

NAME _____

Write the correct form of the verb in parentheses in the space provided. Remember that the first verbs in the passage establish the sequence of tense for the whole. The first one is done for you as an example.

It is understandable that early peoples blamed storms on the gods, praying and sacrificing to them in hopes of calming their violence. More than a thousand years before the modern notion of hurricanes was understood, Asians (think) 1. _thought_ that storms of all kinds were caused by a variety of weather gods. Ancient China (have) 2. _____ a separate god for wind (Feng Po) and for rain (Yu Shih), as well as an enormous dragon god (Lung Wang) whose breath (stir) 3. _____ up storms and to whom the temple priests (can) 4. _____ pray for relief, which they (do) 5. _____ by making his image in wood and paper. Once when Lung Wang (fail) 6. _____ to stop a downpour, the priests (imprison) 7. _____ his image for five days, evidently in the hope that he (will) 8. _____ think twice next time. Rain gods were also asked to ease droughts. And the Japanese (have) 9. _____ a practical punishment for their god if he did not respond: when their prayers (bring) 10. _____ no rain, they (toss) 11. _____ his image into the parched fields to give him a taste of the drought.

Exercise 2–18[7]

If the italicized verb is in the correct tense sequence, write C in the space provided below. If not, write the correct form. Remember that the first verb determines the sequence. The first one is done for you as an example.

Coffee starts out as a bean growing on a windy hill. Thereafter, its life (1) *will get* tougher. The bean (2) *had to be harvested* at just the right time. After it is dried, (3) *it would be roasted*. It (4) *may be processed* to produce decaffeinated coffee. And it certainly (5) *would be ground*, sooner or later, to grains fine enough to suit filter, drip, percolator, or vacuum brewing. These days, drip grind (6) *will be* the best-selling coffee category.

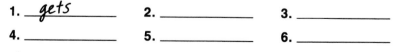

1. _gets_   2. _____   3. _____

4. _____   5. _____   6. _____

Voice: Active and Passive

ACTIVE	PASSIVE
Odysseus *blinded* the Cyclops.	The Cyclops *was blinded* by Odysseus.
Eli Whitney *invented* the cotton gin.	The cotton gin *was invented* by Eli Whitney.
My dog *bit* the guest of honor.	The guest of honor *was bitten* by my dog.

The **voice** of a verb indicates whether the subject does something (*The dog bit*) or has something done to it (*The guest was bitten*). In the **active voice,** the subject is the actor. Eli Whitney did something. He invented the cotton gin. In the **passive voice** the subject names the receiver or the object of the action: *The cotton gin was invented; The guest was bitten.* The direct objects of the active verbs (*cotton gin* and *guest*) become the subjects of the passive verbs.

The passive voice is formed with forms of *be* plus the past participle:

PRESENT:
- Rolls Royces *are made* in England.

PAST:
- Her shoes *were made* in Italy.

FUTURE:
- The bread *will be made* by tomorrow morning.

Passive voice is useful when the actor or agent is unknown or when the thing done is more important than the doer of it. For example, when processes are described, the product is often the focus of interest:

- Cheese *is* often *called* the wine of foods. The diversity of cheese starts with the milk it *is made* from. The fat content *can be adjusted* by skimming the milk or adding cream. Sometimes color *is added.* Grated carrot and crushed marigold petals *were* once *used* to give cheddar and other orange cheeses their color.[8]

The passive voice can be useful for focusing on a product or a process, as the previous paragraph shows; the passive can also be used to correct the indefinite use of *they*:

- **x** They invented the ballpoint pen in 1938.
- The ballpoint pen was invented in 1938.[9]

Ordinarily, however, over- rather than underuse of the passive is the problem you will need to be aware of. To see that the active voice often presents a livelier impression than the passive, compare the two versions of the sentences that follow:

PASSIVE	ACTIVE

Black bears have a rigidly matriarchal society. It is a mother bear's show. *Parts of her own territory are parceled out to her daughters,* who move into their own subdivisions at the age of one-and-a-half years.

She parcels out part of her own territory to her daughters, who . . .

About 4,000 calories a day are burned by sleeping bears, but their fuel is limited to body fat so that their protein reserves can be preserved.

Sleeping bears burn about 4,000 calories a day, but they limit their fuel to body fat while preserving their protein reserves.[10]

SUMMARY

The voice of a verb indicates whether the subject does something or has something done to it. When the verb is in the active voice, the subject is the actor; when the verb is in the passive voice the subject names the receiver or object of the action. Passive voice has various appropriate uses, but to make your writing more vivid, you should generally prefer the active.

Exercise 2—19[11]

NAME _____

The passage below is taken from an account of a space shuttle flight written by the astronauts John Young and Robert Crippen. Indicate whether each of the italicized verbs is active (A) or passive (P). The first one is done for you as an example.

We were 60 miles above Midway and coming home, Crip and I, when we (1) *saw* the reddish pink glow. The space shuttle *Columbia* (2) *was dropping* through deep black night during the last half hour of our phenomenal first flight. Our nose (3) *was pointed* 40 degrees up so that the heat-shielding silica tiles on *Columbia's* underbelly (4) *would bear* the brunt of the scorching temperatures as it (5) *broke* into the upper reaches of Earth's atmosphere.

People (6) *had worried* a lot about this reentry heat. Even our own engineers (7) *had told* us that at least one of the critical tiles on the underside would probably come off. If enough did, they said, the hot plasma outside (8) *could burn* right through *Columbia*.

But we had faith in those tiles, and that tenuous glow (9) *proved* they were out there doing what they (10) *were made* to do. They (11) *were taking* 2300°F and (12) *lighting* up the sky around us.

1. __A__   2. _____   3. _____   4. _____   5. _____

6. _____   7. _____   8. _____   9. _____   10. _____

11. _____

Exercise 2—20[12]

The following paragraph originally had no passive verbs. Underline the passive verbs that appear in the version below, and in the space provided, change them to active, writing both subject and verb. You may use such subjects as *no one, everyone, we,* etc.

Example: Costly on-the-job training is less likely to be needed by a candidate who has already done a bit of governing.

   A candidate . . . is less likely to need . . .

No one expects politicians to win Nobel prizes by thinking up their own "new ideas." Social Security was not devised by FDR all by himself one morning in the library. But a candidate for president should be expected to be thoughtful in two senses. First the dilemmas of the age should have been grappled with seriously, so that when he goes out and talks to academics, policy entrepreneurs, businessmen, and bright young staffers, he can pick and choose with discretion and so that when it comes time to implement those ideas, with all the compromises that entails, he can tell a good compromise from a bad one. Second, our politicians can be asked to have a strong sense of how their various ideas relate to form a coherent whole. A menu of "policies," however comprehensive and sensible, is not enough. Only if a candidate has arrived at some vision of the role of government can it be guessed with any confidence how he will react in the various debates and crises that he will face during a four-year term of office.

_____

_____

_____

_____

_____

_____

_____

Exercise 2—21

NAME _____

If there is a sentence in your own writing in which a passive verb should be changed to active, revise it and write both the original and revised versions below.

1. _____

_____

2. _____

_____

Mood

INDICATIVE
Peanut butter *is* a cheap source of protein.   Who *invented* pencils?

IMPERATIVE
Drive with caution.

SUBJUNCTIVE
If I *were you*, I would leave well enough alone.   If Peter Rabbit *had* not *misbehaved*, no one would have written stories about him.

There are three moods in English: indicative, imperative, and subjunctive. The **indicative**, by far the most common, is used to express simple statements (*Peanut butter is a cheap source of protein*) or questions (*Who invented pencils?*). The **imperative** is used for commands and directions (*Drive* with caution, *Bus* your own tray, *Take* a number and *be* seated). The indicative and the imperative usually pose no problems. The **subjunctive**, however, occasionally causes difficulty: it is used in certain set expressions (So *be* it, Heaven *forbid*) and to express wishes, possibilities, speculations, and formal requirements. Examples of common uses of the subjunctive follow:

UNREAL OR IMPOSSIBLE CONDITIONS:
- If you *had* not *fallen* asleep, you could have seen the eclipse of the moon. (You did fall asleep; therefore you did not see the eclipse. It is an unreal condition.)

IMPOSSIBLE WISHES:
- I wish the Oakland A's *had done* better this year.

CONJECTURES:
- He looks as if he *had seen* a ghost.

THAT CLAUSES EXPRESSING REQUIREMENTS:
- The university requires that everyone *pass* a swimming test or *enroll* in a swimming class.

Except for the verb *be* and the third-person singular of other verbs, subjunctive forms are the same as indicative forms.

PRESENT SUBJUNCTIVE OF *BE*:
- So *be* it.
- If I *were* you . . .
- If you *were* more ambitious . . .
- If he *were* more polite . . .

PAST SUBJUNCTIVE OF *BE*:

- If I *had been* you . . .
- If you *had been* more ambitious . . .
- If he *had been* more polite . . .

For the third person singular omit the *-s* (or *-es*) of the indicative form:

1. The agency required that he provide three references.
   (Compare: Everyone provides three references.)

2. The doctor recommended that she take Vitamin B.
   (Compare: She takes Vitamin B.)

sequence of tenses in impossible conditions and wishes

1. **x** If I *was* you, I would study harder.
   - If I *were* you, I would study harder.

Impossible conditions in the present require the subjunctive form omitted in the example above.

2. **x** If you *would* not *have fallen* asleep, you could have seen the eclipse.
   - If you *had not fallen* asleep, you could have seen the eclipse.

In past impossible conditions, the verb of the *if* clause should be formed from *had* plus the past participle: If you *had* not *fallen* asleep. *Would have* plus the past participle is never the proper choice for the verb of the *if* clause.

3. **x** I wish the Oakland A's *would have done* better.
   - I wish the Oakland A's *had done* better.

Would have plus the past participle cannot be used after the verb *wish*. Again, *had* plus the past participle should be substituted; I *wish* they *had done* better.

SUMMARY

The indicative is the mood for ordinary statements and questions; the imperative mood is used for giving commands and directions; and the subjunctive mood is used to express wishes, impossible conditions, and formal requirements. The subjunctive forms differ from the indicative forms only for the verb *to be* and for the third-person singular of other verbs. Do not use *would have* plus the past participle in an *if* clause or after the verb *wish*.

Exercise 2—22

NAME _____

Indicate whether each of the underlined verbs is indicative (Ind), imperative (Imp), or subjunctive (S).

> *Example:* Take your complaints directly to your dorm counselor. *Imp*

1. He chose to be a conscientious objector. _____

2. Take it or leave it. _____ _____

3. If I had studied, I would not have failed. _____

4. Guess who won. _____

5. Did you give money to the Salvation Army? _____

6. Take the bus to Hollywood and Vine. _____

7. If the man had not been slightly crazy, he would not have tried to make friends with the polar bear. _____

8. A 300-pound policeman sat on the suspect. _____

9. Heaven help him. _____

10. What are the principal parts of *put*? _____

Exercise 2—23

NAME _____

If the verb or verbs in the following sentences are in the indicative mood or if they have correct subjunctive forms, write C in the space provided at the right. If a sentence requires but does not have a subjunctive form, circle the incorrect form and write the correct one in the space provided.

Example: If you (would have asked) for money, we
would certainly have given it to you.   *had asked*

1. The teacher requires that everyone turns in a paper on time and then revise it two weeks later.   _____

2. You may wish that the Mets would have done better, but wishing will not help.   _____

3. "God helps those who help themselves" is a saying that does not offer much hope.   _____

4. "God help him" usually means "No one else can."   _____

5. The swimming coach suggests—and in his case *suggest* means *insist*—that we practice on Saturday from 5:00 to 6:00 a.m.   _____

6. Optimistic voters wished the economy would improve and expected their wishing to have some effect.   _____

7. Computer science might not attract so many students if it was still possible for English and history majors to get jobs.   _____

8. Even if people in the apartment that was demolished would have had renter's insurance, it would not have helped.   _____

9. I wish the change to daylight savings time had never been thought of.   _____

10. What would have happened if we would not have heard the fire alarm?   _____

98

Subject-Verb Agreement

- 1. The <u>difficulty</u> with all your plans <u>is</u> that they cost too much.

- 2. Economic <u>problems</u> in the countries of the West <u>are caused</u> largely by changing oil prices.

- 3. <u>Each</u> of my neighbors <u>has</u> a dog.

- 4. <u>Neither</u> of us <u>is going</u> to class tomorrow.

- 5. My favorite breakfast <u>combination</u> <u>is</u> waffles and eggs.

- 6. The <u>problem</u>—how to identify herself and how to recognize her unknown guests at the airport—<u>was solved</u> by her wearing a red, white, and blue dress and by their carrying small French flags.

- 7. Two basement rooms or a ninth floor <u>apartment</u> <u>is</u> available.

- 8. Do viewers prefer a news anchor <u>who looks</u> attractive to one <u>who is</u> a top-notch news reporter?

- 9. <u>That only a few people show up for volleyball in 100° heat</u> <u>is</u> not surprising.

The subjects and verbs of the sentences above agree. That means that singular subjects are used with singular verb forms and plural subjects are used with plural verb forms. In the following examples pronoun subjects are matched with corresponding verb forms.

I promise	we promise	Do you <u>play</u> the piano?
you promise	you promise	I <u>do</u> not, but she <u>does</u>.
he/she promise<u>s</u>	they promise	And he play<u>s</u> the trumpet.

You can see that the verb form in agreement with he/she/it has an added -s (sometimes -es): *promises, does, plays.* With one exception, this change in verb form occurs only in the present. The exception is the past tense of *be*:

I <u>was</u>	you were
you were	you were
it <u>was</u>	they were

Otherwise, changes in verb form for tenses other than the present affect only the third-person singular forms of *be, do,* or *have,* with which various tenses are formed.

- He *has* tried to learn to swim.
- They *have* tried.
- The layout for the yearbook *was* finished yesterday.
- Their plans for a graduation party *were* met with cheers.

In the first example above—*The difficulty with all your plans is that they cost too much*—the subject and verb are *difficulty is*. Because a phrase ending with a plural noun (*with all your plans*) comes between the singular subject and the verb, writers sometimes make the mistake of using a plural verb: **x** The *difficulty* with your *plans are* . . . Similarly, when a plural subject is separated from the verb by a phrase or clause ending in a singular noun, writers sometimes make the verb singular: **x** *Economic problems in the countries of the West is caused largely by changing oil prices.* Be careful to make the verb agree not with a word that happens to occupy a position close to it, but with the subject.

- The difficulty . . . is . . .

- Economic problems . . . are caused . . .

A similar problem can arise in using such singular pronouns as *each, neither, nothing, everyone, none,* and *something.* When these words are separated from the verbs with which they must agree, writers may make the verb agree with some element in an intervening phrase or clause: **x** *Each of my neighbors have a dog;* **x** *Neither of us are going to class tomorrow.* The word *neighbors,* which is plural, has made the writer forget that the subject is actually *each,* which is singular. And in the next sentence the verb agrees with the plural pronoun *us* rather than the singular subject *neither.* These sentences should be

- Each of my neighbors has a dog.

- Neither of us is going to class tomorrow.

Note that *each* can also modify a plural subject: • *They each want to pay for dinner.* In such a sentence, *each* does not influence the question of subject-verb agreement. The plural subject still requires a plural verb form.

In the fifth example—*My favorite breakfast combination is waffles and eggs*—the subject (*combination*) is singular, but it is followed by a plural complement (*waffles and eggs*). In such a sentence writers sometimes make the verb agree with the plural complement rather than the singular subject: **x** *My favorite breakfast combination are waffles and eggs.* As in the previous examples, this problem too can be solved by locating the subject and matching it rather than other sentence elements with the verb: • My favorite breakfast combination is waffles and eggs.

In the sixth example—*The problem—how to identify herself and how to recognize her unknown guests at the airport—was solved by her wearing a red, white, and blue dress and their carrying small French flags*—a singular subject is followed by a plural appositive. An appositive is a word or phrase whose only function is to identify or restate an immediately preceding noun, pronoun, or nounlike element. Even though the appositive is plural (*how to identify* and *how to recognize*), the subject is singular and requires a singular verb:

- The problem . . . was solved.

When two subjects, one plural and the other singular, are joined by *or*, the verb agrees with the one closest to it:

- A ninth floor apartment or two basement rooms are available.

- Two basement rooms or a ninth floor apartment is available.

In the eighth example—*Do viewers prefer a news anchor who looks attractive to one who is a top-notch news reporter?*—the verb of each of the relative clauses agrees with the relative pronoun *who*. Since the antecedent of *who* is singular (*a news anchor who, one who*), *who* is singular and must be matched with a singular verb form: *a news anchor who looks* and *one who is*.

Noun clauses, for example, *That only a few people show up for volleyball in 100° heat*, are singular and require singular verb forms:

- That only a few people show up for volleyball in 100° heat is not surprising.

SUMMARY

Subjects and verbs are said to agree: singular subjects go with singular verb forms, and plural subjects go with plural forms. With one exception (the past of the verb *be*), a change in verb forms occurs only in the present, third person, singular. When phrases or clauses come between the subject and verb, be sure to make the verb agree not with a word that happens to be located near it but with the subject.

Exercise 2—24

NAME _____

Rewrite the following sentences. Change the subject to third person singular (he, she, it, one, someone, anyone) and make the corresponding change in the form of the verb.

> *Example:*   I have a music stand for sale.
>
> *Someone has a music stand for sale.*

1. Do you sell travel irons?

_____

2. Where are we going for dinner?

_____

3. Have you ever eaten Thai food?

_____

4. I want to hike down into the Grand Canyon.

_____

5. Do you have a telephone in your room?

_____

Exercise 2—25[13]

Circle the correct verb form in each of the following sentences. The first one is done for you as an example.

It (1. is, are) almost impossible to grasp the full meaning of geological time. People (2. remember, remembers) the events of recent years, and (3. have, has) some knowledge of modern history, but the Pharaohs or the Han dynasty (4. seem, seems) unbelievably far in the past. Geological time (5. make, makes) a mockery of all this. While the history of civilizations (6. is measured, are measured) in thousands of years, the age of rocks and fossils (7. is measured, are measured) in hundreds of millions of years. The main Saharan plateaux, the sandstones, (8. is, are) up to 500 million years old. And they (9. is, are) young by the standards of the underlying continental shield, which (10. was formed, were formed) 2,000 million years ago.

In the Sahara you (11. is reminded, are reminded) continually of these facts in a manner that (12. make, makes) them intelligible. Without soil, greenery, or signs of human activity, the evidence of hundreds of millions of years of geological change (13. is laid, are laid) out like an open textbook.

Exercise 2—26[14]

NAME _____

Circle the correct form of the verb.

Example: All the world (is, are) a compass for birds that (migrate, migrates).

A. Excellent weather sensers, birds usually (1. wait, waits) until the passage of fronts that (2. bring, brings) favorable winds.

B. How a bird (3. determine, determines) its position (4. remain, remains) a mystery to man.

C. Each autumn the Tennessee warbler (5. migrate, migrates) some 3,000 miles from nesting sites in Canada and in the northern United States to wintering places in Central and South America.

D. Like many migratory species, it (6. seek, seeks) out the same locale where it wintered the year before.

E. Some small landbirds such as the blackpoll (7. make, makes) a nonstop, overwater flight of more than 2,300 miles lasting an average of 86 hours.

F. Many species of birds (8. set, sets) courses not only by the sun but also by the stars.

G. How birds (9. use, uses) their "instruments," in fact what they are and where they are in those small bodies, (10. remain, remains) unknown.

104

Exercise 2—27[15]

NAME _____

Circle the verbs that do not agree with their subjects and write the correct form in the space provided. If a sentence has no subject-verb agreement error, write C in the space.

> *Example:* Physicists . . . are finding that both history and the fate of the universe (is) (written) in every atom.[16]   *are written*

1. A Swiss company has invented a material that repels water but readily soaks up oil and certain chemicals.   _____

2. The particles, when sprinkled over an oil spill at sea, becomes saturated with oil, swells to the size of kernels of grain, and can then be easily scooped up.   _____

3. Each of the two solid engines used on the space shuttle require over three tons of parachute fabric for a safe ocean splashdown.   _____

4. One of the frightening things about cancer are that cures can be as destructive as the disease.   _____

5. But instead of treating cancer patients by killing malignant cells, it may be possible in the future simply to make those cells behave like normal ones.   _____

6. The hairs on your head grows for a few years and then rests.   _____

7. At any given moment about 85 percent is active; the rest are relaxing.   _____

8. A leprosy vaccine that was developed with the help of a colony of armadillos are being tested on humans for the first time. _____

9. Why armadillos? Their body temperature, lower than that of most animals, provides just the right environment for the virulent microbe. _____

10. The drive between Los Angeles and San Francisco is getting shorter. Because the cities are on opposite sides of the San Andreas fault, they are moving toward each other by about 2.5 inches a year. _____

MODIFIERS

Comparison

1. **x** My accounting course is *more tedious rather than difficult.*
   - My accounting course is *more tedious than difficult.*
   - My accounting course is *tedious rather than difficult.*

2. **x** The problem is *as much or more yours than mine.*
   - The problem is *at least as much yours as mine.*

3. **x** Badminton is somewhat *similar as* tennis.
   - Badminton is somewhat *similar to* tennis.

4. **x** Her *cakes* are *as good as* a professional *cook.*
   - Her *cakes* are *as good as those* of a professional cook.

5. **x** *Like the president said,* everyone has to sacrifice.
   - *As the president said, . . .*

Set expressions such as *more A than B* and *A rather than B* allow us to compare one thing with another. Problems arise when these expressions are used imprecisely or when two of the expressions are mixed. The first sentence above mixes *more tedious than difficult* and *tedious rather than difficult.* The second mixes *as much yours as mine* and *more yours than mine.* If you want to include both ideas, you can say *at least as much yours as mine.* The third sentence mixes *similar to* and *the same as; similar* is followed by *to; the same* is followed by *as.* The two cannot be used together.

Her cakes are as good as a professional cook compares cakes with a cook, which does not have any meaning. The writer's intention was undoubtedly to compare cakes with cakes, but in the sentence as it stands, the writer is *comparing the incomparable.* Another comparison problem is the use of *like* for *as.* You may have gotten used to hearing *Like I said,* but the accepted expression is *As I said. Like* is a preposition and requires an object: *Like a fool, I said I would be on the clean-up committee.*

SUMMARY

Do not mix comparative structures (more A than B; A rather than B); be sure that you are comparing elements that are comparable (cakes with cakes, not cakes with cooks). Do not use *like* for *as.*

Exercise 2—28

NAME _____

Some of the following sentences have problems with comparative expressions. Revise, and in the space provided, rewrite enough of the sentence to make your revision clear. If no revision is necessary, write NR.

> *Example:* The new dean is more willing rather than able to do the job.
>
> *more willing than able/willing rather than able*

1. Like everyone said, it does no good to ask her to change a grade.

   _____

2. Squash is somewhat similar to tennis but much more like handball.

   _____

3. Their mother was more relieved rather than angry when the boys returned two days late from their camping trip.

   _____

4. The student plays the violin at least as well if not better than his teacher.

   _____

5. The solution is as much or more of a problem than the problem it solved.

   _____

6. When summer weather is unbearable, people always say it is the humidity rather than the heat that bothers them.

   _____

7. Many watchdogs are more frightening rather than dangerous to intruders.

   _____

Write three sentences of your own, each using one of the following comparative structures: *more A than B; A rather than B; as much A as B;* and *at least as much A as B.* Look back at the examples on page 107 if doing so would be useful.

1. _____

2. _____

3. _____

Misrelated and Dangling Modifiers

x 1. Water will be served *only if requested because of the drought.*

x 2. He suddenly remembered that he had left the stove on *in the middle of the movie.*

x 3. *Walking* late into the dark theater, *a large hand* descended on his shoulder.

x 4. She asked me *to seriously think* about retiring at thirty.

x 5. Students *only* are satisfied if they get A's.

As you have seen, phrases and clauses often act as modifiers. To be effective, they must clearly relate to the words they modify. Misplacement of modifiers can make your sentences confusing or nonsensical.

Squinting modifiers look in two directions at once. The first example above probably means *Because of the drought, water will be served only if requested,* but it could mean *Only if requested because of the drought, water will be served.* The misplacement of *because of the drought* causes *only if requested* to become a squinting modifier. In order to revise, place *because of the drought* in an unambiguous position.

In the next example, too, a modifier is misplaced. As it stands the sentence says what the writer undoubtedly does not mean—that *in the middle of the movie,* the subject, *he, left the stove on.* The phrase *in the middle of the movie* should be placed so that it will tell us when he remembered that he had left the stove on:

- *In the middle of the movie,* he suddenly remembered that he had left the stove on.

In the third example, *Walking late into the dark theater* is a **dangling modifier**. Although it appears to modify *hand,* it has no relationship to any word in the sentence. Since a large hand could not have been walking into the theater, we can revise by clarifying the relationship between the modifier and an element implied but not stated in the sentence:

- *Walking late into the theater,* he felt a large hand descend on his shoulder.

Now the phrase modifies *he.*

Other modifiers that are sometimes misplaced are such adverbs as *almost, even, just, only,* and *simply:* **x** *Students only are satisfied if they get A's.* To revise, place these adverbs directly before the words, phrases, or clauses they modify:
- *Students are happy only if they get A's.*

split infinitives Modifying words that come between *to* and the base form of the verb result in what is called a **split infinitive** (*to seriously think*). While common in conversation, split infinitives are generally unacceptable in writing. To revise, you can place the modifier somewhere else in the sentence, often just before or just after the infinitive: *She asked me to think seriously about retiring at thirty.*

SUMMARY

Modifiers should be carefully placed so that they clearly relate to the words, phrases, or clauses they are intended to modify. Revise sentences with dangling modifiers so that the relationship between the modifier and some element in the sentence is clear.

Exercise 2—29

NAME _____

Each of the following sentences has a misplaced modifier. Revise and write your revision in the space provided.

> *Example:* After studying all night, the exam should be easy.
>
> *After studying all night, we should find the exam easy.*

1. When learning to ski, falling down is the first lesson.

   _____

2. He is trying to really do a good job.

   _____

3. After locking the door, the key must be hidden in the flower pot.

   _____

4. While standing in line at the bank, reading a book will make the time pass faster.

   _____

5. Anyone who plans to quickly finish that exam will be disappointed.

   _____

6. Like the previous apartment, I moved into this one before it was painted.

   _____

7. Having presented the extreme views, the moderate view can now be appreciated.

   _____

8. Rewrite the following sentences, correcting the problems with modifiers.

   _____

9. By trying to honestly analyze each problem as it arises, roommates can become good friends.

   _____

10. After planting tulips, garlic came up.

   _____

Write five sentences in which you use phrases and clauses as modifiers.

1. _____

2. _____

3. _____

4. _____

5. _____

Write one sentence with an infinitive.

1. _____

Write four sentences, using one of the following words in each: *almost, even, just, only, simply.*

1. _____

2. _____

3. _____

4. _____

PARALLELISM

- 1. Her main goals were *to go* to medical school *and to travel* in South America.
- 2. He looked for his tax refund check everywhere: *in his* room, *in his* car, and *in his* office.
- 3. We must *either meet* the deadline *or face losing* our jobs.

Parallelism is the balanced or matched arrangement of similar sentence elements—whether words, phrases, or clauses. Verbs should be matched with verbs, infinitives with infinitives, gerunds with gerunds, prepositional phrases with prepositional phrases, clauses with clauses, and so on. The use of such balanced elements allows a writer to be more concise and to emphasize important points.

The examples above show three kinds of parallel arrangement. The first illustrates the use of balanced elements joined by the coordinating conjunction *and* (other such conjunctions are *but, or, nor,* and *yet*). *To go* and *to travel* are both infinitives, and *to go to medical school* and *to travel in South America* get equal and balanced emphasis in the sentence. The writer could just as effectively have used a different phrase (for example, *going* to medical school and *traveling* in South America) so long as both goals were expressed in the same structure.

In the second example, one grammatical unit (a prepositional phrase) is repeated to form a **series**. The three places—room, car, and office—work together to define *everywhere*. In this sentence both the preposition and the possessive pronoun—*in* and *his*—are repeated throughout the series, but the construction would still be parallel (though somewhat less emphatic) if it were *in his room, car, and office.* If the writer had written **x** *in his room, car, and in his office,* however, the balanced effect would have been spoiled and the sentence rhythm thrown off. In order to maintain a parallel series, any element repeated in any part of the series must be repeated throughout.

In the third example, a balanced effect is achieved through the use of *either . . . or*: *either* meet the deadline *or* face losing our jobs. In this sentence alternatives are precisely balanced. Because we are used to hearing the two words together, we know as soon as we hear *either* that an *or* is to follow. Such a structure allows us to read efficiently by anticipating the writer's meaning. If the sentence were written **x** *Either we must* meet the deadline *or face losing* our jobs, we would understand the two alternatives, but they would no longer be so precisely balanced. *Either we . . . or face* has lost the immediate clarity of *either meet . . . or face.* The grammatical element that appears after *either* should be repeated after *or.* The same requirement holds for *not only . . . but also, both . . . and,* and other such paired structures. Whatever appears after the second item should be grammatically equal to what appears after the first.

Parallel structures can help a writer or speaker achieve stirring contrasts:

As I would not be a *slave,* so I would not be a *master.*
—Abraham Lincoln

The balanced clauses—*As I would not be a slave* and *so I would not be a master*—are made more emphatic by the repetition of *I would not be.* And the words *slave* and *master* are set off against each other. Because they occupy the same grammatical position and follow the dramatic repetition of *I would not be,* they reinforce the suggestion that slave and master, though essentially opposite, are intimately connected and equally repugnant.

The following sentences would be more effective if nonparallel structures were made parallel:

x 1. *Not only did* he lose his take-home final *but his* girlfriend, too.
x 2. *During* the bus strike *and if* I have very little money, I hitchhike to work.
x 3. We heard on the radio *that the president* will not run for reelection *and his wife* plans to run in his place.

The first sentence might have two quite different meanings:

• He lost *not only* his take-home *final but* his *girlfriend too.*
• *Both he and* his *girlfriend* lost their take-home finals.

In the second sentence a prepositional phrase (*during the bus strike*) and a clause (*if I have very little money*) are joined by a coordinating conjunction. We can revise by using two prepositional phrases:

• *During* bus strikes and *on* days when I have very little money, I hitchhike to work.

The third sentence can be revised by completing the parallel structure begun by the introduction of the *that* clause. *That* should be used to introduce the second clause as well:

• We heard *that* the president will not run for reelection and *that* his wife plans to run in his place.

SUMMARY

Words, phrases, and clauses that are parallel in meaning should also be parallel in form. Elements joined by *and* (*but, or,* etc.) and elements appearing in a series should be carefully matched. The same grammatical structure should follow both units of paired structures such as *not only . . . but also.*

Exercise 2—30[17]

NAME _____

Circle the non-parallel element in each of the following sentences or passages and rewrite it, making it parallel. If no revision is necessary, write NR in the space provided.

Example: The world's largest jellyfish is two-thirds the length of a football field and is composed of only 5 percent organic material; the rest of its body is water. In fact, if the creature were to wash ashore, it would not die so much as (evaporation would take place.)

So much as it would evaporate.

1. Single-parent families and when families have two incomes have made the speed and convenience of microwave ovens particularly desirable.

_____

2. Microwave ovens are famous for being cool, clean, and cooking fast.

_____

3. They are not famous for browning foods or for cooking evenly.

_____

4. No one likes a casserole that is hot in some spots but it's cold in others.

_____

5. In the ovens without a turntable, the pattern of cooked spots is random and unpredictable.

_____

6. For some foods, rotating them, turning, or stirring is not enough to get the desired results.

_____

7. Directions for nearly every oven recommend 120° to 130° for rare roast beef on the assumption undercooking is better than when you overcook.

_____

8. Microwaves tend to bounce around in an unpredictable pattern. The food is hit directly by some, some ricochet off the metal walls and then hit the food, some line up with one another so their effect is strengthened, and some bump into one another so they cancel each other out.

9. With a microwave oven, evenness of cooking depends on the food and the technique as well as on the distribution of the microwaves.

10. Dry foods absorb less energy than if they are liquid.

Exercise 2–31

NAME _____

Write four sentences of your own using (1) *not only . . . but also* or *either . . . or,* (2) a series, (3) parallel phrases connected by *and, but,* or *or,* and (4) parallel clauses. Underline the parallel elements in each.

1. _____

_____

2. _____

_____

3. _____

_____

4. _____

_____

Write another sentence with parallel elements of any kind. Again, underline the parallel elements.

_____

_____

REVIEW TEST

NAME _____

Revise the following sentences, rewriting as completely as necessary while keeping the same meaning. You can make some revisions clear by rewriting only a few words. Others will require you to write out the whole sentence. You may find it helpful to underline the points at which problems occur. Several different revisions will work. There is no *one* correct answer.

> *Example:* Looking through the want ads of the Sunday newspaper, it oc-
> curred to me that looking for a job was going to be harder than I
> had expected.
>
> *Looking through the want ads of the*
> *Sunday newspaper, I realized . . .*

1. Taking surveys, interviewing voters coming out of polling places, and the clean-up committee were my political jobs.

2. If someone would have asked me what movie to see, I would have sug-gested *Gandhi,* if they wanted to learn about a historical figure.

3. Stormy summer weather—thunder, lightning, and rain—often prevent us from going swimming.

4. My main goals are going pro, have a family, and to be rich.

5. The math test is gone about being cheated on in an entirely different manner.

6. If you have a problem that everyone thinks they can solve it, you have many problems instead of one.

_____

_____

7. Even if your boss thinks that you are eligible for a raise, unless it is brought up by you, there is a good chance your pay will stay the same.

_____

_____

8. Because he wanted to save money, my friend decided that he will buy his own phone. He bought a touchtone model from Bell for $60.00 and then finds out that he can get the same phone at the department store for less. But the person who he talked to when he tried to return the phone would not take it back. At Ma Bell's all sales are final. As he discovered too late.

_____

_____

_____

9. Me and my roommate studied all night for an exam, which we did not even have it today.

_____

_____

10. I had to take responsibility for doing my laundry, cooking my meals, and how to manage money.

_____

_____

11. I am going to look for a good job in drafting, which after I work at it for a while I hope to get promoted.

_____

_____

12. After getting the oil changed, buying a new battery, and having all four tires changed, the car was ready to go, and we headed west from Chicago. Our intention being to camp in the Rockies, then the Grand Canyon, then Yosemite, and then the coast of Northern California and Oregon. Unfortu-

nately the new battery died only 50 miles out of town, and we discovered while getting that repaired that the radiator was cracked.

_____

_____

_____

_____

_____

13. My friend asked me to help her with her paper on the birds of North America, but she had made many mistakes that I did not know how to correct them.

_____

_____

14. The greatest disappointment I had was my senior year in high school, on the football team.

_____

_____

15. Every other day we took care of children at the day care center. Our first day we were surprised at them being so relaxed with people who they had never seen before. Even the shy ones seemed to think it was natural to be taken care of by strangers.

_____

_____

NOTES

[1] June Weir, "What It Takes to Be in Fashion: Beautiful Skin," *New York Times Magazine,* 26 Sept. 1983, p. 88.

[2] "Salt and High Blood Pressure," *Consumer Reports,* 44 (1979), 147.

[3] Peter Miller, "Speed Skiing," *New York Times Magazine,* 20 Feb. 1983, p. 32.

[4] Emily Vermeule, "Odysseus at Fenway," *New York Times Magazine,* 26 Sept. 1982, p. 48.

[5] "Inexpensive Pens," *Consumer Reports,* 48 (1983), 229.

[6] A. B. C. Whipple, "Storms the Angry Gods Sent Are Now Science's Quarry," *Smithsonian,* Sept. 1982, p. 89.

[7] "Looking for a Good Cup of Coffee?" *Consumer Reports,* 48 (1983), 110.

[8] "American Cheeses," *Consumer Reports,* 48 (1983), 67.

[9] "Inexpensive Pens," p. 229.

[10] Adele Conover, "Getting to Know Black Bears—Right on Their Own Home Ground," *Smithsonian,* Apr. 1983, pp. 88–89.

[11] John W. Young and Robert L. Crippen, "Columbia's Astronauts' Own Story: Our Phenomenal First Flight," *National Geographic,* 160 (1981), 478.

[12] Robert M. Kaus, "First, Forget the Issues," *Harper's,* Aug. 1983, pp. 15–16.

[13] Jeremy Swift, ed., *The Sahara: The World's Wild Places* (Amsterdam: Time-Life Books, 1975), p. 38.

[14] Allan C. Fisher, Jr., "Mysteries of Bird Migration," *National Geographic,* 156 (1979), 154, 156.

[15] "Update," *Science Digest,* June 1983, p. 24 [Items 1 and 2]; "Technology," *Science Digest,* June 1983, p. 28 [Item 3]; "Mind and Body," *Science Digest,* Aug. 1983, pp. 85, 88 [Items 4–7]; "Update," *Science Digest,* Aug. 1983, p. 29 [Item 10].

[16] Timothy Ferris, "Physics' Newest," *New York Times Magazine,* 26 Sept. 1982, p. 37 [example for exercise; mistake as published].

[17] "Everyday Science," *Science Digest,* June 1983, p. 92 [example for exercise]; "Microwave Ovens," *Consumer Reports,* 48 (1983), 222–223.

PUNCTUATION AND CAPITALIZATION 3

NAME _____

Supply the punctuation and capitalization missing from the following passage. If more than one possibility is correct, choose one. Circle the punctuation marks you supply. Some items have been done for you as examples.

doug lay on an operating table at the university of western ontario hospital as dr⊙ john girvin removed a 2-by-3-inch piece of bone from the back of his skull⊙ the surgeon then carefully placed a one square inch Teflon wafer on the visual cortex of dougs brain. Because the brain has no sensation of pain only local anesthesia had been administered, and doug was awake talking with his surgeon doug could not however see his surgeon he had been unable to see anything since that day in 1966 when a vietcong land mine exploded in front of him⊙

the Teflon wafer contained 64 platinum electrodes each of which was to function as an electrical contact to the visual center of his brain the surgeon attached a small bundle of wires to the wafer and connected it to a computer across the room doug tensed in expectation. As another scientist sent a small burst of current to the electrodes doug immediately saw white points of light

125

before him the first light he had seen in seven years a stream of happy expletives poured from his lips

the electrodes that were temporarily implanted in dougs brain will not fully restore his sight he will never again for example be able to appreciate the smile on the Mona Lisa but he and other blind people may be able to discern that Leonardo's subject was a person possibly even that it was a woman at best if this still experimental system can be perfected the visual world of people like doug will resemble the animated imagery on Yankee Stadiums electronic scoreboard. And with that level of visual acuity they would be able to navigate better in a world whose horizons had been limited to the reach of a cane.[1]

x from the bodys point of view turning tan is not desirable its a defense the warm summer sun may feel friendly but some of its rays are dangerous the part of the suns rays that tan burn and otherwise damage the skin is the ultraviolet or uv rays

x from the Bodys poi'nt of view turning, tan is not. Desirable its a Defense the warm, summer, sun. may Feel Friendly; But some: of its ray's are; dangerous—the Part of the runs rays That. Tan! burn? and otherwise damage: the ski'n! is the Ultraviolet; or uv ray's?

- From the body's point of view, turning tan is not desirable. It's a defense. The warm summer sun may feel friendly, but some of its rays are dangerous. The part of the sun's rays that tan, burn, and otherwise damage the skin is the ultraviolet, or UV, rays.[2]

With no punctuation or capitalization, a passage can be annoyingly hard to read. Incorrect punctuation and capitalization can make it seriously confusing. In both cases, the writer is asking readers to do unnecessary work. Punctuation marks and capitalization are the writer's signs telling the reader how to read efficiently. Without them or with them incorrectly used, writers lose a basic way of making themselves understood.

End Punctuation: Period, Question Mark, and Exclamation Point

period

- Every leaf is a site for photosynthesis⊙That site may be thought of as a solar-powered factory where carbohydrates are assembled out of carbon dioxide and water[3]

A **period** is used to show that a sentence making a statement has come to an end. If you use a comma or no punctuation at all between two independent clauses (in the example above, the first independent clause ends with *photosynthesis*; the second begins with *That site*), you will misdirect your reader. A comma signals only a pause, not a full stop, while using no punctuation at all will make your reader run two sentences together. The first error is called a **comma splice**, the second a **fused sentence**. (Review Chapter 1, pp. 5–6, for the distinction between independent and subordinate clauses.)

In each of the following examples, two independent clauses have been mistakenly separated by a comma:

x 1. Except for coast-to-coast flights, airline travel within the United States is quite expensive, often costing more than the low overseas fares₀ *however,* because of unusually sharp competition between major airlines, there are now several important exceptions.

x 2. You cannot climb Mt. Fuji in December. You will get lost in the fog and snow and freeze to death₀ *besides,* you do not have hiking boots.

When words such as *however, besides, furthermore,* and *therefore* appear at the beginning of an independent clause, they cannot be separated from preceding independent clauses by commas. You could revise both the examples above by supplying periods in place of the commas:

- 1. Except for coast-to-coast flights, airline travel within the United States is quite expensive, often costing more than the low overseas fares₀ However, . . .
- 2. You will get lost in the fog and snow and freeze to death₀ Besides, . . .

(For other ways to punctuate independent clauses, see pp. 135–136.)

A sentence stating an indirect question is no exception; it, too, ends with a period.

- The instructor asked how many people could name five evergreens₀
- The student wanted to know why some trees are evergreen and others deciduous₀

Even though the sentences above contain the idea of a question, their form is that of a statement:

- The instructor asked X.
- The student wanted to know X.

Periods are also used in most abbreviations: *M.D., Tenn.* If a sentence ends with an abbreviation, one period serves to mark the abbreviation and to end the sentence:

- The test results were evaluated by Carole Hansen, M.D.

Names of agencies and some other names are often abbreviated without periods. For example, *FDA* is the abbreviation for the Food and Drug Administration.

question mark

- 1. Are hibiscus and coconuts evergreens⊙
- 2. Most tropical trees are evergreens, aren't they⊙

A **question mark** is used to indicate the end of a direct question. Do not use a question mark with another question mark or with a period, unless an abbreviation occurs at the end of a question:

- Was your paper graded by the instructor or the T.A.?

exclamation point

- Watch out! You're directly under the high diving board!

An **exclamation point** ends an urgent command or an excited statement. As a general rule, you should use it sparingly, letting your words rather than your punctuation convey your meaning.

SUMMARY

Use periods at the end of statements (including indirect questions) and most abbreviations. Use question marks at the end of direct questions. Use exclamation points at the end of urgent commands and excited statements. In most cases, do not use more than one set of these end marks at once, and use exclamation points infrequently.

Beginning Capitalization

- By the time the Old Testament was written, people already knew that many biological functions in animals, reproduction prominent among them, vary with the seasons. . . . But one tantalizing question has received little study. Might the reproductive impulses of humans, too, be influenced by the seasons?[4]

- In an article in *Natural History*, Joel R. L. Ehrenkranz asks, "Might the reproductive impulses of humans, too, be influenced by the seasons?"

A sentence begins with a capital letter. If you quote someone else's sentence, both your sentence and the quoted sentence begin with capital letters.

Exercise 3—1[5]

NAME _____

The following passage has no capitalization at the beginning of sentences and few punctuation marks at the end. Add the necessary capitals and underline each. Add the necessary marks of end punctuation and circle each. The first capital letter is added for you as an example.

I̲
I̲n a fight with Ray ("Boom Boom") Mancini on November 13, 1982, light-weight boxer Duk Koo Kim went down in the ring and never got up knocked unconscious, he was rushed to Desert Springs Hospital, in Las Vegas, where doctors connected him to a respirator his surgeon said, "one tremendous punch to the head gave the young fighter a massive cerebral hemorrhage." a few days later, when tests showed that all brain activity had ceased, the doctors declared Kim dead and turned off the respirator there followed in the press a spate of proposals to ban boxing and, soon after, a round of counter-arguments—all before the fighter's mother, despondent over his death, took her own life on January 30

Exercise 3—2[6]

Write C in the space provided at the right if all beginning capitalization and end punctuation have been provided. If not, underline the mistakes and write the correct punctuation and capitalization in the space at the right. More than one correction may be necessary.

Example: Insects and insect hunters overpower prey with ingenious traps, clever baits, or quick shots of paralyzing
poison_they do not shred flesh or mangle skeletons. ___.T___

1. According to an article in *The Sciences*, "Some styles of killing
amount to sophisticated state-of-the-art displays." _____

2. the toad launches its missile of a tongue from a catapult an-
chored in its mouth the assassin bug coaxes worker termites
from their nest with the bodies of their dead relatives _____

3. And the Venus's flytrap, a most mechanical and covert killer, poisons its prey behind chemically controlled lobes. _____

4. Not long ago, Elizabeth McMahan, of the University of North Carolina, sat beside a termite nest in a Costa Rican rain forest _____

5. she intended to learn which workers repair a broken nest instead, she learned how easily termites are fooled by a dangling corpse. _____

6. Before ambushing a termite nest, the assassin bug camouflages itself with bits of carton, the termite's nesting material. _____

7. The disguise helps the bug avoid soldier termites patrolling the surface of the nest each soldier's pear-shaped head is armed with a "squirt gun" filled with poison _____

8. When at last a worker emerges from the nest, the assassin lunges with its front legs and beak. the bug drags its kicking prey free of the nest. _____

9. it quickly injects the termite with a paralyzing poison and shoots the stiff body with enzymes to soften the meat _____

10. Then putting its long, tubelike mouth parts to the dead worker's body, the killer sips in the termite's liquid innards, as through a straw _____

11. The corpse inflates and collapses in rhythm with the assassin's sucking motion after three or four minutes there is nothing left but an empty, flattened shell _____

12. This shell is perfect bait for the next victim holding the corpse in its front legs, the assassin dangles it over the edge of the nest. _____

13. As soon as another worker reaches up and tries to drag its relative in, the assassin hauls up the living with the dead _____

14. Then, when the live termite is exposed, the assassin drops the bait and begins the next course of its meal. _____

15. McMahan watched one assassin devour thirty-one termites before quitting. _____

16. McMahan says, "it was quite full when it walked away." _____

Exercise 3—3

NAME _____

If you have written sentences with incorrect end punctuation or beginning capitalization, correct and write one of them below.

1. _____

_____

Write four new sentences. Supply correct beginning capitalization and end punctuation for all four.

2. _____

_____

3. _____

_____

4. _____

_____

5. _____

_____

Exercise 3—4[7]

The following paragraphs contain some independent clauses incorrectly joined by commas. In the space provided, revise each of the comma splices by substituting a period and capitalizing the first word of the next sentence. Write only the words immediately preceding and following the period. If a sentence needs no revision, write NR in the space provided.

Example: People used to think black bears were solitary animals, however, we now know that they are highly territorial and that they have a rigidly matriarchal society.

_____*animals. However*_____

(1) People tend to think of black bears as those cute roadside beggars in our national parks, however, black bears are not a bit cuddly. (2) Both male and female can climb a tree with the agility of a cat and have been clocked on the ground at 30 miles per hour. (3) Naturally shy but also amazingly strong, a black bear is nothing to fool with if injured or menaced.

(4) Bears spend much of their time looking for food, they are not choosy. (5) They gorge on insects, berries, nuts, small mammals, ham sandwiches, and garbage with equal relish, nevertheless, the main natural factor limiting a bear population is the food supply. (6) Contrary to popular belief, so-called "garbage bears"—those that visit town dumps or campsites—do not lose their ability to forage successfully for wild foods. (7) These enterprising bears grow faster, mature sooner, and reproduce earlier than those that depend solely on wild foraging. (8) Dump-fed bears are the strongest and largest in the population.

1. _____

2. _____

3. _____

4. _____

5. _____

6. _____

7. _____

8. _____

PUNCTUATION WITHIN A SENTENCE

Independent Clauses

- 1. Students who wish to know their final grades before the registrar posts grade reports should leave stamped, self-addressed post cards with the teaching assistant◯ We will mail the cards in about two weeks.
- 2. The course has three requirements◯the most important one is the research paper.
- 3. Students were not satisfied by the dean's explanation for curtailed library hours◯ *nevertheless,* they agreed to stop their protest activities for one week.
- 4. "Yet" is a coordinating conjunction, *yet* it is often preceded by a semicolon or period rather than by a comma.

As you have just seen in the preceding section on end punctuation, two independent clauses can be separated by a period. The first example above also illustrates this:

- Students should leave stamped, self-addressed post cards with the teaching assistant◯ We will mail the cards in about two weeks.

As the second and third examples show, a semicolon also can be used between two independent clauses.

- The course has three requirements◯ the most important one is the research paper.
- Students were not satisfied by the dean's explanation for curtailed library hours◯ nevertheless, they agreed to stop their protest activities for one week.

A semicolon creates a strong pause but not a full stop. If you want to emphasize the close relationship between the two clauses, use a semicolon instead of a period.

The fourth example shows still a third way to join independent clauses—a comma and a coordinating conjunction—which gives the two clauses approximately equal weight and emphasizes the connection established by the conjunction.

An important distinction to notice is that between coordinating conjunctions (*and, but,* etc.) and sentence adverbs, words such as *however, nevertheless, besides, therefore, indeed,* and *furthermore.* The latter often have meanings similar to the meanings of coordinating conjunctions (*but* and *however,* for example, have similar meanings). Nevertheless, sentence adverbs cannot be used alone or with a comma to join two independent clauses. They must be preceded by semicolons or periods.

SUMMARY

Independent clauses can be separated by a period or joined either by a coordinating conjunction and a comma or by a semicolon. Using commas alone or using no punctuation at all between independent clauses is an error.

Exercise 3—5[8]

NAME _____

Write C in the space provided if beginning capitalization and end punctuation are correct. If not, circle the mistake(s) and write the correct punctuation and the words before and after the punctuation mark. Supply capitalization as necessary. More than one correction may be necessary.

Example: In its first fifty years, the Girl Scouts of the United States had not seen a single year of falling enrollment(,) (i)n 1969 (its peak year) it had a membership of 3,921,000.

enrollment. In

1. In 1971 the numbers started falling, and a few years later, GSUSA had lost fully a million girls. _____

2. Of course many changes had occurred since its founding in 1908, yet despite the changes, much of the Girl Scout program was simply not fashionable in the post-Sixties world. _____

3. It was not surprising that the GSUSA should decide that further changes were necessary, however, what was surprising was the extent and character of this change. _____

4. GSUSA began asking its constituency what it preferred, it began seeking statistics, it held discussion groups, it sent around surveys. _____

5. By 1977 the results were in, it remained only to take action. _____

6. The revisions were complete in 1980, and GSUSA enthusiastically presented its redesigned program to the councils at a series of national program conferences. _____

7. Throughout the process of revision, GSUSA had made a point of saying that it was not going to touch the basics nevertheless, the new program begins with an emphatically new Promise and Law. _____

8. The character of the change in these principles is basic. "Trying to live by the Girl Scout Law" appears, nowadays, to mean thinking about it a lot. _____

9. Scouts are now asked to consider what parts of the Girl Scout Law they value most, they are also urged to ask how "the Girl Scout Promise and Law help you to show your feelings about serving God and your country." _____

10. How to treat religion is something of a problem, for as one leader quite reasonably points out, scouting's nondenominational policy makes religion difficult to take on in any serious way. _____

11. Religion is defused, so is the uncomfortable question of patriotism. _____

12. The patriotic zeal of the early days needed to be toned down, still GSUSA may now have modified it too far in the other direction. _____

13. The new handbooks have such updated titles as *Worlds to Explore* and *You Make a Difference*; they encourage scouts to learn how their communities operate, to think about what they would like to change, and to get busy. _____

14. Girls so young they might not even have memorized the date of Washington's birthday are invited to start considering fundamental changes. _____

15. One of the handbooks says, "Keep a record of all the laws you must follow. Consider changing at least one of these laws so that more people would benefit. Write up your new law, and be able to explain why your law is better." _____

Exercise 3—6

NAME _____

Write two sentences using coordinating conjunctions. Write three sentences using sentence adverbs.

_____

_____

_____

_____

_____

_____

_____

_____

_____

Commas in a Series

- Parsley is in the parsley family, which also includes *celery, caraway, and carrots.*
- *Sage, rosemary, and thyme,* on the other hand, are all in the mint family.
- **x** Benjamin Franklin wrote *Poor Richard's Almanac* invented the Franklin stove and the lightning rod and went to both France and England as a diplomat.
- Benjamin Franklin wrote *Poor Richard's Almanac,* invented the Franklin stove and the lightning rod, and went to both France and England as a diplomat.

A **series** is three or more items linked within a grammatical structure. Each of the items in a series should be separated from the one before it, all except the last by a comma, the last by a comma and a coordinating conjunction:

- sage, rosemary, and thyme
- wrote *Poor Richard's Almanac,* invented the Franklin stove and the lightning rod, and went to both France and England as a diplomat.

The comma before the coordinating conjunction (the comma before *and*: *rosemary,* and) may be omitted and regularly is by many writers. However, using the comma will often clarify your meaning. In the Benjamin Franklin example, the items in the series are long and internally complex enough to cause temporary confusion if you omit the comma after *lightning rod.* Some sentences can be more than temporarily confusing:

- **x** The class elected officers: president, vice president, secretary and treasurer.

We cannot be altogether sure how many officers were elected. If four, an added comma would clarify:

- The class elected officers: president, vice president, secretary, and treasurer.

Commas Between Coordinate Modifiers

USE COMMAS	DO NOT USE COMMAS
relaxed, efficient manner (relaxed *and* efficient manner) minor, temporary problem (temporary, minor problem)	long-established eating habits expensive legal advice

Coordinate adjectives — two adjectives that modify the same noun — can be joined by *and* (relaxed and efficient manner) or separated by a comma (relaxed, efficient manner). Sometimes, however, two adjectives appear together but have unequal status. For example, *long-established* modifies not *habits* but *eating* *habits; expensive* modifies not *advice* but *legal advice.* In such a case the two modifiers should not be separated by a comma.

In order to decide whether or not to use the comma, reverse the order of the modifiers or join them with *and.* If the modifiers make sense, they are coordinate and should be separated by a comma: *minor, temporary problem* and *minor and temporary problem* mean approximately the same as *temporary, minor problem. Eating long-established habits,* on the other hand, does not make sense; nor does *long-established and eating habits.* These modifiers should not be separated by a comma: *long-established eating habits.*

SUMMARY

Items in a series are separated by commas; the last item is separated by both a comma and a coordinating conjunction. The last comma (the one before the coordinating conjunction) may be omitted, but including it will often prevent confusion. Two adjectives modifying the same noun are separated by a comma if they are not joined by *and* (*relaxed, efficient manner*). No comma follows an adjective that modifies an adjective-noun unit: expensive legal advice.

Exercise 3—7[9]

NAME _____

Place a caret (∧) where commas should appear. Several sentences will need more than one comma. Several sentences need none.

Example: Sugar is used not only in sweet baked goods, desserts, and soft drinks, but also in sauces∧ many baby foods∧ almost all fruit drinks∧ salad dressings∧ canned and dehydrated soups∧ pot pies∧ frozen vegetables∧ most canned and frozen fruits∧ fruit yogurt∧ and breakfast cereals.

Food costs so much partly because of the hidden charge for advertising promotion and fancy packaging. Wouldn't it be nice if you didn't have to pay for such frills? In some supermarkets now, you don't have to.

No-name products—also known as no-frills plain-wrap or generic products—consist of everyday grocery items in stripped-down packaging. Wrappers are generally plain white with a stark black legend: "Apple Sauce," "Whole Kernel Corn," "Cut Green Beans," and the like. There is no big advertising and promotion budget concealed in the price of each item. Nor is there a brand name, in the usual sense, to provide whatever security a brand name provides. The appeal is strictly price—and it is appealing enough to cause fear and trembling in the advertising community severe misgivings in the food trade and some cheers from shoppers. It is also the hottest food-marketing trend in years.

Consumer Reports evaluated five no-frills foods: green beans corn apple sauce peanut butter and ketchup. In addition to these, there are generic versions of other canned fruits and vegetables juices jams and jellies soups soft drinks tuna pet food dishwashing detergents laundry products and paper goods.

Exercise 3—8

NAME _____

Write four sentences using the patterns indicated below.

1. Three items in a series: _____

_____

2. Coordinate modifiers: _____

_____

3. Items in a series or coordinate modifiers: _____

_____

4. Items in a series or coordinate modifiers: _____

_____

Modifying Clauses and Phrases

MODIFIERS *BEFORE* MAIN CLAUSE:

- *If a man does not keep pace with his companions,* perhaps it is because he hears a different drummer.[10]

    —Thoreau

- *For many years* I was self-appointed inspector of snowstorms and rainstorms and did my duty faithfully.[11]

    —Thoreau

Modifying clauses and phrases that come before the main clause are usually followed by commas. If the modifier is quite short, the comma may be omitted if omitting it does not cause confusion.

MODIFIERS *AFTER* MAIN CLAUSE:

- If a man does not keep pace with his companions, perhaps it is because he hears a different drummer. Let him step to the *music*[1] *which he hears,*[2] *however measured or far away.*[12]

    —Thoreau

When modifiers appear after the main clause, they should not be separated from it by a comma if they are necessary to the completion of the meaning. In the second of Thoreau's sentences above (*Let him step to the music which he hears, however measured or far away*), the modifying clause—*which he hears*—is necessary to identify the music that Thoreau means. Therefore no comma separates *music* and *which he hears.* The second modifier in the same sentence—*however measured or far away*—tells us something more about the music but is not necessary to identify it. Because the modifier is not necessary to complete the meaning of the main clause, a comma appears after the clause and before the modifier.

MODIFIERS THAT *INTERRUPT* THE MAIN CLAUSE:

- Suddenly, with the number of lawyers doubling in the last decade, legal advice, *at least for common problems,* is becoming more accessible and less expensive.[13]

Interrupting modifiers are parenthetical elements and are, by their nature, not part of the basic meaning of the main clause. They are, therefore, both preceded and followed by commas. (They may also be preceded and followed by parentheses or dashes; see pp. 167–168.)

SUMMARY

Modifying clauses and phrases that come before the main clause are usually followed by commas, especially if they are lengthy. Phrases and clauses that come after the main clause may or may not be preceded by commas, depending on whether or not they are necessary to complete the meaning of the main clause.

145

Interrupting modifiers are parenthetical elements; because they are not part of the main clause, they are both preceded and followed by commas.

Restrictive and Nonrestrictive Elements

- Tests on humans have shown that sugar *eaten as part of a meal* causes less damage to teeth than the same amount of sugar *consumed as a between-meals snack*.[14]

A modifying clause or phrase that is necessary to the meaning of the main clause (the basic meaning would change if the clause or phrase were left out) is said to be **restrictive**, because it restricts the meaning of the main clause. A modifier that follows the main clause and cannot be separated from it by a comma is restrictive. In contrast, a modifying clause or phrase that is *not* necessary (that can be left out without changing the basic meaning of the main clause) is said to be **nonrestrictive**. All interrupting modifiers are nonrestrictive. Modifiers that follow the main clause and can be separated from it by commas are also nonrestrictive. This distinction—between restrictive and nonrestrictive elements—can be applied not just to the main clause and its modifiers but also to all modified words and their modifiers. If the sentence above were written without the phrases that modify sugar, the sentence would read:

- x Tests on humans have shown that sugar causes less damage to teeth than the same amount of sugar.

It does not make sense. The modifying phrases are necessary to identify the two kinds of sugar being talked about: sugar eaten as part of a meal and sugar consumed as a between-meals snack. Because the phrases are necessary to identify or define the words which they modify, there should be no comma separating the modifiers from the modified words.

The same distinction—that between restrictive and nonrestrictive elements—can be applied to **appositives**, words or phrases whose only function is to identify or restate an immediately preceding noun, pronoun, or nounlike element:

RESTRICTIVE—NO COMMAS:
- During the Spanish-American War, the famous U.S. Army doctor *Walter Reed* investigated an outbreak of yellow fever among troops stationed in Cuba.[15]

NONRESTRICTIVE—COMMAS:
- Your actions, *hiding the Bunsen burners and neutralizing the acid,* have made it impossible for the teaching assistant to conduct the lab.

Further examples:

RESTRICTIVE—MODIFIER NECESSARY: NO COMMA
- Is this the picture *that you took while standing on your head?*

- The saliva of the vampire bats contains a chemical *that prevents the blood from clotting.*[16]
- Tuna boats carry small speedboats *that can be dropped into the water within minutes after a tuna school is sighted.*[17]

NONRESTRICTIVE—MODIFIER NOT NECESSARY: COMMAS
- One species of tuna, *the yellowfin,* is considered the pride of the catch by tuna fishermen.
- Porpoises swim near the surface of the water, *above the tuna,* so they can get air.[18]

Although the distinction is in principle a clear-cut one, there are some cases in which a modifier can be seen as either restrictive or nonrestrictive. In the preceding sentence, for example, the phrase *in principle* could be considered either restrictive or nonrestrictive and could therefore be separated by commas from the preceding and following material.

Because clauses require special attention. *I do not swim, because I am afraid* means the reason I do not swim is that I am afraid. Without a comma—x *I do not swim because I am afraid*—the reader might think the sentence means I swim not because I am afraid but for some other reason. The meaning of the main clause is changed according to the use of commas.

After a positive verb, *because* clauses can often be seen as either restrictive or nonrestrictive.

RESTRICTIVE:
- Most people take aerobics classes because the exercise is good for the heart.

If we omit the *because* clause, the sentence is untrue. *Most* people do *not* take aerobics classes.

EITHER RESTRICTIVE OR NONRESTRICTIVE:
- She is taking an aerobics class because she wants to lose weight.
- She is taking an aerobics class, because she wants to lose weight.

If the sentence exists primarily to tell us *why* she is taking an aerobics class, no comma should be used. If the writer primarily wants to establish *that* she is taking the class and wants to add the reason, a comma precedes *because*.

Most cases are not so complicated as this one.

SUMMARY

Modifiers and appositives are either *restrictive* (they define or identify and are essential) or nonrestrictive (they explain and extend but do not define or identify; they are not essential). Restrictive elements should not be set off by commas. Nonrestrictive elements should be set off.

Exercise 3—9¹⁹: COMMAS WITH MODIFIERS

NAME _____

I. In the following sentences, several commas separating modifiers from modified elements have been omitted. Put a caret (ʌ) where commas should be added. (In a few cases, the commas are optional.)

II. Then, in the spaces provided below, indicate whether each of the italicized modifiers is restrictive (R) or nonrestrictive (NR). (In a few cases, a modifier could be viewed as either restrictive or nonrestrictive.)

Example: *Plaintiff* and *defendant* are legal terms: the plaintiff is the person (a) *who sues,* and the defendant is the person (b) *who is sued.*

(a) __R__   (b) __R__

1. An effective small-claims court system is important to consumers (a) *because it provides a simple and inexpensive way to have a complaint fairly judged* (b) *by an impartial third party.*

2. A comprehensive study of small-claims courts was published in 1978 by the National Center for State Courts (NCSC) (c) *a nonprofit organization dedicated to improving state and local courts.*

3. According to the NCSC report about three-fourths of the states have statewide small-claims court systems.

4. The NCSC study focused on courts in 15 metropolitan areas (d) *throughout the United States.*

5. The state laws and the courts were quite different from one another, but the researchers were nevertheless able to provide information on how (e) *in general* the courts work.

6. Most small-claims judges are on temporary assignment (f) *from the parent court.*

7. Typically a judge might spend every tenth week (g) *in small-claims court.*

8. Because the procedures in small-claims courts and formal courts are different the judges have to be fairly flexible.

9. For example in a formal court it is up to the opposing lawyers to look up the relevant law and show how it applies to the case.

10. But in a small-claims court if the plaintiff and defendant are not represented by lawyers the judge has to question both parties to elicit the facts.

11. If one side is represented by a lawyer, the judge may have to protect the other party from the consequences (h) *of not having a lawyer.*

12. Because judges have a lot of control over the trial many people raise the question of whether the outcome will be fair.

13. The NCSC report noted, "It was our subjective impression that most judges are able to achieve fair and even-handed results even though their trial practices differed widely."

14. Plaintiffs have a very good chance of winning their cases. According to the NCSC report about half the defendants did not bother to show up (i) *which usually meant the plaintiff won by default.*

15. Although about one-third of the plaintiffs and a little more than one-third of the defendants contacted lawyers about their cases very few plaintiffs or defendants were actually represented by lawyers in court.

16. Plaintiffs (j) *who had legal advice* were no more likely to win than those (k) *who did not.*

17. On the other hand defendants (l) *who had legal advice* fared better than those (m) *who did not.*

18. For about two-thirds of the plaintiffs the cost of taking a case to small-claims court was $25 or less.

(a) ———

(b) ———

(c) ———

(d) ———

(e) ———

(f) ———

(g) ———

(h) ———

(i) ———

(j) ———

(k) ———

(l) ———

(m) ———

Exercise 3–10²⁰: COMMAS—ALL USES

NAME _____

The following sentences require additional commas. Provide them, writing the comma and the words that precede and follow it. If no commas are required, write NC. (Some commas are optional.)

> *Example:* Whether in packaged salad dressing or in Hostess Twinkies sugar is the leading food additive in the United States. *Twinkies, sugar*

1. Because of overwhelming evidence from animal experiments and human studies there is no longer any controversy about the link between dental cavities and sugar. _____

2. There is not, however, a simple direct relationship between the amount of sugar you consume and the number of cavities you'll get. _____

3. Sticky candy can do far more damage to teeth than a soft drink because the sugar in liquids is more easily washed away. _____

4. Nevertheless, several soft drinks a day might do more damage than one piece of toffee a week. _____

5. Furthermore, the acid content of many soft drinks can also contribute to erosion a chemical wearing away of the teeth at the gum line. _____

6. The bacteria in your mouth do not care whether the sugar has been put there by nature or by industry. _____

7. You can damage a baby's teeth by putting fruit juices or even milk in a bottle at bedtime and allowing the baby to fall asleep while sucking. _____

8. Sugar like all other carbohydrates contains four calories per gram or 113 per ounce. _____

9. But sugar-sweetened foods also tend to be those in which calories are highly concentrated such as in pies, cakes, candy, and the like. _____

10. If you are trying to lose weight reducing your calorie intake without cutting down on sugar will probably prevent you from getting all the nutrients your body needs. _____

Superfluous Commas

x 1. The next questions were to determine whether students thought cheating was wrong‚ and if they had ever done it.

x 2. Some students found it acceptable to let others cheat during exams‚ and often allowed friends to copy homework, labs, etc.

x 3. Only 35 percent of the students who answered‚ believed that cheating was morally wrong.

It is as much a mistake to supply commas where they do not belong as it is to omit them where they are necessary. No comma should separate compound elements. In the first example above, *whether students thought cheating was wrong* and *if they had ever done it* are both objects of the infinitive *to determine:*
• The next questions were to determine *A* and *B*. No comma should appear between compound objects, compound subjects, compound modifiers, or compound verbs. The separation of compound verbs is especially frequent and may through repeated usage become correct, but the preferred practice is still to omit the comma between verbs in such sentences:

• Some students found it acceptable to let others cheat during exams and often allowed friends to copy homework, labs, etc.

Another error is to separate main sentence elements. In the third example above, the subject (*Only 35 percent of the students who answered*) is separated from the verb (*believed*). Even when the subject is followed by long modifiers, as it is in this case, no comma should separate subject and verb:

• Only 35 percent of the students who answered believed that cheating was morally wrong.

SUMMARY

Do not separate main sentence elements (e.g., subject and verb) or compound elements (e.g., compound verbs) with commas.

Exercise 3–11²¹: COMMAS — ALL USES

NAME _____

Supply commas where necessary. Write the comma as well as the words preceding and following it in the spaces provided at the end of the exercise. The first is done for you as an example. (Some commas are optional.)

From outer space there is nothing remarkable about it but to an observer on the earth's surface it is one of the most spectacular of nature's events: a total eclipse of the sun. Slowly and silently out of a clear sky a black arc begins to eat into the sun. An hour passes. The sun which has not failed for a lifetime disappears. During the last few minutes before totality the landscape takes on an eerie slate color stars begin to appear in the darkening sky and an unearthly stillness descends over nature. At the last moment the sun is blotted out entirely. Only then is the dark side of the disk of the moon perceptible as a whole outlined by a halo of light. As many as seven minutes may pass before the sun returns again.

_____*it, but*_____   _____   _____

_____   _____   _____

_____   _____   _____

Exercise 3–12²²: COMMAS — ALL USES

Indicate whether a comma should be supplied at the points marked by each number. If so, write C; if not, write NC (no comma).

> *Example:* Unless the moon's shadow happens to pass over a relatively densely populated area (1) as it did in New York City in 1925 (2) it is unlikely that an individual will see even one total eclipse (3) during a lifetime.
>
> (1) __*C*__   (2) __*C*__   (3) __*NC*__

1. The modern (1) antimosquito war began back at the turn of the century (2) when the famous U.S. Army doctor Walter Reed investigated an outbreak of yellow fever (3) among troops stationed in Cuba (4) during the Spanish-American War.

    (1) _____   (2) _____   (3) _____   (4) _____

2. Using volunteers as guinea pigs (5) Reed confirmed his earlier belief (6) that the disease could be transmitted by a mosquito now known as (7) *Aedes aegypti.*

    (5) _____   (6) _____   (7) _____

3. Thereupon (8) Major William C. Gorgas (9) an Army surgeon and sanitary engineer (10) set about getting rid of the mosquito's breeding places in Cuba (11) and introducing the use of window screens (12) and bed netting.

(8) _____   (9) _____   (10) _____   (11) _____   (12) _____

4. After controlling *Aedes aegypti* there (13) Gorgas went on (14) to all but eliminate (15) yellow fever and malaria in Panama (16) paving the way for construction of the Panama Canal.

(13) _____   (14) _____   (15) _____   (16) _____

5. Subsequently (17) both diseases were pronounced (18) "eradicated" in some other parts of the tropics (19) as well.

(17) _____   (18) _____   (19) _____

6. Reed and Gorgas had mosquitos on the run (20) so to speak.

(20) _____

Exercise 3—13

NAME _____

Write five sentences that require commas.

_____

_____

_____

_____

_____

_____

_____

_____

_____

_____

The Semicolon

A **semicolon** is used between parts of a sentence that are grammatically equal—between two main clauses or between items in a series if at least one of the items contains commas.

independent statements

- The course has three requirements⊘the most important one is the research paper.
- Going to law school was her goal⊘however, going to Nepal was her dream.

Independent clauses—if they are closely related—can be joined by a semicolon, as both examples above show. The semicolon creates a weaker pause than a period does but a stronger one than a comma does. It is sometimes called a weak period. It should not be used to separate a main clause from a subordinate clause:

- x Since I came to college⊘I have begun to get up much earlier than I used to.
- Since I came to college⊘I have begun to get up much earlier than I used to.

series

- Our town's three newspapers—the *Times,* which emphasizes local, national, and international news equally; the *Morning Post,* which concentrates on business news and financial analysis; and the *Evening Gazette,* which features local people and events—flourish in spite of their competition for subscribers and advertisers.

The items in a series can be and often ought to be separated by semicolons if at least one of the items is already punctuated by commas. Because the three items in the series in the sentence above have internal commas, semicolons are used to make clear that there is a series and that there are divisions within the series. Placing commas where semicolons now appear would be confusing:

- x Our town's three newspapers—the *Times,* which emphasizes local, national, and international news equally, the *Morning Post,* which concentrates on business news and financial analysis, and the *Evening Gazette,* which features local people and events—flourish in spite of their competition for subscribers and advertisers.

Using semicolons tells a reader that the three newspaper units are grammatically equal to one another.

The semicolon should not be used to introduce a list. That is the work of a colon (p. 161) and sometimes a dash (p. 167).

- x My job involved several routine activities; carrying supplies, taking specimens to the laboratory, and delivering used bedding to the laundry.
- My job involved several routine activities—carrying supplies, taking specimens to the laboratory, and delivering used bedding to the laundry.

SUMMARY

Semicolons separate grammatically equal units. They are used to separate closely related independent clauses or to separate items in a series if commas appear in at least one of the items. Do not use a semicolon to separate a main clause from a subordinate clause or to introduce a list.

Exercise 3–14[23]: SEMICOLONS

NAME _____

Indicate correctly used semicolons by writing *C* (correct) in the space provided. If the semicolon is not correct, write *NP* (no punctuation) or supply correct punctuation. If more than one punctuation mark would work, choose one.

Example: Presumably, yogurt has achieved its popularity because people see it as; convenient, inexpensive, nutritious, and low-calorie.   *NP*

1. In Egypt, yogurt is made from water buffalos' milk; in other parts of the world, it is made from camels' milk, sheep's milk, goats' milk, or cows' milk.   _____

2. Though yogurt was considered a staff of life in the Near and Middle East, parts of Russia, and the Balkans for centuries; it didn't reach the United States until about 1930.   _____

3. Early commercial production was not exactly a raving success; after all, the product did taste like sour milk.   _____

4. Realizing that sour is not American—sweet is—manufacturers started adding fruit preserves to their yogurt in the late 1940s; the fruit helped.   _____

5. Although yogurt's popularity increased; it was still no smash hit.   _____

6. Then in the late 1960s; it gained some ground with young people.   _____

7. It was convenient, cheap, natural, ethnic, did not pollute the environment; and was fashionably unfashionable.   _____

8. Today, yogurt is the fastest-growing dairy product in the United States, but it has room to grow; in 1976, only about 11 percent of the population ate yogurt regularly.   _____

9. Flavored yogurt is available in the upside-down sundae style; gooey mixture in the bottom of the container, yogurt on top (you get to mix it up yourself).   _____

10. And there's frozen yogurt; on sticks, in cups, or in push-up pops.   _____

Exercise 3–15[24]:   COMMAS AND SEMICOLONS

NAME _____

Indicate whether a comma (C), semicolon (SC), or no punctuation (NP) is required at the points marked by each number. Write your answers in the spaces
provided below. The first is done for you as an example.

   Insect predators attempt to subdue their prey with toxic venoms (1) or to lure
them with seductive perfumes. Unique among the chemically defended insects
is the termite caste of soldiers (2) their heads and bodies are so thoroughly
modified into weapons that they can neither feed themselves nor reproduce.
No other insect species (3) not even the army ants (4) have such a totally specialized and dependent full-time army.
   Termites, often incorrectly called "white ants," evolved quite separately from
ants (5) bees (6) and wasps. Termites have rigidly structured societies in which
specialized individuals execute specific tasks: the king and queen reproduce (7)
the workers forage (8) build the shelter (9) and care for the young (10) fertile
winged pairs fly off to form new colonies (11) and the soldiers defend.

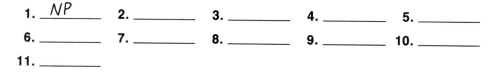

1. _NP_____   2. _____   3. _____   4. _____   5. _____

6. _____   7. _____   8. _____   9. _____   10. _____

11. _____

Exercise 3–16

In the space provided below, write five sentences using semicolons.

_____

_____

_____

_____

_____

_____

_____

_____

_____

_____

The Colon

- 1. With a population of only 75,000, our town manages to support three newspapers: the *Times,* the *Morning Post,* and the *Evening Gazette.*
- 2. People who buy foreign cars are not being disloyal: they are consumers, not patriots.
- 3. In his speech to Asian editors, the president of the East-West Publishing Company declared: "The East and West meet between the covers of every book that comes off our press."

The **colon** is used to introduce lists, restatements or explanation, and formal quotations. The words, phrases, or clauses following a colon are equal in meaning to part or all of the material preceding it. The items of a list following a colon make specific one of the words preceding the colon. In the first example above, the three items—the *Times,* the *Morning Post,* and the *Evening Gazette* —make *three newspapers* specific.

Restated material appearing after a colon is equal to part or all of the material preceding the colon. The restatement is more specific than the first statement. In the second example, *they are consumers, not patriots* explains why people who buy foreign cars are not being disloyal. In some cases of restatement or explanation, a semicolon or a period could be used instead of a colon.

As the third example shows, the colon can be used to introduce formal quotations. This is the only case in which a colon interrupts a sentence pattern. The quoted material is the object of *declared.*

other uses Colons are also used in titles, between main title and subtitle (*The Essential Guide for College Students: How to Complete Assignments in Half the Time*), in time notations (*It's only 4:45*), after the salutation in a letter (*Dear Mrs. Loos:*), and after the abbreviation for carbon copy (*cc: Dean Kenneth Martin*).

when not to use colons

- x 1. You should bring to the exam: a dictionary, several sharpened pencils, and at least two bluebooks.
- x 2. The following common household items are poisonous: bleach, turpentine, insect repellant, and furniture polish, and should be kept out of reach of children.
- x 3. On the morning news report I heard that: it is going to rain for the fifteenth weekend in a row, both the local teams lost their games, and traffic will be diverted from the south side of town on account of a huge chemical spill.

Except for the introduction of quotations, the colon should not be used to separate main sentence elements. In the first sentence, for example, the colon separating the verb (*bring*) from the direct objects (*dictionary, pencils, and bluebooks*) should be omitted:

161

- You should bring to the exam a dictionary, several sharpened pencils, and at least two bluebooks.

The material that follows a colon must end the sentence. In the second sentence a colon is incorrectly used to introduce a list that interrupts the sentence. To correct this, use dashes on each side of the list:

- Many common household items are poisonous—bleach, turpentine, insect repellant, and furniture polish—and should be kept out of reach of children.

A colon is not used to introduce an *indirect* quotation. In the third sentence the colon after *that* should be omitted.

SUMMARY

Colons are used to introduce lists, explanations or restatements, and formal quotations. They indicate that some part of the material preceding the colon is equal in meaning to the material that follows the colon. Colons are also used in dates, titles, and time notations.

Exercise 3–17[25]: COLONS AND OTHER PUNCTUATION MARKS

NAME _____

Supply colons for the sentences that require them. In the space provided, write the colon as well as the words immediately before and after it. Cross out incorrectly used colons, and, in the space provided, write the correct punctuation along with the words preceding and following it. If the sentence is correctly punctuated, write C in the space provided.

Example: From outer space there is nothing remarkable about it a dark speck, sweeping across the surface of our blue-white planet.

it : a

1. But to an observer on the earth's surface, it is one of the most spectacular of nature's events a total eclipse of the sun.

2. The senior year in high school has become a proverbial waste of time students spend too much time taking weak elective courses.

3. Children should start school earlier: at age four, and high school should end after a student completes the eleventh grade.

4. Three proposals for improving the educational system are as follows: (1) We must pay teachers more. (2) Teachers must be regularly recertified in their subject areas. (3) Separate schools of education and departments of education should be abolished.

5. One of these proposals: the last, though old, is still considered very radical.

Exercise 3–18: COLONS—CORRECT AND INCORRECT

Circle the incorrect punctuation in the following letter. In the space provided below, supply colons as necessary and correct incorrectly used colons. Write the correct punctuation and the word immediately preceding it. The first is done for you as an example.

Mr. Takaichi Mano

Yukyo-san-chome, 44 Gai-ku 2

Tokyo, Japan 170

Dear Mr. Mano

Mr. Nakagawa will arrive in Tokyo at 12.00 noon on July 15. He would like to set up a meeting with you on July 16 to discuss the translation of your book *Karate.* We are interested in the possibility of adding a subtitle in the English version and would like you to consider the following suggestions

Karate The Beginner's Step-by-Step Guide

Karate A Practical Guide to Self-Defense

Karate An Introduction to a Method Both Practical and Exotic

Mr. Nakagawa would also like to talk with you about: a short book explaining karate terms, your history of Japanese schools of self-defense, and books by other authors on judo for possible translation.

We look forward to meeting you when you visit the United States in December.

Yours truly,

Jonathan Kishimoto-Smith

Sports & Games Editor

East-West Publishing Co.

cc. Makoto Nakagawa

1. *Mano :* _____ 2. _____ 3. _____

4. _____ 5. _____ 6. _____

7. _____ 8. _____ 9. _____

Exercise 3–19²⁶: COLONS, COMMAS, AND SEMICOLONS

NAME _____

In the space provided, write C if the passage is correctly punctuated. If not, circle incorrect punctuation and, writing the words preceding and following it, supply the correct punctuation.

> *Example:*   Like all folkloric characters, mermaids are described differently in different stories ⃝but most mermaids tend to merge women with fish near or below the waist⃝ where the female torso starts to taper with scaly grace to a fish's tail.
>
> _____*stories, but*_____   _____*waist, where*_____

1. Then things vary. Mermaids have worn: the speckled tails of mackerel, the flukes of dolphins, and the sinewy tails of eels.

   _____

2. A flurry of mermaid sightings, accompanied the early sea explorations.

   _____

3. Mermaids are even mentioned in Christopher Columbus' journal from the voyage of 1492.

   _____

4. He wrote of one of his seamen; "He saw three mermaids; who rose very high from the sea, but they are not so beautiful as they are painted, though to some extent they have a human appearance about the face."

   _____

5. By the middle of the nineteenth century stuffed mermaids had become spectacles in Victorian London.

   _____

6. Showmen bought most of these so-called preserved specimens usually trumped-up monkey-fish composites from Japanese fishermen.

   _____

7. Each came with an individual story of its capture and they sometimes sold for thousands of dollars.

_____

8. One of the most popular versions of these stuffed curiosities came to be known as: the "Feejee Mermaid."

_____

9. It was first shown in a London coffee house; and later brought to Broadway by P. T. Barnum.

_____

10. This Broadway mermaid show was so popular, that it was moved to Barnum's New York American Museum, where, according to Beatrice Phillpotts in her book entitled *Mermaids* the mermaid nearly: "tripled the Museum's takings in the first month of its exhibit."

_____

Exercise 3—20

NAME _____

In the space provided below, write five sentences of your own using colons, two to introduce a list, two to introduce an explanation, and one to introduce a quotation.

1. _____

_____

2. _____

_____

3. _____

_____

4. _____

_____

5. _____

_____

Dashes, Parentheses, and Brackets

dash

- 1. In ten years—perhaps only five—people who do not know how to use a computer will be thought hopelessly old-fashioned.
- 2. IBM features a Charlie Chaplin look-alike in its ads for personal computers—what is the modern world coming to?
- 3. Biology, physics, calculus, and two chemistry courses—these are the basic requirements for premed students.
- 4. There are several basic requirements for premed students—biology, physics, calculus, and two chemistry courses.

Dashes are used to show abrupt changes in thought or to emphasize parenthetical material. In the first example above, the writer suddenly thinks the time might be shorter than ten years and includes the original thought as well as the afterthought to show that the event may be sooner than we expect. In this sentence, the writer could have used either commas or parentheses instead of dashes. The dashes make the interrupting material more emphatic.

In the second example, the question *What is the modern world coming to?* is given an emphatic position by the dash. (The question is already emphatic in content: since Chaplin made a movie in the thirties on the mechanization of modern life [*Modern Times*], it is ironic that his image is used to advertise personal computers.)

Dashes are also used to introduce a series or to introduce a sentence following a series. In the third example above, a colon could not be substituted for the dash; in the second example, either a dash or a colon would be correct.

FREQUENT PROBLEMS

- x 1. It took three weeks to select a jury—unheard of for such a minor case, because the D.A. was suspicious of people under 30 and over 33.
- x 2. If they are really dedicated, astronomers—whether professional or amateur, young or old—nevertheless, they travel anywhere in the world to see an eclipse of the sun.
- x 3. Correct posture while typing will prevent backaches and fatigue—and will allow you to work more efficiently. Your upper arms should be sloped slightly forward —and your forearms should be on the same slope as the keyboard—a table slightly too high will cause muscle tension—your back should be erect—supported by a backrest—and your feet should be flat on the floor. Relax your neck and shoulders—and let your fingers do the typing.

Problems arise when a comma is substituted for the second dash (example 1), when the material set off by dashes makes the writer forget the original sentence structure (example 2), or when the dash is used as an all-purpose punctuation mark (example 3). The three examples can be revised as follows:

- 1. It took three weeks to select a jury—unheard of for such a minor case—because the D.A. was suspicious of people under 30 and over 33.
- 2. If they are really dedicated, astronomers—whether professional or amateur, young or old—will travel anywhere in the world to see an eclipse of the sun.
- 3. Correct posture while typing will prevent backaches and fatigue and will allow you to work more efficiently. Your upper arms should be sloped slightly forward, and your forearms should be on the same slope as the keyboard (a table slightly too high will cause muscle tension). Your back should be erect—supported by a backrest—and your feet should be flat on the floor. Relax your neck and shoulders, and let your fingers do the typing.

parentheses

- 1. Memory improvement courses (their promises are nearly miraculous) appeal to people in every profession.
- 2. Enormous improvement seems available with very little effort (one ad insists that its method requires "no memorization and no word association").
- 3. If such courses could produce the results they promise ("Instant Memory enables you to play any musical instrument, find lost articles, awaken the exact moment you desire, tell jokes and stories without nervousness, improve your typing, think faster, and much more!"), the news would probably spread without advertisements.
- 4. If it were offered by a college, *Instant Memory* might be the most popular course on campus. (Extra work-study students would probably have to be hired to handle registration lines.) But what about the final exam? Would it test the students or the course?
- 5. Can you imagine being promised that you could (1) win at cards, (2) give speeches, (3) overcome stage fright, (4) play any sport better, and (5) learn any skill?[27]

Parentheses are used to enclose interrupting explanatory material that a writer does not want to emphasize. For example, *the promises are nearly miraculous* explains, without emphatically interrupting, the writer's main point—that memory improvement courses appeal to people in every profession. In contrast to dashes, parentheses deemphasize such parenthetical material.

Parentheses are also used to enclose the numbers of a list within a sentence (example 5 above).

PUNCTUATING SENTENCES ENCLOSED IN PARENTHESES

If you place an unquoted sentence in parentheses within your sentence, you should not use a capital letter to begin or a period to end the parenthetical sentence. If the parenthetical sentence ends your sentence, your end punctuation should be placed outside the parenthesis. If the parenthetical material contains quotation marks, you should use them.

Enormous improvement seems available with very little effort (one ad insists that its method requires "no memorization and no word association").

If the parenthetical material ends in a question mark or an exclamation point, you should use it; you should place whatever punctuation your sentence calls for outside the parenthesis.

If the parenthetical material is a quoted sentence, it should begin with a capital letter.

If such courses could produce the results they promise ("Instant Memory enables you to play any musical instrument, find lost articles, awaken the exact moment you desire, tell jokes and stories without nervousness, improve your typing, think faster, and much more!"), the news would probably spread without advertisement.

If the parenthetical sentence occurs between two sentences, it must begin with a capital letter and must have its own end punctuation placed inside the parenthesis:

It might be the most popular course on campus. (Extra work-study students would probably have to be hired to handle registration lines.) But what about the final exam?

brackets

- 1. According to *Science Digest*, "[W]e speak 150 words per minute—twice as fast as most typists type."[28]
- 2. Another nugget in *Science Digest* informs us, "In ancient times [how ancient is not indicated], it was thought that the tides were caused by an angel moving his foot in and out of the ocean."[29]

Brackets are used to enclose a writer's interruption of quoted material. In the second example above, *how ancient is not indicated* did not appear in the original sentence but was inserted by the writer to show that the question could easily arise. Brackets are also used to enclose capital letters or whole words not in the original sentence but necessary to the writer's sentence. The first quotation from *Science Digest* was originally *But, on average, we speak 150 words per minute— twice as fast as most typists type.* By using a bracketed capital, the writer indicates that the quoted sentence included but did not begin with *we*.

SUMMARY

Dashes set off emphatic interruptions and introduce or follow a series attached to a sentence. In the introduction of the series, the use of the dash overlaps with that of the colon.

Parentheses and dashes enclose interruptions and explanations. Use dashes to emphasize, parentheses to deemphasize such material.

Both dashes and parentheses set off material that might be set off by commas. Dashes are more emphatic than commas, parentheses less.

A sentence enclosed in parentheses and incorporated within a sentence does not have its own beginning capitalization or end punctuation unless the parenthetical sentence is quoted or unless the punctuation is a question mark or exclamation point.

Brackets enclose a writer's interruption of a quotation or material not included in the original but necessary to the writer's sentence. The use of brackets does not overlap with that of either dashes or parentheses.

Exercise 3–21[30]: DASH AND PARENTHESES

NAME _____

Choose five of the six items below and indicate whether each should be punctuated by dashes or by parentheses. If either dashes or parentheses would be correct, explain the effect of using each by indicating which part of the sentence would be emphasized. (If the parenthetical material occurs at the end of the sentence, it would, of course, require both parentheses but only one dash.)

Example: Today's ambitious classroom teachers __ if they stay in education __ are usually promoted out of the classroom into administrative posts because of better pay and the promise of advancement.

parentheses: The writer does not want to take our attention from his main point - the promotion of teachers to administrative posts.

dashes: The "if" clause becomes more important, suggesting that ambitious teachers' not staying in education is a serious problem which the writer wants us to consider.

1. In order to keep the best teachers in the school system, promotions and pay incentives __ similar to those in universities __ should be adopted.

_____

_____

_____

_____

2. Yogurt has been around for centuries. Abraham thrived on the stuff until he was 175 __ according to legend, an angel gave him the recipe__.

_____

_____

_____

_____

3. Undertakers frequently claim that embalming will prevent a body from decomposing __ it won't __ or that state law requires it __ only some states do, and then only in special circumstances__.

_____

_____

_____

_____

4. Delaware is a state all right __ and the First State at that, having been the earliest to ratify the U.S. Constitution__.

_____

_____

_____

_____

5. The state began as a confederacy of three counties, and, to hear talk, you might think it remains so, for county loyalty runs deep. Stacked from bottom to top __ descending in size and ascending in population __ are Sussex, Kent, and New Castle.

_____

_____

_____

_____

6. Downstaters paint northern New Castle County as an urban rat race run by aspiring sophisticates who, on the whole, would rather be in Philadelphia __ and should be__.

_____

_____

_____

_____

Exercise 3—22: BRACKETS

NAME _____

Write two sentences quoting material that you interrupt. Enclose your interruption in brackets. In addition write two sentences using quoted material that requires you to include a word or capital not in the original.

1. _____

_____

2. _____

_____

3. _____

_____

4. _____

_____

Exercise 3—23: PARENTHESES AND DASH

Write five sentences using parentheses or dashes.

1. _____

_____

2. _____

_____

3. _____

_____

4. _____

_____

5. _____

_____

The Apostrophe

- "An Adult's Guide to Children's Movies"
- What's new?
- The Spirit of '76
- The Oakland A's
- 6's and 7's
- the 1980s or the 1980's

The apostrophe is used to form the possessive of nouns (*adult's*), contractions (*what's, '76*), and the plural of letters and numbers (*A's, 6's*). The years of a decade can be written with or without an apostrophe (*the 1980's or the 1980s*).

FREQUENT PROBLEMS

x its (*it is*)
x it's (*belonging to it*)
x doesnt (*does not*)
x their's (*belonging to them*)

It's means *it is*; *its* means *belonging to it*. Like *it's*, *doesn't* is a contraction, and the apostrophe marks the omitted letter. Like *its*, *theirs* is a possessive pronoun and cannot be written with an apostrophe.

Exercise 3–24

NAME _____

Supply the missing apostrophes by writing the word(s) that require them in the spaces provided (there may be more than one missing apostrophe in a sentence). If a sentence is correct, write C in the space.

Example: Do you think most of todays high school seniors could do college work?

_____ *today's* _____

1. Dont count your chickens before they hatch.

_____

2. Dot your is and cross your ts.

_____

3. Its useless to cry over spilled milk.

_____

4. Everyone in the class of 84 will undoubtedly be required to read George Orwells *1984.*

_____

5. Historys lessons seem hard to apply in today's situations.

_____

6. TVs power over childrens minds has recently been the topic of many of televisions critics.

_____

7. How much is too much to drink if you're driving?

_____

8. Someone who claims, "Ill be okay as soon as I get behind the wheel" is making a foolish and possibly fatal misjudgment.

_____

9. Her Bs in composition were balanced by her As in organic chemistry.

_____

10. Whos that knocking at the door?

_____

Quotation Marks

- 1. According to a *Science Digest* report on work done at the University of Minnesota School of Dentistry, "Cheddar cheese may prevent cavities."[31]
- 2. Did the weatherperson say it would rain again this weekend?
- 3. Exactly what did she say? She said, "Tomorrow's forecast calls for showers in the morning and heavy rain in the afternoon."
- 4. A *Consumer Reports* article on the funeral industry reports: "Embalming adds an estimated $50 to $150 to the cost of a funeral, and it's an important tool in the sale of additional funeral arrangements. According to one textbook used in the funeral industry, 'without embalming, there would be little demand for beautiful caskets and protective vaults . . . and little need for mortuary service as we know it today.'"[32]

Use quotation marks (" ") to enclose direct quotations (examples 1, 3, and 4); do not use them to report someone's speech indirectly (example 2). Use single quotation marks (' ') to enclose a quotation within a quotation (example 4).

quotation marks with other punctuation

INTRODUCING AND CONTINUING QUOTATIONS

- 1. According to *Science Digest*, "The kidneys work tirelessly: 500 gallons of blood are filtered through these organs every day."[33]
- 2. *Science Digest* comments on babies' cries: "Nature may have intended that certain infants' cries be irritating. To attract attention, malnourished babies can wail a full octave higher than well-fed ones."[34]
- 3. *Science Digest* reports that for some insects "surviving the cold means surrendering to it: At the first signs of excessively frosty weather, the bug causes itself to freeze to death."[35]
- 4. *Science Digest* has a short piece on insects that "survive the cold . . . [by] surrendering to it: At the first signs of excessively frosty weather," the article reports, "the bug causes itself to freeze to death."[36]

Quotations may be introduced by commas or by colons (examples 1 and 2); the colon is more formal. If the quoted material fits into the structure of your sentence (example 3), no punctuation should be used. You may interrupt the quotation in the middle of a sentence. If you do, close the quotation; when you reopen it, use new quotation marks. No capital is necessary unless it was in the original material (example 4).

Use the capitalization of the quoted material or indicate changes by using brackets:

- According to a *Science Digest* report, "[M]alnourished babies can wail a full octave higher than well-fed ones."

179

PERIODS, COMMAS, AND ELLIPSES

- Reporting that some cheddars "may prevent cavities," a *Science Digest* article explains, "Tooth decay is caused by bacteria. . . . The microorganisms produce acid that breaks down tooth enamel, thereby helping to form cavities. The Minnesota scientists have found that some cheeses block this acid production."[37]

Whether or not they appeared in the original material, periods and commas are placed inside quotation marks: *cavities,"* and *production."* Periods and commas in the original give way to the punctuation of your sentence. For example, in the original, *may prevent cavities,* was *Cheddar cheese may prevent cavities.* The period after *cavities* was replaced by the comma needed for the sentence above.

Ellipses (. . .) indicate that material has been omitted. If the omitted section occurs within a sentence, three dots should be used: *" '[W]ithout embalming, there would be little demand for beautiful caskets and protective vaults . . . and little need for mortuary service as we know it today.'"* If, on the other hand, the omitted section occurs at the end of a sentence or between sentences, a period precedes the three dots: *"Tooth decay is caused by bacteria. . . . The microorganisms produce acid that breaks down tooth enamel."*

Ellipses are periods with spaces before, after, and between. Do not crowd the ellipses to save room: ... is incorrect; . . . is correct. When using a period and ellipses, place the period in the usual space, just after the last word.

COLONS AND SEMICOLONS

- 1. "Humpty Dumpty sat on a wall": this is the beginning of a nursery rhyme known to all English-speaking children.
- 2. "Humpty Dumpty sat on a wall"; "Three blind mice, see how they run"; and "Jack and Jill went up the hill" are known to all English-speaking children.
- 3. "Today, yogurt is the fastest-growing dairy product in the United States. But it has room to grow: In 1976, only about 11 percent of the population ate yogurt regularly," according to an article in *Consumer Reports.*
- 4. "Today, yogurt is the fastest-growing dairy product in the United States. But it has room to grow," according to *Consumer Reports.*[38]

Colons and semicolons at the end of quoted material are always placed outside the quotation marks (examples 1 and 2). They are the writer's own punctuation, not the punctuation of the sentence being quoted. A colon or semicolon in the original material gives way to the punctuation of the writer's sentence. In the example above, the colon after *grow* in the original sentence gives way to the comma of the writer's own sentence.

QUESTION MARKS, EXCLAMATION POINTS, AND DASHES

- 1. The teacher's first question—"Who stole the Bunsen burners?"—took all the students by surprise.
- 2. We heard someone shout, "Hurry!"

- 3. Did you hear her ask, "Who stole the Bunsen burners?"
- 4. Did you hear a voice in the back say, "The girls did it"?

Question marks, exclamation points, and dashes are placed inside the quotation marks if they are a part of the quoted material, outside the quotation marks if they are not. If the quoted question ends a question, one question mark ends both (example 3). Do not use periods after quoted questions or quoted exclamation points.

punctuation of titles and words as words

- 1. The word *enigma* is difficult to define.
- 2. The word "enigma" is difficult to define.
- 3. There is an article in *Consumer Reports* on cheese spreads called "Six Ways to Disappoint a Cracker?"[39]

Words as words are usually italicized (*enigma*) but may be enclosed in quotation marks ("enigma"). Titles of movies and works long enough to be published by themselves—books and plays, for example—are italicized. Titles of poems (unless they are long enough to be published by themselves, for example, *Paradise Lost*), chapters in books, articles in magazines, and songs are enclosed in quotation marks.

SUMMARY

Quotations are introduced by commas or colons—or by no punctuation at all if they fit directly into the structure of the writer's sentence. The capitalization of the quoted material is retained unless changes are indicated with brackets. Commas and periods are always placed inside quotation marks, semicolons and colons outside. Question marks, exclamation points, and dashes are placed inside the quotation marks if they are part of the quotation, outside if they are not.

Exercise 3—25[40]

NAME _____

If the quotation marks and the other punctuation marks that accompany them are correct, write C in the space provided. Circle incorrect punctuation and write the corrections in the space provided. Include the word before and after any changes you make. More than one correction may be required in one sentence.

Example: How do you imagine that the writers of *Science Digest* know that "malnourished babies can wail a full octave higher than well-fed ones?"

ones " ?
_____

1. A *Consumer Reports* article, discussing the myths about yogurt, commented on a Dannon advertisement: "Dannon's current advertising campaign shows an elderly man eating Dannon yogurt. An even older woman looks on approvingly. According to the script, the man is in his late 80's; the woman is his mother. They live in Soviet Georgia. The commercial doesn't say that Dannon yogurt will help you live longer. It does say: "But it couldn't hurt".
_____

2. I wonder if the article that said "Cheddar cheese may prevent cavities." increased cheese sales.
_____

3. For the past fifteen weeks the weatherperson has said "there would be rain again on the weekend."
_____

4. Would you respond to an ad for a memory-enhancing method that promised, "Pass exams easily!"?
_____

5. The same ad goes on: "Now you can easily pass every exam with less study, no worry, and no 'test trauma'".
_____

6. A bug that "causes itself to freeze," sounds like a bug with real will power.

---

7. If it is true that "undertakers frequently claim that embalming will prevent a body from decomposing", they are guilty of a highly unethical practice.

---

8. According to *Consumer Reports,* a proposed rule would require undertakers "to state on their price list: 'Embalming is not required by state law in most instances. Unless so required, embalming will not be performed without permission."

---

9. *Consumer Reports* says that an FTC (Federal Trade Commission) report found that "undertakers often call inexpensive caskets "paupers' boxes" or claim that a body might not fit into a low-priced coffin."

---

10. The report on sugar concluded, "(I)f you're concerned about nutrition or your teeth, try to satisfy your craving for sweets with fresh fruits and fresh juices. Brown sugar...and the like offer no health advantage over the undisguised white stuff."

Exercise 3—26

NAME _____

Write five sentences in which you quote material from magazines, books, or newspapers. Use at least one set of dashes, one question mark, and one colon to show that you understand how to use these punctuation marks with quotation marks.

_____

_____

_____

_____

_____

_____

_____

_____

_____

VARIOUS USES OF CAPITALIZATION

Titles and Subtitles

- *Karate: The Fusion of the Exotic and the Practical*
- "Six Ways to Clean House without Doing Any Work"

Capitalize the first letters of the first and last words in a title and subtitle. Also capitalize other important words. Prepositions, conjunctions, and articles (*a, an,* and *the*) should not be capitalized unless they are the first words of the title or subtitle.

Names

Capitalize the names of specific people, places, companies, organizations, and institutions. Do not capitalize general references to geographical locations or unspecified courses or universities.

CAPITALIZE:
- Abraham Lincoln
- St. Louis, Missouri
- The American Society for the Prevention of Cruelty to Animals (ASPCA)
- The North American Treaty Organization (NATO)
- Jupiter
- Atari
- South Carolina
- Economics 3210
- University of Arkansas

DO NOT CAPITALIZE:
- the northeast corner of Arizona
- an economics course
- a university in Arkansas

Units of Time

CAPITALIZE	DO NOT CAPITALIZE
Fall Semester 1984	spring semester, every fall
Friday, October 12	the second of September
Memorial Day	Labor Day weekend

Capitalize names of months, days, and holidays, but do not capitalize the numerical part of a date when it is written out (*the second of September*), seasons, or general references to time (for example, *semester, weekend*).

Ranks and Degrees

CAPITALIZE	DO NOT CAPITALIZE
Chief Justice Earl Warren Chief Justice of the United States	the chief justice
Senator Alan Cranston	the senator from California
President Jane Doe the President of the United States	the first woman president
Benjamin Palmer, Ph.D. Professor Palmer	a doctor's degree in physics a physics professor
Dr. Jessica Palmer	a doctor in Boulder, Colorado

Ranks and titles are capitalized when attached to a specific name; in other cases, they are usually not. (Notice the exceptions: President of the United States, Chief Justice of the United States.) Abbreviations of academic degrees are capitalized.

NAME _____

If the capital or lower-case letter of each of the underlined words is correct, write C in the space provided. If a word is wrongly capitalized, write it below without capitalization; if it should be capitalized, write it below with appropriate capitals. The first is done for you as an example.

Much of the plastic trash washing up on (1) florida (2) beaches facing the (3) atlantic (4) ocean may have started its journey in the (5) caribbean. That's the conclusion of (6) marine biologist (7) judith (8) winston, of the (9) american museum of natural history, in (10) new york city. Winston, who has been collecting plastic beach litter in (11) fort pierce, (12) florida, thinks it becomes tangled in the rafts of *Sargassum* algae that drift (13) north from the (14) Caribbean and is then washed ashore when the (15) Gulf Stream is driven off course by violent (16) winter storms.

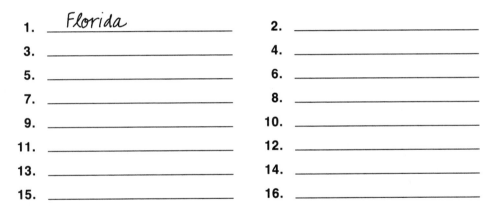

1. _Florida_   2. _____

3. _____ 4. _____

5. _____ 6. _____

7. _____ 8. _____

9. _____ 10. _____

11. _____ 12. _____

13. _____ 14. _____

15. _____ 16. _____

Launched from (17) earth, (18) Voyager 1 flew within 2,500 miles of one of (19) saturn's (20) moons. Such a feat is comparable to shooting an arrow 6 miles and getting it to pass within one inch of an apple.

17. _____ 18. _____

19. _____ 20. _____

189

In (21) june of 1978, the (22) Federal Trade Commission (23) (ftc) proposed a rule that could bring effective regulation to the funeral industry. (24) Under-takers frequently advance payment to florists, pallbearers, and (25) clergy and arrange other third-party payments. According to the (26) FTC, some under-takers pad their bills, resulting in an estimated $40 million a year in over-charges.

21. _____   22. _____

23. _____   24. _____

25. _____   26. _____

NAME _____

Supply the punctuation and capitalization missing from the following passages. Circle the punctuation marks and underline the capital letters you provide. Make use of italics, the dash, colon, and parentheses as well as other punctuation marks. More than one kind of punctuation may be correct; choose the punctuation you think is best. If a comma is optional, choose whether to use it.

Example: agricultural scientists have developed a new strain of potato plant that may need almost no help from pesticides instead the new spud may be able to dispatch on its own destructive insects that chance to alight on its leaves.

1. the thermos company popularized vacuum bottles so thoroughly that the word thermos became a generic term even the competition which is mainly aladdin industries uses the word thermos in describing its products

2. the heart of an old-fashioned thermos bottle that silvery glass double envelope that breaks so easily actually has another name the dewar flask it was named after the scottish scientist sir james dewar who invented it in the 1890s to contain the cold gases he had liquified

3. there are small-mouthed bottles for liquids and wide-mouthed bottles for soups stews potato salad and such besides the traditional glass vacuum bottles there are unbreakable bottles made of foam-lined plastic much cheaper than the glass bottles or of steel much more expensive there are also large inexpensive plastic jugs made of foam-lined plastic and meant for holding liquids

4. in the days when energy was more abundant turning up the thermostat was the usual way to keep warm but now with homeowners landlords and employers alike cutting back on the heat people have to cope with lower temperatures at home and at work

5. winter sports enthusiasts and people who work outdoors have known about long underwear for years but it took an energy crisis and a brutally cold winter to alert others to the advantages of long johns shirts and drawers sold separately are available in an array of colors patterns and fabrics consumer reports had no trouble finding 62 different models for both men and women for their report on long underwear

6. any time you try to change your writing, you do things that look unnatural says gary herbertson chief of the fbi laboratorys document section. "A forgers writing does not have the speed the fluidity or the smoothness of natural writing you can see blunt beginnings and ends of strokes rough curves inappropriate breaks and little tremors. two letters may be the same shape but you can tell if one is written quickly and the other is carefully drawn it may sound subjective but if you give two experienced examiners the same documents they will come to the same opinion nearly every time

7. according to many physicians and health experts alcoholism is the most urgent public health problem in the country three to ten percent of the population will become alcoholic at one time or another in their lives affecting one out of three families but the exact number of alcoholics at any given time is impossible to determine for one thing doctors are understandably hesitant to stamp a patients record with a diagnosis of alcoholism

8. unfortunately says james r milam a seattle treatment specialist author and lecturer alcoholism is not considered a medical diagnosis by most people it is considered a personal slur

9. if you approach early-stage alcoholics says morris hill and tell them that they have a problem, they will tell you to go take a hike they know for a fact that they can handle their drinking better than most of their friends they can drink their friends under the table they dont know he continues that an early high tolerance for alcohol is not a talent its a symptom

10. its not exactly a fetal position but the leaves of many plants assume a compact vertical sleeping posture peanut and tobacco leaves bend skyward white clover and flowering bean plants drop their blades toward the ground. on the basis of recent experiments behavioral physiologist james enright of the scripps institution of oceanography in la jolla california offers a new explanation for the nighttime positions sleep movements he says enhance leaf growth by keeping the leaves warm at night

NOTES

[1] Adapted from Stephen Solomon, "Spare-Parts Medicine," *New York Times Magazine,* 28 Nov. 1982, p. 120.

[2] "Sunscreens," *Consumer Reports,* 48 (1983), 275.

[3] Roger B. Swain, "The Secret Life of the Familiar Evergreen," *New York Times Magazine,* 13 Mar. 1983, p. 78.

[4] Joel R. L. Ehrenkranz, "A Gland for All Seasons," *Natural History,* June 1983, p. 18.

[5] Adapted from Louis Lasagna, "Death in the Ring," *The Sciences,* May/June 1983, p. 61.

[6] Adapted from Sarah Boxer, "The Subtlest Assassins," *The Sciences,* May/June 1983, p. 7.

[7] Adapted from Adele Conover, "Getting to Know Black Bears—Right on Their Own Home Ground," *Smithsonian,* Apr. 1983, pp. 87–88.

[8] Adapted from Rachel Flick, "The Truth about Girl Scouts," *Harper's,* Mar. 1983, pp. 43–46.

[9] Adapted from "Too Much Sugar?" *Consumer Reports,* 43 (1978), 136 (exercise example) and "Big Savings in Small Packages," *Consumer Reports,* 43 (1978), 315 (body of exercise).

[10] Henry David Thoreau, *Walden: A Writer's Edition* (New York: Holt, Rinehart and Winston, 1966), p. 251.

[11] Thoreau, p. 14.

[12] Thoreau, p. 251.

[13] "Paying Less for a Lawyer," *Consumer Reports,* 44 (1979), 522.

[14] "Too Much Sugar?" p. 139.

[15] David Zimmerman, "The Mosquitoes Are Coming—And They Are Among Man's Most Lethal Foes," *Smithsonian,* June 1983, p. 30.

[16] Adapted from Donald Dale Jackson, "Close Encounters with the Creatures of Another World," *Smithsonian,* Nov. 1982, p. 78.

[17] "Tuna vs. Porpoises: The Survival of an Endangered Species," *Consumer Reports,* 44 (1979), 11.

[18] Ibid.

[19] Adapted from "Alternate Legal Services—Part II: The Role of the Small-Claims Court," *Consumer Reports,* 44 (1979), 66.

[20] Adapted from "Too Much Sugar?" p. 137.

[21] Adapted from Laurence A. Marschall, "The Compleat Eclipse-Chaser," *The Sciences,* May/June 1983, p. 24.

[22] Adapted from Zimmerman, p. 30.

[23] Adapted from "Yogurt: Will It Keep You Fit? Can It Help You Live Longer? How Low-calorie Is It?" *Consumer Reports,* 43 (1978), 7.

[24] Adapted from Glenn D. Prestwich, "The Chemical Defenses of Termites," *Scientific American,* Aug. 1983, p. 78.

[25] Adapted from Marschall, p. 24 (exercise example and exercise item 1) and Leon Botstein, "Nine Proposals to Improve Our Schools," *New York Times Magazine,* 5 June 1983, pp. 63–64, 66 (exercise items 2–5).

[26] Adapted from Carrol B. Fleming, "Maidens of the Sea Can Be Alluring, But Sailor, Beware," *Smithsonian,* June 1983, pp. 86, 88–89, 92.

[27] Adapted from an advertisement appearing in *Science Digest,* July 1983, p. 93.

[28]"Mind and Body," *Science Digest,* July 1983, p. 86.

[29]"Everyday Science," *Science Digest,* July 1983, p. 92.

[30]Adapted from Botstein, p. 66 (exercise example and exercise item 1); "Yogurt: Will It Keep You Fit?" p. 7 (exercise item 2); "Funerals: The FTC's Halfhearted Reform," *Consumer Reports,* 44 (1979), 492 (exercise item 3); and Jane Vessels, "Delaware: Who Needs to Be Big?" *National Geographic,* 164 (1983), 172 (exercise items 4–6).

[31]"Mind and Body," *Science Digest,* Apr. 1983, p. 90.

[32]"Funerals: The FTC's Halfhearted Reform," p. 492.

[33]"Mind and Body," *Science Digest,* Apr. 1983, p. 88.

[34]"Everyday Science," *Science Digest,* Apr. 1983, p. 92.

[35]"Update," *Science Digest,* Apr. 1983, p. 24.

[36]"Update," p. 24.

[37]"Mind and Body," *Science Digest,* Apr. 1983, p. 90.

[38]"Yogurt: Will It Keep You Fit?" p. 7.

[39]"Six Ways to Disappoint a Cracker?" *Consumer Reports,* 48 (1983), 63.

[40]Adapted from "Everyday Science," *Science Digest,* Apr. 1983, p. 92 (exercise example); "Yogurt: Will It Keep You Fit?" p. 8 (exercise item 1); "Mind and Body," *Science Digest,* Apr. 1983, p. 90 (exercise item 2); Advertisement for "Instant Memory," *Science Digest,* July 1983, p. 93 (exercise items 4–5); "Funerals: The FTC's Halfhearted Reform," pp. 492–493 (exercise items 7–9); and "Too Much Sugar?" p. 139 (exercise item 10).

[41]Adapted from "Update," *Science Digest,* July 1983, p. 23 (exercise items 1–16); "Technology," *Science Digest,* July 1983, p. 27 (exercise items 17–20); and "Funerals: The FTC's Halfhearted Reform," p. 492 (exercise items 21–26).

[42]Adapted from "Update," *Science Digest,* July 1983, p. 24 (Review Test example); "Thermos Bottles and Picnic Jugs," *Consumer Reports,* 48 (1983), 304 (Review Test items 1–3); "Long Underwear: A Personal Way to Save Energy," *Consumer Reports,* 43 (1978), 46 (Review Test items 4–5); John Tierney, "Handwriting Analysis: More Art than Science?" *Science 83,* Aug. 1983, p. 14 (Review Test item 6); and Michael Watterlond, "The Telltale Metabolism of Alcoholics," *Science 83,* June 1983, pp. 72, 74 (Review Test items 7–10).

WORDS 4

"But 'glory' doesn't mean 'a nice knock-down argument,'" Alice objected.

"When *I* use a word," Humpty Dumpty said, in rather a scornful tone, "it means just what I choose it to mean—neither more nor less."

"The question is," said Alice, "whether you *can* make words mean so many different things."

"The question is," said Humpty Dumpty, "which is to be master—that's all."[1]

— Lewis Carroll, *Through the Looking Glass*

The spelling and the meaning of words are based on the agreement of people who use them. Even when English spelling was far less regular than it is now, variations were within a recognizable range. And although established by general consent, the conventions of spelling are now rather firmly established. In order to be "master," that is, in order to communicate efficiently, it is necessary to conform to the general agreement. That general agreement is the basis of the spellings provided by a dictionary.

Meaning is more complex, but it too is based on usage. Alice is right, of course —*glory* does not mean *a nice knock-down argument*—and Humpty Dumpty's treatment of words as if they were his private domain would make the simplest communication impossible. But words are not so stable as Alice thinks or so immune to change by their users. They continually gain new meanings, and new words enter the language.

In an interview on a morning news program, the editor of *Webster's Dictionary* listed some words that have entered the language recently. Prominent among them are words for food that many Americans now eat—*kiwi fruit, sushi, zuppa inglese,* and *burrito.* Computer technology has added many new words, such as *microchip, videotex, cursor,* and *PASCAL.* And our changing lifestyles account for the creation of still other new words: *open marriage, survivalist, house husband.*

People who write dictionaries (lexicographers) are always looking for new words and new applications of old words. The first step in their job is to read and listen. A dictionary's authority is based on lexicographers' careful study of how writers and speakers have used and are using words.

USING YOUR DICTIONARY

Let's look at a typical entry in *The Random House College Dictionary* (Revised Edition, 1982).

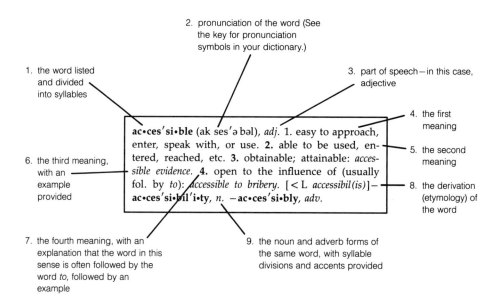

2. pronunciation of the word (See the key for pronunciation symbols in your dictionary.)

1. the word listed and divided into syllables

3. part of speech — in this case, adjective

4. the first meaning

6. the third meaning, with an example provided

ac•ces′si•ble (ak ses′ə bəl), *adj.* 1. easy to approach, enter, speak with, or use. 2. able to be used, entered, reached, etc. 3. obtainable; attainable: *accessible evidence.* 4. open to the influence of (usually fol. by *to*): *accessible to bribery.* [< L *accessibil(is)*] — ac•ces′si•bil′i•ty, *n.* —ac•ces′si•bly, *adv.*

5. the second meaning

8. the derivation (etymology) of the word

7. the fourth meaning, with an explanation that the word in this sense is often followed by the word *to*, followed by an example

9. the noun and adverb forms of the same word, with syllable divisions and accents provided

Your dictionary gives you the spelling, part of speech, pronunciation, meaning(s), and origin of a word. It lists principal parts of verbs, indicates whether a verb is transitive or intransitive (pp. 27–28), gives synonyms (words with the same meaning) and antonyms (words with the opposite meaning), and often gives examples of the meanings it provides. It also lists usage labels such as *slang* to guide you in choosing appropriate language.

In order to use your dictionary efficiently, you must learn its abbreviations and symbols. You will find a key or table of explanation in the front section. In the entry above, the symbol *n.* means *noun: accessibility* is the noun formed from *accessible.* "L" means *Latin,* and "< L *accessibil(is)*" means that *accessible* is derived from the Latin word *accessibilis.*

You should also get in the habit of using the guide words—the words printed in boldface type at the top of each column on every page. The guide word at the head of the left column is the first word listed on that page, while the guide word at the top of the right column is the last word listed on that page. In *The Random House College Dictionary*, *accessible* is found between the guide words *acaridan* and *access time*. In *Webster's New World Dictionary*, the guide words for the page on which *accessible* is listed are *accentual* and *acclivous*. You will find words much faster by using the guide words than by running your eye down page after page, and you may become a better speller, since the guide-word system causes you to think precisely about the spelling of the word you are looking up.

1. **Get'tysburg Address'**, the short speech made by President Lincoln on November 19, 1863, at the dedication of the national cemetery at Gettysburg.

2. **Kil•i•man•ja•ro** (kil'ə mən jär'ō), *n.* a volcanic mountain in N Tanzania: highest peak in Africa. 19,321 ft.

3. **Rob•in•son** (rob'in sən), *n.* **1. Edwin Arlington**, 1869–1935, U.S. poet. **2. Jack Roosevelt** ("Jackie"), 1919–72, U.S. baseball player.

As you can see from the above examples from *The Random House College Dictionary*, the dictionary also has entries for especially noteworthy events, some geographical locations, and famous people. As example 3 shows, biographical entries are under the last name and more than one person may be listed. Many dictionaries also have other information, such as a list of proofreader's symbols, a list of colleges and universities in the United States and Canada, and a table of weights and measures. Some also provide a general guide to style (including information about the use of punctuation, capitalization, and abbreviations).

SUMMARY

The authority of a dictionary is based on a careful study of how writers and speakers have used and are using the language. The dictionary gives you the spelling, part of speech, pronunciation, meaning(s), and origin of a word, as well as other information. To use the dictionary efficiently you need to learn its labels and symbols and its guide words.

Use your own dictionary to do the following exercises.

NAME _____

Title of dictionary _____

Publisher _____

Date of publication _____

Exercise 4—1: SYMBOLS AND ABBREVIATIONS

Find your dictionary's explanation of its labels and explain the meaning of the following items.

Example: obs. _____ *obsolete* _____

1. i.e. _____	6. syll. _____
2. pl. _____	7. sing. _____
3. dial. _____	8. = _____
4. n. _____	9. v.t. _____
5. cf. _____	10. v.i. _____

Look up five words and explain one of the accompanying labels for each word. Write the word, the label, and the meaning of the label in the space provided below.

Example: _____ *among, prep. preposition* _____

11. _____

12. _____

13. _____

14. _____

15. _____

Exercise 4—2: PRONUNCIATION

Use your dictionary to divide the following lists of words into syllables. Provide the stress mark over the proper syllable. List the guide words (GW) for each.

Example: nutrition _nu·tri·tion_   GW _numerosity/nutritive_

1. bibulous _____ GW _____
2. buckle_____ GW _____
3. desuetude _____ GW _____
4. manipulate _____ GW _____
5. saturate _____ GW _____
6. flourish _____ GW _____
7. decade _____ GW _____
8. legendary _____ GW _____
9. ferocious_____ GW _____
10. unheralded_____ GW _____

Write the pronunciation(s) given by your dictionary for each of the following words. Sound each out according to the pronunciation key supplied at the bottom of the page or at the front of the dictionary.

Example: caffeine _ka fēn´; kaf´ēn; kaf´ē in_

11. flaccid_____
12. defensible _____
13. sedentary _____
14. desultory _____
15. exemption _____
16. competitive_____
17. lieutenant _____
18. succumb _____
19. contraband _____
20. charivari _____

Exercise 4–3: DERIVATION

NAME _____

Give the derivation or etymology of each of the following words as given in your dictionary. Explain any symbols and write out all abbreviations in full.

202

Example: mob <u>*short for Latin mobile vulgus* the movable (that</u>
<u>*is, changeable, inconstant*) common people</u>

1. gobble _____

_____

2. bedlam _____

_____

3. Scrooge _____

_____

4. Kleenex _____

_____

5. bluestocking _____

_____

6. flabbergast _____

_____

7. bamboozle _____

_____

8. nature_____

_____

9. chartreuse _____

_____

10. Mason jar _____

_____

Exercise 4—4:   MEANING: SYNONYMS AND ANTONYMS

NAME _____

Give the synonyms provided by your dictionary for the following words.

Example: hardy <u>*vigorous, robust, hale, stout, sound*</u>

1. vague _____

2. hungry_____

3. harmony _____

4. incompatible_____

5. joy _____

Give the antonyms provided by your dictionary for the following words.

Example: authentic: _spurious, counterfeit, sham_____

1. power _____

2. poverty _____

3. sacred _____

4. harmful _____

5. monotonous_____

Exercise 4—5: OTHER FEATURES OF THE DICTIONARY

NAME _____

If your dictionary contains the following sections, give one item of information found in each.

Example: signs and symbols: ___☄ = comet_____

1. directory of colleges and universities _____

_____

2. English given names _____

_____

3. basic manual of style or guide to punctuation and mechanics _____

_____

4. tables of weights and measures _____

_____

5. proofreader's marks and sample copy _____

_____

Adding Prefixes

PREFIX AND ROOT	COMBINED WORD
mis + spell	misspelled
mis + understand	misunderstand
un + neighborly	unneighborly
un + reasonable	unreasonable
il + legal	illegal
ir + regular	irregular

Adding prefixes (*mis-*, *un-*, *in-*, *pro-*, *pre-*, *non-*) does not change the spelling of the word. Words such as misspell and unneighborly have double consonants only because the same consonant appears both at the end of the prefix and at the beginning of the word (mis + spell and un + neighborly). The prefix *il-* (meaning *not*) only appears before a word beginning with *-l*; the result is always a double letter (illegal). Likewise, *ir-* (meaning *not*) only appears before a word beginning with *-r*; the result is a double letter (irregular).

Adding Endings (Suffixes)

single and double consonants

ROOT	ROOT AND SUFFIX
run	running
tan	tanned
jog	jogger
seal	sealing
sprint	sprinted
control'	controlled'
occur'	occúrring, occúrrence
refer'	reférring, *but* réference
commit'	committed, *but* commitment
trável	tráveled

When adding *-ing, -ed, -er,* or *-ence* to a *one-syllable* word ending in a single consonant, double the final consonant if it is preceded by one vowel: run — running; jog — jogger. Do not double the final consonant if it is preceded by two vowels (seal — sealing) or by a consonant (sprint — sprinted).

When adding *-ing, -ed, -er, -en,* or *-ence* to a word of two or more syllables that ends in a consonant (trável, contról), double the final consonant if the accent falls on the last syllable of the stem after the ending is added: controlled, referring, committed. Do not double the final consonant if the accent falls on any other syllable: réference, tráveled.

When adding *-ment, -ness, -less, -ly,* and other endings that begin with a consonant, do not double the final consonant of the word. Meanness may look like an exception but it is not: one *n* comes from the stem (mean), the other from the ending (-ness).

final -e

love	loving	lovable	lovely
manage	managing	manageable	management
argue	arguing	arguable	argument
notice	noticing	noticeable	
knowledge		knowledgeable	
acknowledge	acknowledging	acknowledgeable	acknowledgment
judge	judging	judgeable	judgment

KEEP THE *-E*

Keep the *-e* when adding an ending that begins with a consonant: lovely, management. However, when the final *-e* is preceded by a vowel (argue, due), the *-e* is often dropped: *argument, duly.* Other exceptions are *acknowledgment, judgment.* In British spelling the *-e* is kept, but in American spelling it is dropped when *-ment* is added to *acknowledge* and *judge.*

DROP THE *-E*

Drop the *-e* when adding an ending that begins with a vowel (for example, *-ing, -ed, -er*): *arranging, argued, manager.* Exception: *dye — dyeing.* Although *dyeing* may look strange, *dying* would be confusing, since it would look like *die — dying.*

ADDING *-ABLE* TO WORDS ENDING IN *-E*

When *-able* is added to a word, the *-e* is usually dropped: *lovable, arguable.* Keep the *-e* when the word ends in a soft *c* sound (for example, *notice, noticeable*) or when the word ends with a soft *g* sound (when the *g* sounds like *j*, for example, *manage, manageable*).

final -y

cr<u>y</u>	cr<u>ies</u>	cry<u>ing</u>	cr<u>ied</u>
monke<u>y</u>	monke<u>ys</u>	monke<u>ying</u>	monke<u>yed</u>

When the *-y* is preceded by one or more consonants, change it to an *-i* and add *-es* or *-ed* (*cries* and *cried*), but keep the *-y* before *-ing* (*crying*). When the *-y* is preceded by a vowel, keep the *-y* for all endings: *monkeys, monkeying,* and *monkeyed.*

final -ie

lie	lying
die	dying

Change the *-ie* of a verb to *-y* when adding *-ing.*

Ie versus ei

-IE	-EI
believe	receive
friend	weigh

The old rule is useful: "*I* before *e* except after *c* or when pronounced *ay* as in ne<u>igh</u>bor or we<u>igh</u>." (Exceptions: *their, height, foreign, leisure, seize.*)

Frequently Misspelled Words

Some words cause confusion because they sound the same or quite similar:

accept	except	loose	lose
affect	effect	precede	proceed
all ready	already	prejudice	prejudiced
alter	altar	there	their
dual	duel	whether	weather
hear	here	you're	your
lessen	lesson		

Other frequently misspelled words:

-S OR -C
absence
license
supersede

DOUBLE OR SINGLE CONSONANT
accommodate
aggressive
harass
occasion
parallel
recommendation

-ABLE	-IBLE
lovable	incredible
likable	irresistible
desirable	responsible
respectable	reversible

-ANT/-ANCE	-ENT/-ENCE (Y)
resistant	dependent
relevant	consistency
maintenance	existence
attendance	tendency
appearance	apparent

Although there are no simple rules to follow in order to decide whether a word is spelled with -ant/-ance or -ent/-ence, most words that have both an -nce and an -nt form are consistent: relevant/relevance; dependent/dependence. Appearance/apparent is an exception. Notice that there is also an internal spelling change: the e of appear is retained in appearance but dropped in apparent. Another word that has an internal spelling change with the addition of *-ance* is *maintenance*: *maintain* + *ance* = *maintenance*.

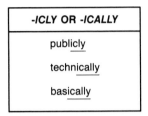

-ATION	
explain + tion	explanation
pronounce + ation	pronunciation

When *-ation* is added to *explain* the *i* is dropped: *explanation*. When *-ation* is added to *pronounce*, the *o* of the second syllable is dropped and the final *-e* changes to *i*: *pronunciation*.

-ICLY OR -ICALLY
pub<u>licly</u>
techni<u>cally</u>
basi<u>cally</u>

Add *-ly* to the original word: *public* + *ly* = *publicly*; *technical* + *ly* = *technically*. *Basically* is an exception: *basic* + *ally* = *basically*.

SUMMARY

1. Adding prefixes does not change the spelling of a word.
2. a) One-syllable words ending in a single consonant preceded by a single vowel double that consonant when endings such as *-ing, -ed, -er,* or *-ence* are added. Example: *run, running*.
   b) Do not double if final consonant is preceded by more than one vowel. Example: *sealed*.
   c) Words of two or more syllables double the consonant if (and only if) after the ending is added the accent falls on the last syllable of the base word. Examples: *contrólled, tráveled, reférring, réference*.
   d) Do not double the consonant before adding *-ment, -ness, -less, -ly,* or other endings beginning with a consonant.
3. Final *-e*
   a) Keep the *-e* when adding endings that begin with a consonant. Example: *lovely, management*. (Exception: *truly, argument*.)
   b) Drop the *-e* when adding an ending that begins with a vowel.
   c) When adding *-able*, keep the *e* if the word ends with a soft *c* sound (*notice*) or a soft *g* sound (*manage*): *noticeable, manageable*. Otherwise, drop the *-e*.

4. Final -*y*
   a) When the -*y* is preceded by a consonant, change it to *i* and add -*es* or -*ed*.
   b) Keep the *y* before adding -*ing*. Examples: *cries, cried, crying.*
5. Final -*ie*
   Change *ie* of a verb to *y* when adding -*ing*: *lying.*
6. *Ie* versus *ei*
   "*I* before *e* except after *c* or when pronounced *ay* as in *neighbor* and *weigh.*"
   Examples: *believe, friend, receive, weigh.* (Exceptions: *height, their, seize.*)
7. Some words are easily confused because they are pronounced alike: *proceed, precede.*

Exercise 4—6

NAME _____

Add each of the endings indicated to the words that follow. After completing the exercise, check the words in the dictionary.

Example: notice + ing   ___*noticing*___

              notice + able   ___*noticeable*___

1. manage + able   _____

    manage + ing   _____

    manage + ment   _____

2. commit + ed   _____

    commit + ing   _____

    commit + ment   _____

3. appear + ance   _____

    appear + ent   _____

4. like + ing   _____

    like + able   _____

5. advise + ing   _____

    advise + able   _____

6. try + s   _____

    try + ing   _____

7. explain + able   _____

    explain + ation   _____

8. rely + able   _____

    rely + s   _____

    rely + ing   _____

9. pronounce + ment _____

    pronounce + ation _____

10. change + ing   _____

      change + able   _____

11. acknowledge + able   _____

      acknowledge + ment   _____

12. maintain + ed   _____

      maintain + ance   _____

13. love + ly   _____

      love + able   _____

14. die + ing   _____

      die + s   _____

15. peace + ful   _____

      peace + able   _____

Exercise 4—7

NAME   _____

In the space provided, give the correct spelling of the word indicated. After forming the word, check it in your dictionary.

     Example: ir + re + place + able   *irreplaceable*

1. judge + ment   _____

2. solve + ing   _____

3. true + ly   _____

4. il + legal   _____

5. commit + ment   _____

6. un + change + able   _____

7. argue + ment   _____

8. die + ing   _____

9. try + ed   _____

10. refer + ence   _____

11. apply + ed   _____

12. control + ed   _____

13. squint + ing   _____

14. ir + responsible   _____

15. appear + ent   _____

16. occur + ed   _____

17. desire + able   _____

18. ir + regular   _____

19. travel + ing   _____

20. notice + able   _____

Exercise 4—8

NAME   _____

Fill in the blanks by forming the word or choosing the letter(s) indicated in parentheses. The first one is done for you as an example.

If you have a food processor, making recipes that require (1. chop + ing) _chopping_, (2. grate + ing) _____, (3. knead + ing) _____, (4. mince + ing) _____, (5. shred + ing) _____, and (6. slice + ing) _____ becomes very easy.

Although there are important differences between models, those differences are (7. in + significant) _____ for most basic recipes.

Gazpacho (8. pronounce + ation _____: gäz pä′ chō) requires only about 30 minutes. You need a small onion (9. peel + ed) _____ and (10. quarter + ed) _____, two cloves of garlic, three green peppers (11. seed + ed) _____ and (10. quarter + ed) _____, four tomatoes, one cucumber (9. peel + ed) _____ and cut into six (12. ie or ei) p____ces, chili powder, olive oil, lemon juice, tomato juice, and sherry. After processing the vegetables (13. separate + ly) _____, blend in the rest of the ingredients. Then chill and serve with sour cream or plain yogurt.

The food processor could be called a time- (14. manage + ment) _____
(15. apply + ance) _____. It allows you to leave the kitchen and (16. ie
or ei) l_____surely enjoy time with your guests.

Some (17. basic + ly) _____ simple but important precautions should
be followed:

a. Read all instructions before (18. use + ing) _____ the food processor.

b. Use only the (19. attach + ments) _____ (20. c or cc; m or mm)
re_____o_____ended by the manufacturer.

c. Handle blades (21. careful + ly) _____.

d. Never place blades on base without first (22. put + ing) _____ container properly in place.

e. Keep the cord where no one will trip over it (23. accidental + ly)
_____.

f. If mechanical (24. adjust + ments) _____ are necessary, return the
processor to an (25. authorize + ed) _____ service company.

Exercise 4—9

NAME _____

Circle the words that are spelled correctly and write them in the space provided.

Example: (informal)   *informal*

likeable   _____

(referring)   *referring*

1. manageable   _____

2. accommodate   _____

3. judgement   _____

4. arguement   _____

5. shopping   _____

6. writing   _____

7. commitment   _____

8. occasion   _____

9. planned   _____

10. existance   _____

11. basicly   _____

12. receive   _____

13. their   _____

14. license   _____

15. foreign   _____

16. friend   _____

17. recommendation   _____

18. beleive   _____

19. groceries   _____

20. monkeys   _____

There are five words in the list above that are misspelled. Give the correct spelling in the spaces provided below.

Example: *likable*

1. _____   2. _____

3. _____   4. _____

5. _____

Exercise 4—10

NAME _____

If there are words that you often have difficulty remembering how to spell, write sentences with as many as five of them, spelling each troublesome word correctly and circling it.

1. _____

_____

2. _____

_____

3. _____

_____

4. _____

_____

5. _____

_____

If there are words that you have recently learned how to spell, write sentences with as many as five of them, circling the word in question.

1. _____

_____

2. _____

_____

3. _____

_____

4. _____

_____

5. _____

_____

Spelling Plural and Possessive Forms

SINGULAR	PLURAL
1 pancake	18 pancakes
1 flavor	31 flavors
1 glass	2 glasses
1 church	6 churches
1 child	12 children
1 mouse	several mice
1 foot	six feet
1 life	2 lives

Most nouns are made plural by the addition of -s or -es (18 pancakes, 2 glasses), but some irregular nouns require an internal spelling change (*children, mice, lives, feet*).

Nouns ending in -y or -o require special attention:

SINGULAR	PLURAL
monkey	monkeys
1 potato	2 potatoes
French fry	French fries
1 patio	2 patios

If the -y is preceded by a consonant, it changes to -i before the addition of -es: *fry—fries*. If the -y is preceded by a vowel, however, the word becomes plural with the simple addition of -s: *monkeys*. If the -o is preceded by a consonant, the plural is formed by adding -es: *potatoes*. If, however, the -o is preceded by a vowel, the plural is formed by adding -s: *patios*. There are some exceptions: several words in which the -o is preceded by a consonant form plurals by adding -s: *sopranos, altos, solos, pianos*. Some words have both forms: *zeros* or *zeroes*.

Compound nouns usually form plurals by the addition of -s to the second word of the compound: *fire hoses, cut-outs, market places, arm loads*. When a clearly more important word appears first, it has the plural form: *brothers-in-law, passers-by*.

Words that end in -*ful* are made plural by the addition of -s: *spoonfuls, cupfuls*.

possessive of nouns

POSSESSIVE SINGULAR	POSSESSIVE PLURAL
the child's toys	the children's toys
the monkey's cage	the monkeys' cage

The possessive of nouns is made by adding an apostrophe or an apostrophe plus -s (-'s). An apostrophe plus -s is added to singular nouns (*monkey's* cage) or to nouns whose plural forms do not end in -s (*children's* toys). An apostrophe by itself is used for the possessive form of plurals that end in -s (*monkeys'* cage). Do not confuse plural and possessive forms. An apostrophe is the sign of the possessive, not the plural.

When two people share ownership of the same thing, only the second name is made possessive: *Tom and Nadina's apartment* means that Tom and Nadina share an apartment. *Kathy's and Carey's keys,* on the other hand, means that Kathy and Carey have different keys; both names are made possessive.

possessive of pronouns

SINGULAR POSSESSIVE		PLURAL POSSESSIVE	
my	mine	our	ours
[thy]	[thine]	your	yours
his	his	their	theirs
her	hers		
its	—		

Personal pronouns have the possessive forms listed above and should *not,* therefore, have an apostrophe: not **x** *their's* but *theirs* is correct. Pay special attention to the difference between *its* (belonging to it) and *it's* (it is).

Other pronouns such as *somebody* and *anyone* and *each other* are made possessive by the addition of an apostrophe plus -s (-'s):

- *Somebody's* pet raccoon is destroying the laundry room.
- *Anyone's* guess is as good as mine.
- Roommates should respect *each other's* privacy.

Exercise 4—11

NAME _____

Give the plural forms of each of the following words. Use your dictionary as necessary.

Example: soprano _____*sopranos*_____

1. country _____
2. ax _____
3. ox _____
4. leaf _____
5. tomato _____
6. key _____
7. enemy _____
8. sister-in-law _____
9. belief _____
10. tornado

Give the singular and plural possessive forms of the following words.

Example: child __*child's*__   __*children's*__

1. mouse _____   _____
2. life _____   _____
3. soprano _____   _____
4. I _____   _____
5. he _____   _____

Give the possessive form of the following words.

6. no one _____
7. one another _____
8. it _____
9. friends of Carol and Denny's _____
10. pets of Molly's and Patrick's _____

219

Exercise 4–12[2]

NAME _____

For each of the underlined words, give either the plural, the singular possessive, or the plural possessive as appropriate. Write your answers in the blanks provided at the end of the exercise. The fourth one is done for you as an example.

Much of modern (1) beer flavor comes from hops, a European variety of nettle now also grown in the U.S. (2) Gourmet generally agree that the really world-class hops are the Bohemian variety, from Czechoslovakia. Most American (3) brewer use the home-grown kind, sometimes blended with imported hops.

If American (4) beer are blended for mildness, are they all (5) taste-alike? Do foreign (4) beer offer something extra?

If you look at a textbook, you'll find that 12 fluid (6) ounce of beer contain about one-half ounce of alcohol, another half-ounce of carbohydrate material, and (7) trace of protein and nutritive salts. The rest, about 90 percent of it, is water.

Like cigarette (8) advertiser, beer (8) advertiser are quick to protest that (9) they increased spending is merely intended to introduce new (10) product or to gain a larger share of the market. They say the ads don't encourage people to drink more or encourage young people to start drinking. (11) Critic of the industry contend that the ads do encourage drinking. Beer-consumption (12) figure do not prove the case one way or the other, but there is hardly any denying the beer (13) company effort to reach college students.

A large proportion of advertising in college newspapers is for beer and other alcoholic (14) beverage. The beer (15) company go far beyond mere (16) commercial during (17) broadcast of college team contests. Beer-drinking contests and free beer before big football games and other big events are part of most (13) company marketing (18) strategy. With brewers acting as (19) host at the party, it is no wonder that college officials are worried about alcohol abuse among students.

1. _____ 2. _____ 3. _____

4. _beers_____ 5. _____ 6. _____

7. _____ 8. _____ 9. _____

10. _____ 11. _____ 12. _____

13. _____ 14. _____ 15. _____

16. _____ 17. _____ 18. _____

19. _____

Hyphenation

dividing words at the end of a line

ap-pal-ling	lath-er
call-ing	or-gan-i-za-tion
clut-ter	tried

Words broken at the end of a line should be divided at the syllable break. Check your dictionary to be sure of where that break occurs, and practice sounding words out in syllables. Double consonants are usually divided (ap-pal-ling). The double consonants that end a one-syllable word, however, are not divided (call-ing). Endings such as *-able, -tious, -tion,* and *-tial* should not be divided. Hyphenated words should be divided only where the hyphen occurs: *self-respect.* Do not divide a one-syllable word (• *tried* not **x** *tri-ed*) and do not leave a single letter stranded at the end of a line: **x** *a-lone.* (In the latter case, the whole word should be written on the next line). Although not wrong, try to avoid carrying only two letters to the next line (• *lather* rather than **x** *lath-er*).

prefixes

NO HYPHEN	WITH HYPHEN
antisocial	anti-British
antiwar	anti-intellectual
midwinter	mid-Atlantic

Prefixes such as *anti-, mid-, non-, pro-,* and *un-* are usually joined to common nouns without hyphenation. When joined to a noun beginning with a capital letter, however, the prefixes are followed by a hyphen: *anti-British, mid-Atlantic.*

When the same vowel ends the prefix and begins the word, a hyphen is sometimes used in order to avoid confusion in pronunciation: *anti-intellectual.* This practice is infrequent, however, and you should check your dictionary in each case. *Co-ordination,* which used to be written with a hyphen, is now regularly written as *coordination.*

The prefix *ex-* is followed by a hyphen when it indicates a former title or status. The prefix *self-* is almost always followed by a hyphen: *ex-husband, self-confidence.*

compound modifiers

WITH HYPHEN	NO HYPHEN
hand-to-mouth existence	to live hand to mouth
well-dressed man	a man who is well dressed
eighteenth-century literature	literature of the eighteenth century
well-guarded secret	carefully guarded secret

When compound modifiers precede a noun, they are usually joined by a hyphen; when they follow, no hyphen is used: *well-dressed man, man who is well dressed*. If the first part of the compound modifier ends in *-ly,* no hyphen is used (*carefully guarded secret*).

other compound words

thirty-six
cross-examine
cease-fire

Compound numbers between twenty-one and ninety-nine are hyphenated when they are written out. Many other compound words also require hyphens. Since there are no helpful rules (and dictionaries sometimes disagree), you should check your dictionary and then be consistent in your practice.

SUMMARY

Words should be divided at a syllable break. Do not leave one letter stranded at the end of a line. Avoid carrying only two letters over to the next line. Hyphenated words should be divided only where the hyphen occurs. Most prefixes are joined directly to words except when those words begin with capital letters (*pro-Canadian*). The prefix *ex-* is followed by a hyphen when it indicates a former title or status. The prefix *self-* is almost always followed by a hyphen. Compound modifiers preceding a noun are usually joined by a hyphen (*well-dressed woman*).

Exercise 4–13³: HYPHENATION

NAME _____

Divide each of the underlined words into syllables and write it in the space provided below. Use your dictionary to check your answers. Number 1 and number 10 are done for you as examples.

(1) <u>Several</u> (2) <u>thousand</u> years ago (3) <u>prehistoric</u> (4) <u>artists</u> in Tanzania, East Africa, (5) <u>produced</u> a (6) <u>priceless</u> and (7) <u>detailed</u> record of (8) <u>various</u> events in their lives. On the (9) <u>sheltered</u> (10) <u>surfaces</u> of cliffs and rock faces these Stone Age (11) <u>painters</u> (12) <u>recreated</u> the world around them in scenes (13) <u>reminiscent</u> of the great prehistoric cave paintings of Europe.

Neither the (14) <u>identity</u> of the artists nor the date of their work is (15) <u>known</u>. It is (16) <u>doubtful</u> that any of the paintings could have (17) <u>survived</u> in open air more than several thousand years, although carbon-14 tests (18) <u>indicate</u> that the (19) <u>coloring</u> (20) <u>materials</u> could be much older.

In many (21) <u>respects</u> the paintings tell us more than we can learn from the bones and stone tools and other artifacts that form the basis of much of our archeological study of man's (22) <u>distant</u> past. Those long-ago works of art tell us, for example, that Stone Age man in Africa wore (23) <u>clothing</u>, had a (24) <u>variety</u> of hairstyles, (25) <u>hunted</u>, (26) <u>danced</u>, sang, played (27) <u>musical</u> (28) <u>instruments</u>, and may even have known the secret of fermenting spirits.

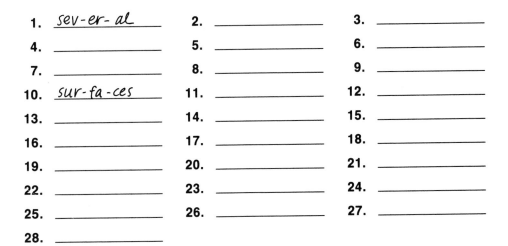

1. _sev-er-al_   2. _____   3. _____

4. _____   5. _____   6. _____

7. _____   8. _____   9. _____

10. _sur-fa-ces_   11. _____   12. _____

13. _____   14. _____   15. _____

16. _____   17. _____   18. _____

19. _____   20. _____   21. _____

22. _____   23. _____   24. _____

25. _____   26. _____   27. _____

28. _____

If you needed to divide each of the following words between two lines, which syllable breaks could you use?

Example: prehistoric __pre-historic__

1. several _____

2. various _____

3. surfaces _____

4. identity _____

5. hunted _____

Exercise 4—14

NAME _____

Combine the prefixes and words below, adding hyphens where needed. Use your dictionary as necessary.

1. pro French   _____

2. pro feminist   _____

3. self explanatory   _____

4. mid day   _____

5. mid August   _____

6. re heat   _____

7. better than usual prospects for success   _____

8. six year presidential term   _____

9. mid term elections   _____

10. cure all   _____

MEANING

Confusing Words

accept, except	formally, formerly
affect, effect	imaginary, imaginative
amount, number	imply, infer
brake, break	predominant, predominate
complement, compliment	replace, substitute
disinterested, uninterested	sit, set

Some words are confusing because they sound alike or have closely related meanings. *Predominant* and *predominate* sound very much alike, but the first is an adjective while the second is a verb: *Among students, the predominant attitude toward politicians seems to be a mild suspicion. Who now predominates in the Senate, liberals or conservatives? Imply* means to suggest a meaning without saying it directly: *The biology teacher implied that the final would be easy; infer* means to draw a conclusion that someone else implies: *Because the biology teacher said that the final would cover only half the course material, the students inferred that it would be easy.* And *imaginary* means *unreal* or *imagined* (for example, ghosts are imaginary), while *imaginative* means *showing imagination* (a child of three who writes poetry is imaginative). Use your dictionary to learn the differences between confusingly similar words.

Roots and Prefixes

roots

trans*port*	*spect*acle
im*port*	*spect*ator
ex*port*	*spect*acles

If several words have the same root, their meanings are probably closely related. The *-port* of *transport, import,* and *export* means *to carry.* The *specta* of *spectacle, spectator,* and *spectacles* means *to see.* Although you cannot tell exactly what a new word means by noticing its similarity to other words, you can make some intelligent guesses.

prefixes   Knowing the meaning of standard prefixes can help you to see relationships between words and can help you to guess at the meanings of words that are new to you. For example, the *mal-* of *malpractice* and *malnutrition* means *bad.* The next *mal-* word you see might be related, for example, *maladjusted.* Some prefixes have more than one meaning; for example, *in-* may mean *not* (*insane*) or *in* (*insert*). With some practice, you can use prefixes as a guide to meaning.

PREFIX	MEANING	EXAMPLE
a-	without, not	amoral, amorphous
ante-	before	antebellum
anti-	opposite, against	antiseptic, antibiotic
auto-	self	autograph, autobiography
col-, com-, con-	with	conspiracy, commiserate, colleague
dis-	not	disservice, dissimilar
ex-	from, out of	extend, expell, exterior
il-, im-, in-, ir-	not	illegal, irregular, inorganic, insane
in-	in	insert, inspire
mal-	wrong, bad	malpractice, malnutrition

Context[4]

- 1. Many North American birds change their behavior entirely each year in order to survive in the tropics. Some become aggressively *territorial*; others that were solitary join flocks.

- 2. If a cough lasts longer than a week following a cold, a doctor's help should be sought. A *persistent* cough can be sign of pneumonia, bronchitis, or other illness, and it warrants medical examination.

- 3. His *desultory* lecture was especially disappointing to those who had traveled some distance to hear him. They expected something more than a random set of observations.

Before looking a word up in the dictionary, try to guess its meaning from its similarities to other words and from its context. In the first example above, *territorial* looks very much like *territory* and in fact describes the behavior of an animal defending its territory. A *persistent* cough appears from the context to mean a cough that lasts longer than a week. Its meaning is *lasting, enduring, continued*. If the second sentence in example 3 (*They expected something more than random observations*) explains why the people were disappointed, then *desultory lecture* is close in meaning to *random set of observations*. And the dictionary's definition confirms the guess from context: *desultory* means *lacking in consistency, disconnected, fitful, random*.

After you have guessed at the meaning of a word, look it up in order to confirm or revise your guess.

SUMMARY

Use your dictionary to learn the distinctions between confusingly similar words (*disinterested, uninterested*). If words have the same root, their meanings are usually related (*spectacle, spectator*). Knowing the meanings of standard prefixes can help you guess at the meanings of words that are new to you, and you can often guess the meaning of a new word from its context.

Exercise 4—15

NAME _____

Using your dictionary as necessary, explain the differences between the following words.

Example: accept, except *Accept is a verb meaning receive.*
Except is a preposition meaning excluding; except
is also sometimes a verb meaning exclude.

1. disinterested, uninterested _____

_____

2. complement, compliment _____

_____

3. affect, effect _____

_____

4. replace, substitute _____

_____

5. council, counsel _____

_____

Write sentences showing that you know the meaning of the words listed below.

6. affect _____

7. effect _____

8. replace _____

9. substitute _____

10. disinterested _____

Exercise 4–16

Circle the correct word in each of the following sentences.

Example: (Who's, (Whose)) dirty laundry is piled in the living room?

1. What is the (principal, principle) difference between an A paper and a B paper?

2–3. (2. Proceed, Precede) with the exam unless you have questions about the (3. proceeding, preceding) explanation.

4–5. The prosecutor claimed that he would have no difficulty in handling the case in a(n) (4. disinterested, uninterested) manner, but the judge and the defense lawyer thought that his wife's being the defendant would cause him to be somewhat (5. prejudice, prejudiced) in the matter.

6–10. (6. You're, Your) (7. oral, verbal) presentation (8. affected, effected) (6. you're, your) audience so strongly that they could not refrain from expressing (9. their, there, they're) anger. Why did you have to insult the most (10. eminent, imminent) man in the community? The committee has decided to (11. replace, substitute) you as the keynote speaker for next year. You've made your bed. Now (12. lie, lay) in it.

Exercise 4–17

Listed below are the words given as examples on page 228. Circle the ones that are new to you (or those whose meanings you are unsure of). Look them up and write sentences with ten of them.

amoral, amorphous	conspiracy, commiserate, colleague
antebellum	disservice, dissimilar
antiseptic, antibiotic	extend, expel, exterior
autograph, autobiography	illegal, irregular, inorganic, insane
insert, inspire	malpractice, malnutrition

1. _____

2. _____

3. _____

4. _____

5. _____

6. _____

7. _____

8. _____

9. _____

10. _____

Exercise 4—18

NAME _____

Using your dictionary, supply the meaning of the following prefixes and give two examples of each. The first is done for you as an example.

Prefix	Meaning	Examples
1. hyper-	*excessively*	hyperactive, hyperventilate
2. inter-	_____	_____
3. intra-	_____	_____
4. post-	_____	_____
5. pre-	_____	_____
6. pro-	_____	_____
7. semi-	_____	_____
8. sub-	_____	_____
9. super-	_____	_____
10. sym-, syn-	_____	_____
11. un-	_____	_____

Use five of your examples in sentences.

1. _____

2. _____

3. _____

4. _____

5. _____

Exercise 4–19[5]

NAME _____

Guess the meaning of the underlined words from their similarity to other words you know and from the context. Then look the words up in the dictionary. First, rewrite the dictionary definition in your own words, and then write a sentence with each word, showing that you understand the meaning.

> *Example:* Proponents of a single six-year presidential term say that not having to run again would eliminate some of the political pressures on a president.
>
> proponent *A person who is for or who supports a cause or idea. Proponents say that total disarmament is the only reliable way to prevent a third world war.*

The idea was debated in the Constitutional Convention. Andrew Jackson (1) revived it 40 years later. Most 19th-century Presidents favored it, and in 1913 Woodrow Wilson had to (2) intervene personally to stop Congress from approving it. The idea of electing the President of the United States for only one term of six years won't die.

Why has this (3) perennial reform proposal, as old as the Republic and at least as hearty, refused to go away? Probably because it reflects a view that's just as (4) persistent—the American (5) conviction that (6) unseemly "politics" somehow stands too often in the way of "good government" by pure-souled "statesmen" dedicated only to "the public interest."

Andrew Jackson was not generally considered in his day such a (7) paragon of nonpolitical government, but he nevertheless gave Congress in 1830 a (8) resounding statement of this attitude. He recommended a single term "in order that [the President] may . . . be placed beyond the reach of any improper influences . . . and that the securities for this independence may be (9) rendered as strong as the nature of power and the weakness of its possessor will admit."

But the single-term idea has never (10) prevailed because of an equally strong belief of similar persistence that such "good government" is (11) elitist in (12) concept and unrealistic in practice, while grubby politics (13) reconciles the necessarily conflicting interests of a democracy and makes the wheels of government turn, even if slowly.

Harry Truman said to a Congressional hearing on the single-term issue: "You do not have to be very smart to know that an officeholder who is not (14) eligible for re-election loses a lot of influence."

1. revived _____

_____

_____

2. intervene _____

_____

_____

3. perennial _____

_____

_____

4. persistent _____

_____

_____

5. conviction _____

_____

_____

6. unseemly _____

_____

_____

7. paragon _____

_____

_____

8. resounding _____

_____

_____

9. rendered_____

_____

_____

10. prevailed _____

_____

_____

11. elitist _____

_____

_____

12. concept _____

_____

_____

13. reconciles _____

_____

_____

14. eligible _____

_____

_____

Exercise 4—20

NAME _____

In a book, magazine, or newspaper, find five words that are new to you. In the spaces provided below copy the phrases or clauses in which they are used and make a guess about meanings from the contexts; then, after looking each word up in the dictionary, write a sentence of your own with each word, showing that you know its meaning.

1. New word: _____

Context in which it appeared: _____

_____

New sentence using the same word:_____

_____

2. New word: _____

Context in which it appeared: _____

_____

New sentence using the same word:_____

_____

3. New word: _____

Context in which it appeared: _____

_____

New sentence using the same word:_____

_____

4. New word: _____

Context in which it appeared: _____

_____

New sentence using the same word:_____

_____

5. New word: _____

Context in which it appeared: _____

_____

New sentence using the same word:_____

_____

Connotation

hair stylist	beautician
salon	beauty shop
childlike	childish

In addition to its dictionary definition—which is called the **denotative** meaning—a word often implies associated or secondary meanings. The implied meanings are called **connotations**. For example, a *beautician* and a *hair stylist* may give the same haircut, but the greater skill and elegance implied by the term *hair stylist* contribute to the higher cost of a cut at a *salon* than of one at a *beauty shop*. *Childish* and *childlike* both refer to characteristics of childhood, but *childish* has unfavorable connotations while *childlike* refers to admirable traits.

Diction

FORMAL	MIDDLE	INFORMAL
adumbrate	foreshadow	
ignoble	mean-spirited	
repudiate	disown or reject	
admonition	warning	
colleague	coworker	
suitor	boyfriend	fellow
	silly	goofy
	nonsense	bunk

Some words are more formal than others; for example, *admonition* and *colleague* are more formal than *warning* and *coworker*. Less formal than either of these are words like *fellow, goofy,* and *bunk*. On the whole, you should get into the habit of choosing a middle level of diction in order to write lively, straightforward essays. The middle level of formality is neither impersonal on the one hand nor chummy and casual on the other. Essays that are too formal may sound pretentious, while essays that are too informal may not be taken seriously. A second objection to too great a degree of informality is that such words may soon sound dated. For example, although all three are still quite recognizable informal words, *fellow, goofy,* and *bunk* probably sound old-fashioned to you.

SUMMARY

In addition to its denotative meaning, a word often implies associated or secondary meanings called connotations. Some words are more formal than others. Choose your level of diction according to the tone you want to create; in most cases you should use the middle level of diction.

Exercise 4–21

NAME _____

Using your dictionary, explain the different connotations of the following sets of words.

Example: naïve: *implies a genuine, innocent simplicity or lack of artificiality but sometimes connotes an almost foolish lack of worldly wisdom*

unsophisticated: *like naive, implies a lack of worldly wisdom, but connotes that this is the result merely of a lack of experience*

1. apparent _____

   evident _____

   obvious _____

   clear _____

   plain _____

   ostensible _____

2. indulge _____

   humor _____

   pamper _____

   baby _____

   spoil _____

3. item _____

   detail _____

4. custom _____

   practice _____

   habit _____

5. pensive _____

   meditative _____

   reflective _____

6. separate _____

   divide_____

7. strength _____

   power_____

   force _____

   might _____

8. mystery _____

   enigma _____

   riddle _____

   puzzle _____

9. rough _____

   harsh _____

   uneven _____

   rugged _____

10. soft_____

    bland _____

    mild _____

    gentle_____

Exercise 4—22

NAME _____

Using the distinctions learned from your dictionary, write sentences with the following words.

1. apparent_____

2. obvious _____

3. indulge _____

4. pamper _____

5. pensive _____

6. reflective_____

7. custom _____

8. habit _____

9. enigma _____

10. puzzle _____

Exercise 4—23

NAME _____

Identify words that are formal or informal. Then change each that you identified to its middle-level equivalent.

Example: Though the answers in the survey varied, they can be (split) into
two categories.

_____ *informal; divided* _____

1. With almost no exceptions, students had no trepidations about getting
caught while cheating.

_____

2. Many years ago, as a small child, I witnessed a fire in our home.

_____

3. The roadrunner is the goof-off of the desert.

_____

4. You're nuts.

_____

Exercise 4—24

Using your dictionary as necessary, identify the level of diction of each of the following words. Give the middle-level equivalent (if there is one) of formal and informal words or phrases. Some words have both informal and middle-level meanings.

Example: olfactory organ _*formal; nose*_____

1. penurious _____

2. lightweight_____

3. inimical _____

4. bluster _____

5. hang-out_____

6. imitate _____

7. jam_____

8. domicile _____

9. fuzz _____

10. super _____

Use five of the middle-level words in sentences.

1. _____

_____

2. _____

_____

3. _____

_____

4. _____

_____

5. _____

_____

HOLDING YOUR READER'S ATTENTION

Conciseness

WORDY	CONCISE
x Due to the fact that	• Because
x To have a preference for	• Prefer
x At this point in time	• Now
x As far as I am concerned . . .	[Omit]
x It seems to me that . . .	
x There are those who	• They
x It is not unlikely that he will win.	• It is likely that he will win.
	• He will probably win.

When you revise your rough drafts, you should prune away all unnecessary words. Holding your reader's attention requires that you be concise. Some expressions (for example, the first three above) should nearly always be replaced by their shorter, more direct equivalents. You can pare away some unnecessary words by making positive rather than negative statements: *It is likely that* rather than *It is not unlikely that*. Some sentence structures naturally lead to wordiness (for example, *there are [X] who*) and should be stated more directly. Some sentence openers—for example, those that allow the writer to hedge—should generally be omitted; *as far as I'm concerned* and *it seems to me that* add nothing to your sentence and get in your reader's way.

x It seems to me that due to the fact that financial aid funds are decreasing, it is clear that there is a certain percentage of students who will find it difficult or impossible to be able to continue in school.

REVISION:
• Because financial aid funds have decreased, some students will not be able to stay in school.

x Upon recognizing the political advantage of receiving more network air time, many candidates structure their campaign behavior around the television medium.

REVISION:
• Because being seen on network television is a political advantage, many candidates plan their campaigns for television coverage.

Exercise 4—25

NAME _____

Underline the words or phrases that seem essential. Rewrite the sentence omitting unnecessary words and phrases.

> *Example:* One example of my efforts to <u>avoid mowing the lawn</u> occurred when <u>I told my father</u> that I had become <u>allergic to the lawn clippings.</u> *To avoid mowing the lawn, I told my father I was allergic to lawn clippings.*

1. This attitude—either cheat or fail—has a tendency to surface more often among students in technical courses than among those in humanities courses. _____

_____

2. When considered in light of the quantity and quality of housing at comparable colleges, the housing on our campus is worth the high cost burden on the student. _____

_____

3. I like movies of this nature because of this reason—that they take my mind off my worries. _____

_____

4. The fact that this job was a necessity was the only force compelling me to show up every morning. _____

_____

5. It seems to me that in debating national issues, the use of empty rhetoric by political figures to influence their listeners to adopt a certain point of view is a common occurrence. _____

_____

Exercise 4—26

NAME _____

If there are sentences in your own writing that could be written more concisely, revise and write as many as five in the space provided below.

1. _____

_____

2. _____

_____

3. _____

_____

4. _____

_____

5. _____

_____

Figurative Language

- Dictionaries are like watches; the worst is better than none, and the best cannot be expected to go quite true.

  —Samuel Johnson

- Biographies are but the clothes and buttons of the man—the biography of the man himself cannot be written.[6]

  —Mark Twain

In order to speak or write about objects and ideas precisely and vividly, writers often use figurative language. Two kinds of figurative expressions, similes and metaphors, allow a writer to make comparisons between two things that are essentially unlike but that have suggestive or revealing similarities. Dictionaries are not very much like watches, or so we think until the comparison is drawn. Then are reminded that we can neither keep track of time nor define words so precisely as we sometimes think. Such a comparison (one that uses the words *like* or *as*: *Dictionaries are like watches*) is called a **simile**. In the second example, a comparison is made without the use of *like* or *as*. Mark Twain says that biographies *are* the clothes and buttons of a man. Figurative language that states that two things are the same or that one is the other does so by means of a **metaphor**.

Figurative language does not always state a comparison or an identification. Without saying that mountain goats *are* or *are like* kings, for example, a *National Geographic* writer conveys their seemingly regal power by using the word *reign*:

- In bold defiance of gravity, mountain goats *reign* with eagles across a no-man's-land of rock and ice stretching from the northwestern United States through Canada to Alaska.[7]

Though it is often associated with poetry, figurative language is a regular feature not only of prose but of ordinary conversation as well. If we considered just a few of the figurative expressions concerned with parts of the body, we could develop a long list:

the head on beer	face card
head over heels in love	type face
keep one's head above water	to fly in the face of
to lose one's head	to face up to
to give someone a hand	to put one's foot in one's mouth
to win hands down	to foot the bill
to eat out of someone's hand	to land on one's feet
to be out of one's hands	to get off on the right foot

clichés

- x He washed his hands of the whole problem.
- x Communication is a two-way street.

Clichés are figurative expressions that once were vivid but have become trite. The first example above refers to the ritual washing of one's hands in order to show that one is no longer responsible for a matter. The second example may once have suggested important ideas about communication but now creates hardly any impression at all. Neither of the examples suggests a vivid image and cannot, therefore, catch and hold the reader's attention.

Clichés are at best unnoticeable but can be ridiculous, especially if two or more are mixed. Because they are handy expressions, we use them without thinking and are therefore often not in control of their suggestiveness. The result can be unintentionally comic:

x He watched his horse come in last and his dream of living in the fast lane go down the drain.

SUMMARY

Figurative expressions are a natural part of the language and often make writing precise and vivid. Avoid using clichés, trite figurative expressions.

Exercise 4—27

Underline the clichés in the following sentences. (There may be more than one cliché in one sentence.)

> *Example:* There we were, <u>packed like sardines in a can</u> in an elevator that wouldn't move.

1. I took the whole experience in stride and wrote it off as a lesson in how not to get taken in New York City.
2. Since I was a sophomore with only a few political science courses under my belt, I was naturally scared when I went into the majors' seminar. I wouldn't say I was quiet as a mouse, but I didn't roar like a lion either.
3. He thought he was going places, but he got a job that was a real dead end: there was no ladder to climb.
4. He's as honest as the day is long and his word is as good as gold, but he tells jokes that are as old as the hills.
5. This cookbook has a section on nutrition called "Food for Thought," and it promises to get readers back on the right track on the road to good health.
6. You get what you pay for when you take advantage of the rock-bottom prices at the local discount store, where most things are a dime a dozen.
7. When I dropped Latin and started taking statistics, I went from the frying pan into the fire.
8. He met a sea of trouble on the highway of life.
9. If life is like a mountain railroad, our train got derailed at the last curve.
10. Well, that's a pretty kettle of fish; how do you propose to fry them?

Rewrite sentences 4 and 7, keeping the meaning suggested by the clichés without using them.

> *Example:* *There we were, pressed shoulder to shoulder in an elevator that wouldn't move.*

4. _____

_____

7. _____

_____

Exercise 4–28[8]

NAME _____

Locate and underline the key words in six figurative expressions in the following passage. Name the source of one of the figurative expressions.

Example: America's <u>love affair with the automobile sparked decades</u> of prosperity for U.S. car manufacturers.

_____*source : love (and marriage)*_____

I began a year of studying the automotive world with a number of preconceptions, shared, I believe, by many Americans:

I. The U.S. auto industry has been left in the dust of foreign competition; the automobile as we know it is doomed by dwindling fuel supplies; the American love affair with the automobile is dead. All contain elements of truth; all are misleading.

II. American automakers, grown fat by past successes and tripped up by oil prices and a lingering recession, lost an edge. They now struggle to regain ground lost to aggressive competitors.

III. Fuels will change, but the end of cars is not even in sight. Other fuels are waiting in the wings for the day when burning gasoline is no longer practical.

IV. We appear to have lost a love affair with the automobile only because it has become a marriage. Now familiar with and dependent upon this mechanical mate, we have taken it for granted and become impatient with its shortcomings. One thing appears certain: The honeymoon is over.

The source of one figurative expression: _____

_____

Exercise 4—29⁹

NAME _____

Explain what the underlined figurative language seems to suggest.

Example: Fourscore and seven years ago our fathers <u>brought forth</u> on this
continent a new nation, conceived in liberty and dedicated to the
proposition that all men are created equal.
                                                —Abraham Lincoln, *The Gettysburg Address*

Brought forth suggests that the fathers gave birth to the
country. This idea is continued with the word conceived
and perhaps with dedicated, which may in this context
suggest a child's dedication when christened.

1. It is our true policy to <u>steer clear</u> of permanent alliances with any portion of
the foreign world.
                                —George Washington, *Farewell Address* (September 17, 1796)

_____

_____

2. Fear is the <u>foundation</u> of most governments.
                                —John Adams, *Thoughts on Government*

_____

_____

3. I have but one lamp by which my feet are guided, and that is the <u>lamp of
experience</u>.
                                —Patrick Henry, *Speech at First Continental Congress,*
                                Philadelphia (October 14, 1774)

_____

_____

4. Mind is the great <u>lever</u> of all things; human thought is the process by which
human ends are ultimately answered.
                                —Daniel Webster, *Address on Laying the Corner-Stone of the
                                Bunker Hill Monument* (June 17, 1825)

_____

_____

251

5. The almighty dollar, that great object of universal devotion throughout our
   land, seems to have no genuine devotees in these peculiar villages.
                                             —Washington Irving, *Wolfert's Roost*

_____

_____

Exercise 4—30

NAME _____

In a newspaper, book, or magazine find a sentence or two that you think uses
figurative language effectively. Copy it in the space provided below and explain why the language is effective.

_____

_____

_____

_____

_____

_____

NAME _____

I. Choose the word, add the ending, or otherwise follow the directions given in parentheses. Write your answers in the corresponding spaces below.

If *potato* (1. plural) had feelings, they'd be (2. *terrify* + ed) by (3. their, there) trip through a modern packing plant. First, (4. they're, their, there) (5. *smother* + ed) under thousands of other *potato* (1. plural). Then they fall onto a conveyor chain and are pulled up a steep incline to a sheer drop. They *plummet* (6. divide into syllables) onto a second chain, rumble over a table full of rollers, and (7. *final* + ly) are (8. *swallow* + ed) by a (9. *bag* + ing) machine. A fifth of them are so badly (10. *bruise* + ed) they end up in the trash heap or the starch factory.

With *profit* (11. plural) at about a penny a pound, smart packers are eager to know exactly where in (12. their, there, they're) systems the damage is (13. *occur* + ing). A couple of *agricultural* (14. divide into syllables) engineers have (15. *try* + ed) finding out, with a potato that broadcasts pain.

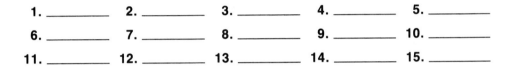

1. _____   2. _____   3. _____   4. _____   5. _____

6. _____   7. _____   8. _____   9. _____   10. _____

11. _____   12. _____   13. _____   14. _____   15. _____

II. Choose the correct word or letter or add the ending indicated in parentheses. Write the complete word in the corresponding spaces below.

(1. It's, its) hard to imagine how this improb___ble (2. a, i) beast *manage* (3. -s) to survive. It can (4. *bare* + ly) see or (5. here, hear); it has very little muscle; it cannot walk or even stand; it spends most of (6. it's, its) life hanging upside down, sleeping.

Everything it does seems to be in slow motion. It may take as long as 30 seconds to shift one leg a few inches. It even sneezes slowly—when it sneezes at all.

If you were to fire a gun next to one of these creatures, it would do no more than turn (7. it's, its) head and blink. (8. It's, Its) incred___ble (9. a, i) sluggishness is (10. *true* + ly) "one of the wonders of nature," says an American zoologist. Yet it is one of the most successful mammals alive today. Despite (11. it's, its) laz___ness (12. y, i), it is bel___ved (13. ie, ei) to be the most abund___nt (14. a, e) tree-dwelling mammal in South America (15. 's, s) tropical forests.

What is (16. it's, its) secret? To find out, see page 107 of the July 1983 issue of *Sc____nce* (17. ie, ei) *Digest*.

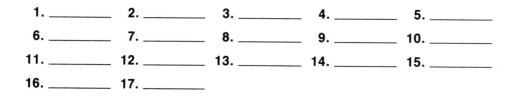

1. _____ 2. _____ 3. _____ 4. _____ 5. _____

6. _____ 7. _____ 8. _____ 9. _____ 10. _____

11. _____ 12. _____ 13. _____ 14. _____ 15. _____

16. _____ 17. _____

III. Choose the correct word or letter, add the ending, or otherwise follow the directions indicated in parentheses or in the answer spaces below.

When one roadrunner ventures onto *another* (1. possessive) (2) *turf,* the reaction is either fight or flight. For an experiment, I presented a (3) *decoy* to several nesting birds. Males either attacked the model (4) *viciously* or courted it royally, depending on (5. they're, their, there) stage in the (6) *reproductive* cycle.

My model was of neither (7) *gender*; to humans, male and female appear *identical* (8. divide into syllables), with (9) *iridescent* plumage of dark green, blue, or black, depending on the angle of light, and an orange patch of skin behind the eye.

When a roadrunner passes a parked car, it will attack (10. its, it's) own reflection in the hubcap. Such attacks often increase in a__re__iveness (11. g or gg, s or ss) since the "rival" always refuses to back down.

Roadrunners (12) *rush in where* most desert dwellers, including humans, (12) *fear to tread*—into a *rattlesnake* (13. possessive) reach. The lore of the West contains many stories of roadrunners killing rattlesnakes. I had never (14) *witnessed* such battles until I released several rattlers in roadrunner territory during my field study.

I found the two (15) *predators* a good match in quickness. The bird struck repeatedly at the *snake* (16. possessive) head, avoiding injury by *leap* (17. -ing) up and spreading (18. its, it's) wing feathers, which are unharmed by counter strikes. Eventually the snake coiled and hid (19. its, it's) head. Unable to see the target, the bird finally gave up and left.

1. _____

2a. *turf:* level of diction:_____

2b. effect of this level of diction:_____

3a. Probable meaning of *decoy* from context: _____

3b. Dictionary definition: _____

NOTES

[1]Lewis Carroll, *Through the Looking Glass* in *The Works of Lewis Carroll*, ed. Roger L. Green (Middlesex: The Hamlyn Publishing Group Ltd., 1965), p. 174.

[2]Adapted from "Beer," *Consumer Reports*, 48 (1983), pp. 342–344, 348–349.

[3]Adapted from Mary D. Leakey, "Tanzania's Stone Age Art," *National Geographic*, 164 (1983), 86.

[4]Roger F. Pasquier and Eugene S. Morton, "For Avian Migrants a Tropical Vacation Is Not a Bed of Roses," *Smithsonian*, Oct. 1982, p. 170 (example 1); "Cough Remedies: Which Ones Work Best?" *Consumer Reports*, 48 (1983), 59 (example 2).

[5]Adapted from Tom Wicker, "Six Years for the President," *New York Times Magazine*, 26 June 1983, pp. 16–18.

[6]Mark Twain, *Mark Twain's Autobiography* (New York: Harper & Brothers, 1924), I, 2.

[7]Douglas Chadwick, "Mountain Goats: Guardians of the Heights," *National Geographic*, 154 (1978), 284.

[8]Noel Grove, "Swing Low, Sweet Chariot!" *National Geographic*, 164 (1983), pp. 1, 6.

[9]John Bartlett, *Familiar Quotations* (Boston: Little, Brown, 1955), pp. 540, 367–368, 443, 446.

[10]Adapted from Terry Dunkle, "Talking Potatoes," *Science 83*, June 1983, p. 86 (Review Test, Part I); Rachel Wilder, "The Challenge: When Laziness Pays Off," *Science Digest*, July 1983, p. 112 (Review Test, Part II); and Martha A. Whitson, "The Road Runner: Clown of the Desert," *National Geographic*, 163 (1983), 698–700 (Review Test, Part III).

[11]Both advertisements appear widely.

SENTENCE REVISION

MAIN ASSERTIONS

Recognizing Main Assertions

- 1. *Humans have always been susceptible to the charms of birds.*
- 2. *The beauty of birds' plumage, the loveliness of their songs, and the grace of their flight have been extolled by poets and other writers from the Greeks to the present.*[1]
- 3. Favorite subjects in popular art and fables, *owls have been cast in many roles*—from messenger of death and evil omen to symbol of wisdom and good luck.
- 4. (a) *Few people,* however, *actually see owls in the wild,* and (b) *fewer still are familiar with their habits.*[2]

The main assertion is the basic statement made by a sentence. It includes the subject and verb, any objects or complements, and other sentence elements that cannot be set off by commas. Any material that can be set off by commas, dashes, or parentheses is not part of the main assertion.

In the first two examples above, the whole sentence is the main assertion. The subject, verb, and complement of the first are *humans have been susceptible,* and the phrases that follow *susceptible* are necessary to its meaning (susceptible to what? to the charms of birds). Nothing here could be set off from the subject–verb–complement by commas. In the second example, the subject and verb are *beauty/loveliness/grace have been extolled.* The modifying phrases that follow the three subjects (beauty *of birds' plumage,* loveliness *of their songs,* and grace *of their flight*) are necessary to establish the meaning of those subjects. Similarly, the modifying phrases that follow the verb complete the meaning of the sentence. Extolled by whom? By poets and other writers from the Greeks to the present.

In the third sentence, on the other hand, the main assertion—*owls have been cast in many roles*—is preceded by introductory material set off from the subject by commas (*Favorite subjects in popular art and fables*, owls . . .). In addition, this sentence includes explanatory material that follows the main assertion and is set off from it by a dash (*—from messenger of death and evil omen to symbol of wisdom and good luck*). Neither the introductory nor the extending explanatory material is part of the basic statement made by the sentence.

A sentence may make more than one main assertion; in fact, all compound sentences do.

- (1) *Few people,* however, *actually see owls in the wild,* and (2) *fewer still are familiar with their habits.*

This sentence makes one basic statement about *few people* and another basic statement about *fewer people.* Notice also that the first of these main assertions is interrupted by the word *however.* The commas that precede and follow it show that it is not part of the main statement made by the sentence.

A single subject and a compound verb, on the other hand, make only one basic statement. For example, the following sentence, which has one subject (*earthquakes*) and a compound verb (*have leveled and killed*), makes one main assertion:

- *Earthquakes have leveled cities and killed as many as 800,000 people.*[3]

In the following paragraph, all main assertions are italicized:

At eleven o'clock on Sunday morning, September 8, 1974, one month after taking office, (1) *President Gerald R. Ford announced that he had granted Richard M. Nixon a full pardon for any offenses against the United States he might have committed while serving as the thirty-seventh President.* With that act, (2) *Ford made a political blunder that would haunt his presidency and submerge his campaign two years later.* (3) *The pardon immediately raised speculation that he and Nixon,* working through Alexander M. Haig, Jr., the Army general who served as chief of staff to both, *had struck a deal for the presidency.*

(4) *Many of the aides who worked closely with Haig and Ford still assume that there was a deal of some kind.* (5) *Whether there was may never be known,* because the men involved have yet to give a full account.[4]

SUMMARY

The main assertion is the basic statement made by a sentence and includes the subject, verb, any objects or complements, and other elements that cannot be set off by commas, dashes, or parentheses.

Exercise 5–1

NAME _____

Underline the main assertions in the following paragraphs. If a sentence contains more than one main assertion, number them.

Example: ① The warm summer sun may feel friendly, but ② some of its rays are dangerous.[5]

When Europeans first arrived on the eastern shores of North America, they faced a virtually unbroken forest stretching for more than a thousand miles. Within three centuries, less than one percent of the virgin forest remained; the land had been cleared for farms, timber, highways, and housing. Cleared tracts, however, were often permitted to grow back into forest. Today, although some primeval woodlands persist, second-growth woods, which vary in size from immense national forests to small backyard woodlots, are the principal remains of the once imposing eastern wilderness.

Only a few bird species, such as the ivory-billed woodpecker and perhaps the Carolina parakeet, became extinct because of deforestation. But in many forest tracts, especially the smaller patches, the mix of bird species that once existed has changed. In particular, those birds that breed in North America but winter in the Caribbean and Latin America—Neotropical migrants—have declined in numbers and variety in many areas where the forest has been severely fragmented. Migrants are no trivial component of the avifauna; in large forests, they account for up to 90 percent of the breeding pairs.[6]

Everyone knows what bird migration is in some sense, but the tendency is to emphasize a few, admittedly extraordinary cases. The arctic tern, for example, journeys from arctic to antarctic waters and back each year, thus spending most of its life over open oceans and seeing more sunlight than any other animal. The great albatrosses of the Southern Hemisphere circumnavigate the globe in the roaring forties, and several species of shearwaters and petrels also circle the oceans during the nonbreeding seasons. The feat of the blackpoll warbler—which breeds in the coniferous forests of North America, all the way to the tree line—is perhaps even more remarkable. In the fall, most individuals of this species move southeastward from their breeding grounds to Canada's Maritime Provinces and the northeastern United States. When winds from the northwest arise, the birds continue their journey, apparently making a nonstop ocean crossing to their wintering grounds in northern South America. During this three- to four-day flight, these tiny 20-gram birds have no place to alight for water, food, or rest.[7]

Align Meaning with Grammatically Important Words

    x For students who study a foreign language in their own country, *one* of the most frustrating difficulties encountered *is* a *lack* of opportunity to apply what they learn and to practice by talking to people who are native speakers of the language.

    • *Students* who study a foreign language in their own country often *feel frustrated* by not being able to talk with native speakers.

In order to write clear assertions, you should use the grammatically important positions (subject, verb, objects, and complements) for words that convey important elements of meaning. In the first sentence above, the subject, object, and complement are *one is lack*; almost none of the writer's meaning is revealed. In order to clarify, locate the important words, put one of them in a grammatically important position, and revise the sentence accordingly. What is the sentence about? *Students*. Make that the subject and experiment to see what happens. The revised sentence might be that suggested above: *Students who study a foreign language in their own country often feel frustrated by not being able to talk with native speakers*. Now the subject, verb, and complement are *students feel frustrated*, an obvious improvement over *one is lack*.

In clarifying an assertion, focus on important points and simplify. After revising an unclear assertion, read it again to see whether you have omitted anything important. In the sentence above, the revision no longer mentions *difficulties*, *lack of opportunity*, *apply what they learn*, and *practice*. The idea of *difficulties* is expressed in *frustrated by not being able . . .* ; *lack of opportunity* is taken care of by *not being able*; *practicing* a language and *applying what they learn* are the same in this case, and both are expressed by *talk with native speakers*. As you can see, clarifying an assertion may solve problems of wordiness, vagueness, and repetition.

Some clues that your sentence may have an unclear assertion:

1. the verb is a form of *to be* (*is, are, was, were, had been*);
2. the sentence conveys action through a noun rather than a verb (*there was a reorganization* instead of *they reorganized*);
3. the verb is in the passive voice (editorial policies *are reviewed*);
4. the sentence begins with a delaying formula (for example, *It was she who*—*it was the woman in the Houston Astros T-shirt who had cause to be unhappy*);
5. the sentence contains two or more *that* clauses.

Of course, not all uses of the verb *to be* are to be avoided, but if you depend almost exclusively on its various forms, your writing will lack energy. Likewise, the passive voice has appropriate uses, but overused, it keeps your sentences from being vivid. Keep these clues in mind, not as rules but as guidelines.

With these guidelines in mind, we can revise the following sentence.

    x It seems to me that the money that is allotted to the student newspaper by the college should be used for other purposes unless its editorial policies are reviewed and a reorganization is carried out by the staff.

DELAYING FORMULA:
It seems to me that . . .

TWO RELATIVE CLAUSES:
that the money . . . which is allotted . . .

FOUR PASSIVE VERBS:
is allotted, should be used, are reviewed, is carried out.

ACTION LOCATED IN NOUN RATHER THAN VERB:
reorganization rather than *reorganize.*

What is the sentence about? *The student newspaper, money,* and the *college's spending policies.* With *newspaper* as the subject and with an active verb, the revised sentence might read as follows:

- Unless the staff reviews its editorial policies and reorganizes itself, the student newspaper does not deserve financial support from the college.

If the context for this sentence were a discussion of the college's spending policies, *college* instead of *newspaper* might be the subject, and the revision might be

- The college should not support the student newspaper unless the staff reviews its editorial policies and reorganizes itself.

The subject, verb, and object of the first revision are *newspaper does (not) deserve support* and of the second, *college should (not) support newspaper,* both more meaningful than *It seems that,* which can be used at the beginning of almost any sentence.

SUMMARY

In order to write clear assertions, you should use the grammatically important positions (subject, verb, objects, and complements) for words that convey important elements of meaning.

Exercise 5–2[8]

NAME _____

Locate the important sentence positions by underlining and labeling the subjects (S), verbs (V), direct objects (O), and complements (C) in the following paragraph. The first sentence is done for you as an example.

    S   V   C

<u>Voices</u> built of computer bits <u>have become</u> <u>commonplace</u>. They chatter through video games, announce fuel levels from car dashboards, and bellow warnings from airplane instrument panels. In the future they may teach English speakers a second language, usher moviegoers out of the theater in an emergency, and even dictate the day's chores in the morning. Still, the talking computer's main role in the here and now is to help illuminate the mysteries of speech.

Exercise 5–3

Underline the subjects, verbs, objects, and complements of the following sentences and then, in the spaces provided, rewrite, clarifying indistinct assertions. Several revisions will work; there is not one "right" answer. If a sentence does not need revision, write *NR* (no revision) in the space provided.

Example: The <u>truth</u> of Murphy's laws <u>is found</u> in the fact that they are only remembered when they are confirmed by our experience.

> *Murphy's laws seem true because we only remember them when they apply.* OR *Murphy's laws seem true because we only remember them when our experience confirms them.*

1. The old maxim "You get what you pay for" may not always hold true, but from my experiences, I can conclude that, for myself, it does most of the time.

_____

_____

2. My best example is that two summers ago, I decided to visit a close friend at Lake Placid.

_____

_____

3. The fact that I had very little money meant that I had to look for the cheapest possible room.

_____

_____

4. After arriving late in the evening, I found a "skater's inn," a cheap housing arrangement for athletes.

_____

_____

5. It was not to be expected that such a room would be very big, but I did expect to get some sleep.

_____

_____

6. At 3:00 a.m., after I had been asleep for two hours, however, a drunk man stumbled into my room, waking me up.

_____

_____

7. He then proceeded to occupy a narrow bed adjacent to mine.

_____

_____

8. He not only woke me up but kept me up all night.

_____

_____

9. His snoring and grunting all night were not the only thing that was objectionable; another thing the matter with him was that he smelled like the garbage in the back alley.

_____

_____

10. At 7:00 a.m., I got dressed, packed my bags, paid my bill, and left, resolving never again to travel without money for a decent room.

_____

_____

Exercise 5—4

NAME _____

Find five sentences with unclear assertions in your own writing or elsewhere, clarify them, and write your revisions in the space provided below.

1. _____

_____

2. _____

_____

3. _____

_____

4. _____

_____

5. _____

_____

SUBORDINATION

- The most famous quake to hit this country may be the San Francisco earthquake of 1906; the most far-reaching, *however,* appears to be a series of three near New Madrid, Missouri, *in 1811 and 1812, which changed the course of the Mississippi River and stopped clocks as far away as Boston.*[9]

Subordinate elements can be single words (*however*), phrases (*in 1811 and 1812*), or clauses (*which changed the course of the Mississippi River and stopped clocks as far away as Boston*). (See Chapter 1 for a review of the function of subordinate elements in sentences.)

Coordination versus Subordination

TWO SENTENCES:

- In the winter, some bats migrate to warm climates. Others hibernate in their caves.

COMBINED SENTENCE USING COORDINATION:

- In the winter, some bats migrate to warm climates, *but* others hibernate in their caves.[10]

TWO SENTENCES:

- Nearly half the packaged foods in the U.S. carry a nutrition label. Few people take the time to read those labels carefully.

COMBINED SENTENCE USING SUBORDINATION:

- Although nearly half the packaged foods sold in the U.S. carry a nutrition label, few people take the time to read those labels carefully.[11]

When two sentences are joined with a coordinating conjunction (*but, and, or, for,* or *yet*) the two parts of the new sentence are of approximately equal importance. In the first example above, the combined sentence gives bats that migrate and bats that hibernate equal emphasis. When two sentences are joined with a subordinating conjunction, on the other hand, the main assertion is emphasized while the subordinate clause is used to provide background or further information. In the second example above, the writer wants us to concentrate not on the existence of nutrition labels but on the fact that few people read them. As you saw in Exercise 1–5, the writer went on to discuss why people do not read the labels and what can be done about making them more readable. Even though *but* and *although* have similar meanings (both sets of sentences above could logically be combined with either), the effects they produce in a sentence are quite different: *but* opposes two things equally; *although* opposes two things and emphasizes one of them.

Subordinate to Clarify Assertions

Subordination, then, is used to emphasize the writer's main point. If the nutrition-label sentence were subordinated differently (*Although few people take the time to read carefully, nearly half the packaged foods sold in the U.S. carry a nutrition label*), the new sentence could introduce a paragraph about the valuable information supplied by the labels; such a paragraph might even go on to criticize consumers who fail to make use of the information. In order to direct your reader precisely, it is necessary to put your main point in the main assertion and to subordinate the other information.

Subordinate to Establish Relationships

RELATIONSHIP ESTABLISHED BY SUBORDINATION	EXAMPLE
Time	*In the next century*, it may be possible to travel frequently in space.
Place	*At Four Corners*, it is possible to be in four states at once.
Cause	*Because of the doctor's incompetence*, the patient had to have a second operation.
Concession	*Although nearly half the packaged foods sold in the U.S. carry a nutrition label*, few people take the time to read those labels carefully.
Condition	*If you forget to take water*, a hike to the bottom of the Grand Canyon will be miserable.
Exception	*Except for the reading list, the papers, and the exams*, the course was enjoyable.
Purpose	*In order to stay in shape*, many people are taking aerobics classes.
Description	She stood hesitantly, *looking several times in both directions*.

Subordinate material, whether in a phrase or a clause, describes one or more sentence elements or makes clear such relations as concession, time, place, and cause. In the nutrition-label sentence, the *although* clause concedes that packaged foods have labels and prepares us for the writer's point that few people read them. *In the next century* gives the time at which frequent space travel can be expected to happen, and *Except for the reading list, the papers, and the exams* states the exceptions to the main assertion, which follows.

SUMMARY

Subordination allows a writer to emphasize a main point. Subordinate material describes one or more sentence elements or makes clear such relations as concession, time, place, and cause.

Exercise 5—5[12]

NAME _____

Combine the following sentences, subordinating as appropriate. The subordinate element may be a phrase or a clause.

Example: Cockroaches can sample food with "taste hairs" before it enters
their mouths.
They learn to shun foul-tasting poison.

Because cockroaches can sample food with "taste hairs"
before it enters their mouths, they learn to shun
foul-tasting poison.

Example: Virgin female Suriname cockroaches clone themselves.
They produce generation after generation of genetically identical females.

Virgin female Suriname cockroaches clone themselves,
producing generation after generation of genetically
identical females.

1. We call them water bugs, Croton bugs, palmetto bugs, and a half a dozen
other "we-don't-really-have-cockroaches" names.
These glossy black or tan pests stubbornly remain true to themselves—
and to us.

_____

_____

_____

2. They have come from their ancestral homes in Africa and Central Asia.
They have fanned out over the globe in camel caravans and slave ships,
in airplanes and submarines.

_____

_____

_____

3. These were the trailblazers.
Cockroaches abound everywhere but in polar regions.

_____

_____

_____

4. Stolid Madagascar roaches are more tolerable than most.
   They cannot flit up a sleeve and are less likely to carry the universal baggage of common cockroaches: bacteria, viruses, and worms.

   _____

   _____

   _____

5. The pest species are nocturnal.
   People seldom see them or fully realize how serious a potential health menace cockroaches are.

   _____

   _____

6. They are not incubators of infection as mosquitoes are.
   They harbor bacteria causing typhoid, leprosy, plague, food poisoning, and a legion of other ills.

   _____

   _____

   _____

7. Termites are more destructive, rats more dangerous.
   Cockroaches are an exterminator's bread and butter.

   _____

   _____

8. Sometimes sanitation is poor.
   Then cockroaches quickly get out of hand.

   _____

9. Scientists have catalogued about 3,500 roach species.
   Probably as many remain unidentified.

   _____

   _____

10. Most of the 3,500 known species flee from danger.
    One rolls up into a ball when threatened, and one sprays attackers with an irritating fluid.

   _____

   _____

   _____

Exercise 5—6

NAME _____

In the space provided below, write five sentences with subordinate clauses or phrases, and underline the subordinate material.

1. _____
   _____

2. _____
   _____

3. _____
   _____

4. _____
   _____

5. _____
   _____

Exercise 5—7

Find five sentences in your own writing or elsewhere that you think could be improved by combining through subordination. Revise and write them below.

_____

_____

_____

_____

_____

_____

_____

_____

_____

Bound and Free Subordinate Elements

BOUND ELEMENTS:
- Sugar *eaten as part of a meal* causes less damage to teeth than the same amount of sugar *consumed as a between-meals snack.*[13]

Bound elements are subordinate parts of the main assertion that cannot be omitted or moved without changing its basic meaning or structure. In the example above, the modifying phrases *eaten as part of a meal* and *consumed as a between-meals snack* are necessary to identify two kinds of sugar consumption. If the modifying phrases were left out, the sentence would make no sense: **x** *Sugar causes less damage to teeth than the same amount of sugar.* If one of the phrases were moved, we would have to change the structure of the sentence: • *When eaten as part of a meal, sugar causes less damage than when it is consumed as a between-meals snack.* Such modifiers are *restrictive* (see pp. 144–145) and may be said to be *bound* to the main assertion.

BOUND	FREE
1. The Wright brothers made the first controlled flight in a power-driven airplane *near Kittyhawk eighty years ago.*	1. *Eighty years ago, near Kittyhawk,* the Wright brothers made the first controlled flight in a power-driven airplane.
2. You will have to find a different lawyer *if you keep lying to me.*	2. *If you keep lying to me,* you will have to find a different lawyer.

Free elements are subordinate words or phrases that are *not* part of the main assertion. Some modifiers can become free by being moved—often from the end of the sentence to the beginning. In both the examples above the relocation of the modifier shortens the main assertion and creates a context for it—in the first case a context of time and place (when and where the event took place: *eighty years ago, near Kittyhawk*) and in the second case a context of condition (the condition under which the main assertion will happen: *if you keep lying to me*).

Such introductory modifying clauses and phrases are free from the main assertion simply because they precede it. Since we have the information they provide before we read the main assertion, we mentally supply whatever is necessary to complete the meaning of the sentence as we read. Therefore, even when the modifying phrase or clause is essential—*on the sleeping child's lap, the snake lay coiled*—it becomes free from the main assertion when placed in the introductory position. (If placed after the verb, the same phrase would be bound: *The snake lay coiled on the sleeping child's lap.*)

Some modifiers are free in either position:

- The cat paused for a long time on the window sill, *testing the latticed ironwork first with one paw, then the other.*

- *Testing the latticed ironwork first with one paw, then the other,* the cat paused for a long time on the window sill.

Testing the latticed ironwork first with one paw, then the other provides important descriptive details but is nonrestrictive (pp. 144–145) or free whether placed before or after the main assertion.

Free elements are set off from the main assertion by commas, dashes, or parentheses. (Exception: as you saw in Chapter 3 [p. 143], the comma may be omitted after short introductory modifiers.)

clarifying sentences by reducing bound elements

x *Measles and rubella are like many other formerly devastating infectious diseases that have been brought under control and all but disappeared in the United States.*

- Like many other formerly devastating infectious diseases that have been brought under control, *measles and rubella have all but disappeared in the United States.*[14]

Understanding the distinction between bound and free elements can help solve important sentence problems. First, subordinate material bound to the main statement in the form of a *that* clause may invade the subject–verb–object alignment, causing the assertion to be vague, wordy, or repetitious. For example, *Measles and rubella are like diseases* does not tell us much, while *Measles and rubella have all but disappeared in the United States* is informative and clear. Second, the longer the main assertion, the more work there is for the reader. When as much subordinate material as possible is moved to a free position, the assertion itself is emphasized, and the relationship between the assertion and the subordinate material becomes easier to grasp. For example, in *Like many other formerly devastating infectious diseases that have been brought under control, measles and rubella . . . ,* the free modifier efficiently establishes a relationship of similarity between *devastating infectious diseases* and prepares us for the now clarified main assertion.

SUMMARY

Bound refers to subordinate material that is part of the main assertion, *free* to subordinate material that is not. By reducing bound elements, you can clarify main assertions and establish immediately understandable sentence relationships.

placement of free subordinate elements

- 1. *According to a 1980 report issued jointly by the U.S. Department of the Treasury and the Surgeon General,* approximately one-third of the deaths resulting from traffic accidents are alcohol-related.

- 2. The National Transportation Safety Board puts the figure even higher, *estimating that roughly half of all fatal accidents involve drunk drivers.*[15]
- 3. Alcohol's ability to overcome inhibitions and produce euphoria—*a feeling of well-being*—probably accounts for much of its widespread popularity.[16]

Free subordinate elements may introduce, extend, or interrupt the main assertion, from which they are set off by commas, parentheses, or dashes. (Exception: Short introductory elements may or may not be followed by commas.)

INTRODUCTORY ELEMENTS

Introductory elements give the reader information useful in understanding or evaluating the main assertion. In the first example above, the introductory phrase tells us the source of the statistic that follows. When we read that one-third of the deaths resulting from traffic accidents are alcohol-related, we already know the two sources for that information and therefore know how to evaluate it. If the statistic appeared alone, we might well ask "Who says so?" or "According to whom?" By anticipating our need for the information, the writer allows us to read smoothly.

EXTENDING ELEMENTS

Extending elements come after the main assertion and refine it, making the whole assertion or part of it more specific. In the second example above, the main assertion contrasts two authorities on deaths resulting from alcohol-related traffic accidents. The extending element—*estimating that roughly half of all fatal accidents involve drunk drivers*—makes specific the position held by the second authority.

COMMON EXTENDING ELEMENTS	
-ing modifier	She stood hesitantly, *looking several times in both directions.*
absolute construction	She studied her map for a long time, *her forehead wrinkled, her shoulders slumped.*
appositional words and phrases	She pulled out her purse and counted the coins—*two quarters, one dime, and three pennies.*
	I introduced him to my neighbor, *a famous naturalist who studies hummingbirds.*

Extending elements give the impression that we are following the writer's thoughts as they occur. Often we seem to be following a sequence of events as it happens or to be studying a situation longer and seeing it in greater detail. In the first example, *looking several times in both directions* allows us to follow the girl's movements in time. In the second, on the other hand, the extending element (*her forehead wrinkled, her shoulders slumped*) creates a more detailed picture of her, apparently possible as a result of closer observation.

Many sentences have both introductory and extending subordinate elements:

- *Once outside the subway station,* she stood hesitantly, *looking several times in both directions.*
- *Sighing with discouragement,* she pulled out her purse and counted the coins—*two quarters, one dime, and three pennies.*
- *After discovering that my friend was an avid bird watcher,* I introduced him to my neighbor, *a famous naturalist who studies hummingbirds.*

INTERRUPTING ELEMENTS

Interrupting subordinate elements give additional (sometimes even emphatic) but not essential information about part of the main assertion. The interrupting elements are either modifiers or appositives, and they are usually placed next to the word, phrase, or clause that they modify. In the sample sentence *Alcohol's ability to overcome inhibitions and produce euphoria—a feeling of well-being—probably accounts for much of its widespread popularity, a feeling of well-being* is an appositive defining *euphoria.* It gives us helpful information but is not essential to the main assertion.

In the following sentences interrupting subordinate elements are italicized.

- One species of tuna, *the yellowfin,* is considered the pride of the catch by tuna fishermen.
- Porpoises swim near the surface of the water, *above the tuna,* so they can get air.[17]

SUMMARY

Free subordinate elements may introduce, extend, or interrupt the main assertion. Introductory elements give the reader information useful in understanding or evaluating the main assertion, while extending elements make the whole assertion or part of it more specific. Interrupting elements give additional information about part of the main assertion, usually the part they immediately follow. Free subordinate material is set off from the main assertion by commas, parentheses, or dashes.

Exercise 5—8[18]

NAME _____

Decide whether the material in parentheses should be used to introduce, interrupt, or extend the main assertion. In the space provided, rewrite enough of
the sentence to show how you would incorporate the subordinate material.
More than one arrangement may be appropriate.

> *Example:* Most parents everywhere were keenly aware of the devastating
> effects of such diseases as smallpox, diphtheria, and poliomyelitis.
> (1. often from firsthand knowledge 2. before the 1950s)
>
> *1. aware, often from firsthand Knowledge*
> *2. Before the 1950s, most parents*

1. Such diseases as measles and rubella were in those days considered to be
inevitable but relatively unimportant maladies of childhood.
(1. commonly known as German measles 2. unlike smallpox, diphtheria,
and poliomyelitis)

   _____

   _____   _____

2. Measles was recognized as a disease more than eleven centuries ago.
(when it was described by Rhazes, an Arabian physician)

   _____

   _____

3. Measles was predominantly a disease of infants and young children.
(1. during the prevaccine era 2. affecting the most susceptible among them)

   _____

   _____

4. It was rare for adults to contract the disease.
(since one attack of measles provided lasting immunity)

   _____

5. The consequences are often disastrous for both children and adults.
(1. however 2. when measles has been introduced into isolated communities that have not experienced the disease for many years)

   _____

   _____

6. The 1875 measles epidemic in the Fiji Islands was responsible for 20,000 deaths.
(a loss of about one-fifth of the native population)

---

7. Measles had a tremendous impact on the Civil War.
(1. in the United States 2. affecting about 75,000 soldiers and causing approximately 5,000 deaths)

---

8. Measles continued to be a serious infectious disease in infants and children in the United States and was an even greater threat in the less developed areas of the world.
(despite the widespread use of antibiotics)

---

9. Approximately 500,000 cases of measles and 300 to 400 cases of measles encephalitis were reported in the United States each year.
(prior to the licensing of the vaccine)

---

10. The extensive use of vaccine has been associated with a progressive decline in the number of reported cases.
(from 500,000 each year during the prevaccine era, to an all-time low of about 3,000 cases in 1981)

Exercise 5—9[19]

NAME _____

Combine the following sentences, using the second to extend the first according to the instructions given in parentheses. Circle the words and punctuation that show where you joined the two sentences. Omit words, phrases, or clauses from the second sentence as appropriate.

> *Example:* In 1886 an earthquake shook Charleston, South Carolina, for more than eight minutes. The earthquake killed about sixty people. (Use an -*ing* form for the second verb.)
>
> *In 1886 an earthquake shook Charleston, South Carolina*
> *for more than eight* (*minutes, killing*) *about sixty*
> *people.*

> *Example:* In 1976 as many as 700,000 people may have died. Most of these people died in a single earthquake in China that was not predicted. (Omit the verb of the second sentence.)
>
> *In 1976 as many as 700,000 people may have*
> (*died, most*) *in a single earthquake in China*
> *that was not predicted.*

1. An earthquake is the shaking that occurs when a slowly accumulated strain in the earth's crust is suddenly released. The strain is typically released along preexisting fracture lines called faults. (Omit the second verb, making the second sentence a modifying phrase.)

   _____

   _____

   _____

2. Boston was rattled just 17 days after the great Lisbon quake in 1755. In that earthquake, walls and chimneys collapsed, stone fences fell apart, and fish were killed in the harbor. (Use a colon.)

   _____

   _____

   _____

3. To be able to talk about earthquakes, scientists, disaster-agency planners, and the rest of us need ways to measure and compare them. Most familiar is the Richter magnitude scale. This scale measures the height of earthquake-generated waves recorded on seismographs. (Combine the last two sentences by making the second a modifying clause with *which*.)

_____

_____

_____

_____

4. The scale is logarithmic. This means that a quake of magnitude 7 produces waves ten times larger than one of magnitude 6. (Use a colon; omit unnecessary words.)

_____

_____

5. Geophysicists believe that when rocks are stressed to about half of their breaking point, they begin to expand. At this point, they fill with numerous small cracks. (Use an *-ing* form for the second verb.)

_____

_____

_____

Exercise 5–10[20]

NAME _____

Using the information supplied below, write ten sentences, five with extending elements, five with interrupting elements. Any of your sentences may also have introductory material.

1. Amazonia is the world's largest remaining jungle.
2. In Amazonia, extensive clearing of forest and overfishing of rivers are relatively recent.
3. The harvesting of resources was restrained in the past.
4. There were aboriginal beliefs in supernatural game wardens and forest demons.
5. Most Amazonian tribes have become extinct.
6. Aboriginal ideas about the spiritual dimension of nature have trickled into the cultural reservoir of rural people.
7. These ideas continue to play a conservation role.
8. The rural population of Amazonia is known as *caboclos* in Brazil.
9. It includes small-scale farmers, sharecroppers, ranch hands, hunters, fishermen, and itinerant miners.
10. *Caboclos* are descended largely from Indian tribes.
11. They are intermixed to varying degrees with Europeans and blacks.
12. They are nominally Catholic.
13. These country people firmly believe in a bewildering cast of supernatural creatures that daily influence their behavior.
14. They think that the forest is full of spirits.
15. Some spirits watch over game.
16. Some harass those who venture deep into the woods.
17. Several ghosts live in trees.
18. Others take on human form and punish those who abuse nature's providence.
19. Rubber has dominated much of the economic history of Amazonia in the last one hundred years.
20. Rubber's economic domination has made the graceful, gray-barked rubber tree the focus of folklore.
21. Sometimes rubber tappers drain too much sap from the trees.
22. Then *mae de seringa* sometimes intervenes.
23. *Mae de seringa* means the "mother of rubber trees."
24. She may appear along forest trails at any time.
25. Most commonly, she appears on Good Friday.
26. She is a short woman with long hair.
27. Her arms and legs are gashed in a herringbone pattern.
28. This pattern is similar to that on the trunks of harvested rubber trees.
29. She only challenges those who slice her children too deeply.
30. A fantastic array of monsters and spirits also lurks in the region's waters.
31. Many of them help to conserve the forest as well as the fish.

SENTENCES WITH EXTENDING ELEMENTS

Example: <u>Rubber has dominated much of the economic history of</u>
<u>Amazonia in the last one hundred years, making</u>
<u>the graceful, gray-barked rubber tree the focus</u>
<u>of folklore.</u>

1. _____

_____

2. _____

_____

3. _____

_____

4. _____

_____

5. _____

_____

SENTENCES WITH INTERRUPTING ELEMENTS

Example: <u>The rural population of Amazonia, known as *caboclos*</u>
<u>in Brazil, includes small-scale farmers, sharecroppers,</u>
<u>ranch hands, hunters, fishermen, and itinerant</u>
<u>miners.</u>

1. _____

_____

2. _____

_____

3. _____

_____

4. _____

_____

5. _____

_____

Exercise 5–11

NAME _____

Find five sets of sentences in your own writing or elsewhere that you think could be improved by being combined. Revise—using subordinate material to introduce, interrupt, or extend main assertions as appropriate—and write both the original and the combined versions below.

1. Original: _____

_____

_____

1. Revision: _____

_____

_____

2. Original: _____

_____

_____

2. Revision: _____

_____

_____

3. Original: _____

_____

_____

3. Revision: _____

_____

_____

4. Original: _____

_____

_____

4. Revision: _____

_____

_____

5. Original: _____

_____

_____

5. Revision: _____

_____

_____

Exercise 5—12[21]

NAME _____

Rewrite the following sentences to reduce bound elements and/or increase free elements. (It may be necessary to rewrite only part of the sentence.) More than one revision is possible. If no revision is necessary, write *NR*. Number 6 is done for you as an example.

1. Captain Richard H. Truly was beset by the fear that he was developing motion sickness only hours before he flew the space shuttle Columbia to a safe landing on a dry lake bed in California two years ago.

_____

_____

2. Indeed, at least a third of the astronauts who have flown in space have been beset by feelings of dizziness and nausea, and for centuries, many otherwise dauntless travelers, from skippers of ocean-going vessels to racing car drivers, have been similarly humbled.

_____

_____

3. However, a new method for administering drugs that uses neither pills nor injections but lets the medicine seep through the skin has now been developed, and this procedure is called transdermal medication.

_____

_____

4. Not only is it helping astronauts and other travelers overcome their occasional bouts of motion sickness, disorientation, and malaise, but its apparent success in that area has encouraged at least six pharmaceutical houses to work toward using transdermal medication for cancer chemotherapy,

duodenal ulcers, glaucoma, asthma, allergies, hypertension, diabetes, and contraception.

_____

_____

_____

5. The case of Captain Truly was that he simply opened the shuttle's medical kit, took out a flexible patch resembling a Band-Aid, peeled the protective coating off the thumbnail-sized disk, and placed its adhesive side on the skin behind his ear.

_____

_____

6. Five micrograms of a drug called scopolamine, which combats the effects of motion sickness, dripped through his skin into his bloodstream each hour the patch was in place.

Each hour the patch was in place, it dripped five micrograms of

scopolamine, a drug that combats the effects...

7. *Transdermal* is a medical term that was all but unheard of before the 1980s but that has suddenly become a buzzword, from the space center at Cape Canaveral to the America's Cup races at Newport, R.I.

_____

_____

8. Over the centuries physicians have used just about every organ to transmit drugs into the body, but only rarely have they used the largest of all—the skin.

_____

_____

9. The major problem that the researchers have had was not getting the drugs through the pores and different levels of skin but controlling the amount.

_____

_____

10. Scopolamine is one of the best drugs available to control motion sickness, but high doses of it may cause a wide variety of side effects up to and including hallucinations.

_____

_____

11. Therefore, the problem became one of controlled release, trickling just the right amount of scopolamine through the skin over just the right period of time.

_____

_____

Subordination in a Paragraph

x This territory is dotted with sparkling ponds and lakes, and it is considered the primeval heart and soul of the Pine Barrens. That name is a curious misnomer. The region is full of pitch pines, short-leaf pines and even pygmy pines. It is anything but barren. It sustains more than 80 bird species, dozens of reptiles and amphibians, and many deer, fox raccoons, and other creatures. The pine trees are ubiquitous. The diverse vegetation also includes varieties of oak, cedar, and magnolia, shoulder-high blueberry shrubs, myrtle, azaleas, and a great many wild herbs.

• This territory, *dotted* with sparkling ponds and lakes, is considered the primeval heart and soul of the Pine Barrens. That name is a curious misnomer, *because although* the region is full of pitch pines, short-leaf pines and even pygmy pines, it is anything but barren. It sustains more than 80 bird species, dozens of reptiles and amphibians, and many deer, fox, raccoons, and other creatures. The diverse vegetation includes, *in addition to* the ubiquitous pine trees, varieties of oak, cedar, and magnolia, shoulder-high blueberry shrubs, myrtle, azaleas, and a great many wild herbs.[22]

By comparing the two versions of the paragraph, the first without subordination, the second with subordination restored, you can see how a whole paragraph becomes more readable when a writer subordinates to clarify relationships between ideas and to give emphasis to main assertions. For example, descriptive details included in an *-ing* or *-ed* modifying phrase emphasize rather than compete with the main assertion, as you can see in the first sentence. And the *because* and *although* clauses clarify what seems otherwise to be little more than listlike information.

NAME _____

Combine the sentences of the following paragraph as directed, and write them in paragraph form in the space provided below. The first is done for you as an example.

(1) There is an unfortunate fluke of nature in Brazil. (2) Brazil is unlike its neighbors. (3) Brazil has no significant oil reserves. (4) What it does have is something else. (5) It has been importing almost a million barrels of oil every day. (6) It has a $90 billion foreign debt. (7) This debt is the biggest in the world. (8) It also has the Amazon Basin. (9) The Amazon Basin is a 1.3 million-square-mile tract of forest. (10) This forest has for the past century or more defied almost all attempts at development. (11) Now Brazil's leaders think they have finally discovered a way to make the Amazon pay.

1. Combine sentences 1, 2, and 3.
   Make 3 the main assertion.
   Use *because of* to make 1 a subordinate phrase.
   Use 2 as a modifier that interrupts the main assertion.

2. Combine sentences 4, 5, 6, and 7.
   Make 4 and 6 the main assertion.
   Use 5 as a subordinate element that interrupts the main assertion. Change the verb to an *-ing* form and introduce this subordinate phrase with *primarily as a result of*.
   Use 7 as a modifier which extends the main assertion. Omit the verb.

3. Combine sentences 8, 9, and 10.
   Make 8 the main assertion.
   Make 9 and 10 a modifier that extends the main assertion.
   Combine 9 and 10, making 10 a clause modifying *forest*, the last word of 9.
   Make the combined 9 and 10 a modifier that extends the main assertion.

4. No revision necessary for 11. Write it as it is at the end of the paragraph.

1. *Because of an unfortunate fluke of nature, Brazil, unlike its neighbors, has no significant oil reserves.*

2. _____

   _____

   _____

3. _____

_____

_____

4. _____

_____

_____

MATCHING

- 1. (A) The (a) *most famous quake* to hit this country may be the San Francisco earthquake of 1906, but (B) the (b) *most far-reaching* appears to be a series of three near New Madrid, Missouri.[24]
- 2. The cat paused on the window sill, (A) extending (a) *first one* paw, (b) *then the other*, (B) testing the latticed ironwork of the fire escape, (C) looking as if she wanted (1) *both* to advance (2) *and* to retreat.
- 3. (A) (a) Termites are (1) *more* destructive, (b) rats (2) *more* dangerous, but (B) cockroaches are an exterminator's (x) bread and (y) butter.[25]

The word *matching* describes how words, phrases, and clauses can be paired, brought together in a series, or balanced against each other in a sentence. Matching is a process of putting words with related meaning into related structures. In compound sentences, for example, independent clauses are matched: two clauses are coordinated, each given the same emphasis as the other. In the first and last sentences above, clauses *A* and *B* are matched. Similarly, in the last sentence, two words (*bread* and *butter*) occupy matching positions as complements, while in the second sentence, a series of phrases (*extending . . . , testing . . . ,* and *looking . . .*) are matched modifiers.

Some very familiar anticipatory structures are also examples of matching: *not only . . . but also, both . . . and, neither . . . nor,* and the like. The proper use of such matching formulas allows readers to grasp quickly the meaning of the sentence. In the second example above, as soon as we have read *both to advance*, we wait for *and* and a parallel item: *both to advance and to retreat*. Similarly, when we read *first*, we expect *then* or *second*. Since *one* and *the other* are also matching words, *first one* almost has to lead to *then the other*. Such structures allow the reader to anticipate the writer's next move.

Using matching elements in a sentence results in parallel structure (see pp. 113–114), which can be used to emphasize both similarities and differences. In the first sample sentence, within the matching clauses (*A* and *B*), there is another parallel structure—*most famous* and *most far-reaching* (*a* and *b*). Occupying the same grammatical position, the two phrases show further parallelism through repetition. *Most* emphasizes that both earthquakes were significant and sets us up for the contrast between two kinds of significance: *famous* and *far-reaching*. So controlled is this structure that the word *quake* can be omitted in the second clause.

The last example deserves special attention because it illustrates several matched elements:

(A) Termites are more destructive, rats more dangerous,
(B) but cockroaches are an exterminator's bread and butter.

The two clauses in (A) are coordinated with clause (B), allowing for the contrast of termites and rats on the one hand and cockroaches on the other.

293

(a) termites are more destructive
(b) rats more dangerous

Within (A) is another set of clauses, marked (a) and (b). *Termites* contrasts with *rats, destructive* with *dangerous* because they occupy parallel grammatical positions. And the repetition of the word *more* aligns termites and rats by placing them in contrast with something to follow (cockroaches). So closely controlled are the first two clauses that the verb *is* can be omitted from the second (rats more dangerous). Parallel structures allow a reader to see immediately relationships that are not fully stated. Compare this sentence as it might be without the condensation allowed by parallelism:

Termites are more destructive than cockroaches are.

Rats are more dangerous than cockroaches are.

Nevertheless, cockroaches are an exterminator's bread and butter.

Exercise 5—14

NAME _____

The following passage is taken from the Declaration of Independence. Indicate in the space provided below which of the numbered elements are parallel with one another. The first is done for you as an example.

When, in the course of human events, it becomes necessary for one people (1) to dissolve the political bands which have connected them with another, and (2) to assume among the powers of the earth the separate and equal station to which the laws of nature and of nature's God entitle them, a decent respect to the opinions of mankind requires that they should declare the causes which impel them to the separation. We hold these truths to be self-evident: (3) that all men are created equal; (4) that they are endowed by their creator with certain inalienable rights; (5) that among these are (6) life, (7) liberty, and the (8) pursuit of happiness; (9) that to secure these rights, governments are instituted among men, deriving their just powers from the consent of the governed; (10) that whenever any form of government becomes destructive to these ends, it is the right of the people (11) to alter or (12) to abolish it, and (13) to institute a new government, (14) laying its foundations (15) on such principles, and (16) organizing its powers (17) in such form, as to them shall seem most likely to effect their (18) safety and (19) happiness.

PARALLEL ELEMENTS

_____#1 and #2_____   _____

_____   _____

_____   _____

_____   _____

Exercise 5—15[26]

NAME _____

The following sentences are famous quotations without their original parallel structures. Rewrite the italicized sections, following the pattern set up in the first part of the sentence.

Example: (Always do right.) This will gratify some people, and *the rest will be astonished.* (Mark Twain)

_____*astonish the rest*_____

1. Every sweet has its sour; *evil is also balanced by good.* (Emerson)

---

2. They are too proud to beg, and *stealing is out of the question because they are too honest.* (Folk saying)

---

3. The time to stop a revolution is at the beginning; *the end is not the time.* (Adlai Stevenson)

---

4. Humility must always be the portion of any man who receives acclaim earned in the blood of his followers *and because his friends sacrificed.* (Eisenhower)

---

5. Man's capacity for justice makes democracy possible, but *because man also has an inclination to injustice, democracy is necessary.* (Reinhold Niebuhr)

Significant Pauses

- Drunk drivers are a distinct menace both to themselves and to others. According to a 1980 report issued jointly by the U.S. Department of the Treasury and the Surgeon General, approximately one-third of the deaths resulting from traffic accidents are alcohol-related. The National Transportation Safety Board puts the figure even higher, estimating that roughly half of all fatal traffic accidents involve drunk drivers. In 1982, nearly 44,000 people were killed in traffic accidents in the U.S.[27]

Sentences should work together not only logically but also rhythmically. As you can see from the paragraph above, a careful arrangement of subordinate elements creates a series of pauses, and those pauses create a smooth and interesting rhythm. The first sentence above, which has no pauses, is followed by a sentence beginning with a long introductory modifier. Between the modifier and the main assertion, readers pause, not only in reading but also in thinking, as they prepare for the relationship set up by the *although* clause. The third sentence begins with a main assertion, which is extended and made more specific by the modifying phrase. Once again, the reader can easily grasp the relationship established between the main assertion and the subordinate element. Carefully arranged free subordinate elements, then, allow the reader both to rest and to see relationships precisely. The paragraph is pleasing and easy to read because of the variation in rhythm and the clarity with which it establishes relationships.

Compare the two versions of the following paragraph. The first is a series of main assertions, with very few free subordinate elements. It does not allow the reader to pause, nor does it clarify relationships. The second version is the paragraph as it appeared in *Natural History*. The subordinate relationships – and along with them significant pauses – have been restored.

x There are engineering and logistical problems. Only a few dams have been built in rain forest areas anywhere in the world. Their history has not been a happy one. The first one was completed in 1964. It created Lake Brokopondo in the former Dutch colony of Suriname. Suriname is just north of Brazil. Five hundred seventy square miles of dense, virgin rain forest were flooded for this reservoir. The trees decomposed. They produced hydrogen sulfide. The resultant stink brought complaints from people many miles downwind. For two years workers at the dam had to wear gas masks. Another aspect of the decomposing vegetation was even worse. It made the water more acidic and corroded the dam's expensive cooling system. The cost of extra maintenance and of repairing and replacing damaged equipment was estimated in 1977 to have totaled $4 million. This is more than 7 percent of the total cost of the project.

- Because of engineering and logistical problems, only a few dams have been built in rain forest areas anywhere in the world, and their history has not been a happy one. The first one, completed in 1964, created Lake Brokopondo in the former Dutch colony of Suriname just north of Brazil. Five hundred seventy square miles of dense virgin rain forest were flooded for this reservoir. As the trees decomposed, they produced hydrogen sulfide, and the resultant stink brought complaints from people many miles downwind. For two years workers at the dam had to wear gas masks. The worst aspect of the decomposing vegetation was that it made the water more acidic and corroded the dam's expensive cooling system. The cost of extra maintenance and of repairing and replacing damaged equipment was estimated in 1977 to have totaled $4 million, or more than 7 percent of the total cost of the project.[28]

SUMMARY

Sentences in a paragraph should work together not only logically but rhythmically as well. Carefully arranged free subordinate elements create variety in sentence rhythm and clearly establish sentence relationships.

Vary Your Sentence Patterns

SENTENCE PATTERN	EXAMPLES
Cumulative	1. Once outside the subway station, she stood hesitantly, *looking several times in both directions.* 2. She studied her map for a long time, *her forehead wrinkled, her shoulders slumped.* 3. She pulled out her coin purse and counted—*two quarters, one dime, and three pennies, not enough for a bus, let alone a taxi.*
Periodic	4. She seemed to be asking herself, *as she stood examining approximately every third passer-by,* whether she could possibly, *even in this emergency,* manage to overcome her embarrassment enough to say to a stranger, *even a kind stranger,* those words *to which she had sometimes responded but which she had more often hurriedly ignored:* "Spare change, spare change, please."
"False start"	5. *Good walking shoes, one nice dress, toothbrush, airline ticket, map, even one subway token given to her a year ago by her cousin—* these she had remembered, but she had left behind her wallet, her traveler's checks, and the unlisted phone number of her friend.
Interruption	6. Other traveling stories—*she had lost her suitcase in Washington, she had gotten on a plane for Chicago by mistake, she had been left behind by the tour bus at Grand Canyon—*came to her mind, making her smile to think that this was no worse. She might even write a story: "How to Manage in New York City on 63¢."

The sentences above illustrate various sentence patterns. The first—the cumulative sentence—is familiar to you from the exercises in the subordination section. Whenever you extend an already complete sentence with a free subordinate element (for example, an *-ing* modifier or an absolute phrase), you have written a **cumulative sentence**. In each of the sentences above, the italicized element extends the sentence without becoming part of the main assertion.

The cumulative pattern gets its name from the way a sentence *accumulates* parts by simply adding them on. It gives readers the impression that they are watching a writer add to the sentence as he or she thinks. As the second and third examples show, more than one extending phrase can be added. In the third sentence, one extension—*two quarters, one dime, and three pennies*—looks back to the main assertion, while the second extension modifies not the main assertion but the first extension. In the second sentence, on the other hand, both extensions look back to the main statement. In this case, they must be parallel.

The **periodic sentence** also gives the impression that the reader is watching the writer think—but think analytically or remember rather than follow a natural or observable process. The extensions of a periodic sentence occur within the sentence, interrupting and delaying the completion of the main assertion as the writer mulls over particular details or their significance. The writer withholds the completion of his or her thought until the reader has had enough time to analyze or appreciate particular parts.

The sentence with the "false start" begins with the items on a list that we expect to function as the subject. Instead, these items are in apposition (p. 144) either to the subject or to an object. In the sentence above, the list is equal to *these*, which is the object of *had remembered*. This sentence also shows another kind of sentence pattern, called **inversion**: instead of subject–verb–object (*she had remembered these*), the order here is inverted and we have object–subject–verb: *these she had remembered*.

The **interrupting sentence** is like an interrupting modifier except that it is a full continuous sentence on its own, with no structural connection to the sentence it interrupts. The interrupting sentence provides vivid details that help the reader to appreciate or understand a part of the main assertion. The interruption—when punctuated with dashes—creates a dramatic pause in the sentence rhythm, catching the reader's attention and creating variety. Notice that the extending element makes the sample sentence (6) cumulative as well.

Another variation in sentence pattern that you have probably used is the question. Although questions can appear at any point, they are more frequent at the beginning or end of paragraphs:

- But why become flightless? To most people, birds symbolize flight, and most of the evolutionary history of the class Aves has indeed revolved around the opportunities created by flight, on the one hand, and the physical constraints of flight, on the other. Yet the Hawaiian Islands are not unique; flightless birds occur on islands throughout the world's oceans. What great selective pressure spurs the development of flightlessness on islands?[29]

Exercise 5–16[30]

NAME _____

Supply and circle commas in the following paragraphs in order to show where pauses occur. The first is done for you as an example. (Commas in a series have already been supplied.)

Nothing succeeds like a cockroach when it comes to surviving. Lacking food, a roach can subsist on glue, paper, or soap. With nothing to eat the American roach can draw on body stores and live as long as three months. It can last a month without water. Lightning-fast responses and receptors sensitive even to another roach's footfall enable cockroaches to thwart a human heel in hot pursuit. They can tolerate many times more radiation than man perhaps because of their thick body walls and one species can survive freezing for 48 hours.

World travelers roaches thrive everywhere but in the polar regions having hitchhiked aboard ships, submarines, and planes. The United States harbors about 55 species.

But this irrepressible insect is a health menace. Roaches carry viruses and bacteria that cause such diseases as hepatitis, polio, typhoid fever, plague, and salmonella which they may track from one place to another.

Exercise 5–17[31]

The following paragraph has been written with few or no significant pauses. Rewrite it, subordinating where possible and arranging free subordinate elements to produce significant pauses. (In the article on damming the Amazon, this paragraph comes immediately after the sample paragraph on p. 298.)

The dam was built. Up to then water hyacinth had been rare in the Suriname River. It began to spread over the surface of the lake. It impeded navigation and got entangled in machinery. A lake in which decaying trees are releasing nutrients is an attractive habitat for waterweeds. They appear first on the edges of the lake. They are fed by the nutrient-rich water lapping up and down on the shores. Eventually they break loose and float into the main part of the lake. They form dense mats. They anchor in the branches and on the trunks of still standing trees. Within a year a 50-square-mile carpet of water hyacinth was floating on Lake Brokopondo. By 1966 almost half the reservoir was covered by the weed. There was also a floating fern. It is called *Ceratopteris.* It covered another 170 square miles.

Exercise 5–18[32]

NAME _____

Read the paragraph on earthquake prediction that follows, and in the space provided below, list the features that create variety.

> *Example:* Just what is an earthquake? It is the shaking that occurs when a slowly accumulating strain in the Earth's crust is suddenly re-leased, typically along preexisting fracture lines called faults.
>
> *Use of question at the beginning of paragraph*
> *Use of extending modifier which creates a pause*

The scientists face not only virtually impossible technical problems—they cannot afford to instrument all of the Earth's fault systems with creep-meters, tiltmeters, and level lines—but knotty ethical issues as well, for the conse-quences of an erroneous prediction can be serious indeed. One bad prediction could cause unnecessary pandemonium—a series of them the same effect as the boy who cried "Wolf!"

_____

_____

_____

_____

_____

_____

_____

_____

_____

_____

Exercise 5—19[33]

NAME _____

Using the following information and any information you want to add, write five sentences, two cumulative, two periodic, and one inverted. (You may make up details if you want to, and you may use the same information in different sentences.)

1. Kangaroos are marsupials.
2. They raise their young in body pouches.
3. The young kangaroo can count on the pouch until it is 8–11 months old.
4. They are born the size of a lima bean.
5. They can grow to seven feet tall and weigh as much as 200 pounds.
6. A female kangaroo can hold an embryo in reserve for several months.
7. She can hold it until conditions are right for its development.
8. This arrested state is called embryonic diapause.
9. If a nursing kangaroo dies young, the reserve is jolted into development.
10. A young kangaroo is called a joey.
11. Full grown males are called boomers.
12. Groups of five to several hundred are called mobs.
13. They cruise at 12–15 miles an hour and can go twice that fast if necessary.
14. The dominant male usually fathers most of the offspring.
15. Males do not help to raise the young.
16. The kangaroo tail is prized for soup and meat.
17. The tail bends at the end while the kangaroo is running and acts as a counter balance. It keeps the creature on an even keel.
18. Normal life span is about 7 years.
19. They can reach the age of 20.
20. The best known ones both in Australia and abroad are probably the big ones, the grays, reds, and wallaroos.
21. Kangaroos were a major source of food and skins for centuries for native Australian aborigines.
22. Their hunting had little effect on the kangaroo population.
23. Sheep ranchers and cattlemen had a great effect on the kangaroo "census."
24. They created grasslands and water holes for livestock.
25. They inadvertently created a kangaroo paradise for the bigger grazers and destroyed the habitat of smaller ones.

CUMULATIVE

1. _____

_____

_____

2. _____

_____

_____

PERIODIC

1. _____

_____

_____

2. _____

_____

_____

INVERTED

_____

_____

_____

Exercise 5—20

NAME _____

Find a paragraph in your own writing that you think would be improved by increasing subordination and varying sentence patterns. Revise it and write your revision in the space provided below.

_____

_____

_____

_____

_____

_____

_____

_____

_____

_____

_____

REVISION EXERCISES

In the following exercises, several revisions are possible. There is not one "right" answer.

I. Rewrite the main assertions of the italicized sentences to make them more distinct.

(1) *The fact remains that no matter how just a test the SAT may be, such a convenient tool is used by many college administrators who then neglect all other methods of screening applicants.* But the problem may go deeper. (2) *The widespread notion exists that intelligence can be quantified.* Does that blue and white package truly represent the sum of twelve years of schooling? Is intelligence made up of the factors that test makers say it is? (3) *The belief that our intelligence can be represented numerically would seem to hinder us from giving the proper emphasis to creativity.*

1. _____

_____

_____

2. _____

_____

_____

3. _____

_____

_____

II. Combine sentences and subordinate to highlight main assertions. Vary sentence rhythms and use parallel structures where appropriate.

My roommate is from Indonesia. She is studying chemical engineering. One of her classes is at 8:00 a.m. She is careful not to wake me up when she gets ready for class. She always moves quietly about the room, and when she leaves, she shuts the door very carefully. I usually do not see her again until dinnertime, but we always eat dinner together. At dinner, we talk about our experiences during the day, and we invariably joke about the poor quality of cafeteria food. We study in our room after dinner, and she often helps me with my chemistry homework. We normally take several breaks from studying during the evening. Sometimes we just stay in the room and talk, and sometimes we go downstairs to play a few games of ping-pong.

III. Condense the sentences of this paragraph as much as possible, omitting repetitious statements and clarifying and highlighting main assertions. Vary your sentence rhythms. (You may decide to leave some sentences as they are.)

Finally there is the big question of safety. Many people say getting on one of these bikes is taking your life into your own hands. In a way it is. Your safety is up to you. It is true that a major accident on a bike is bad news. The whole idea is to avoid accidents. Even in a car there are things one can do to help prevent wrecks, and the problem is that people do not always take them seriously. On a bike you either take them seriously or you face the consequences. It is not hard to remember that there is nothing but cloth between your skin and whatever you hit. If you are careful, a bike is safe. You just have to keep an eye out for the rest of the world and assume that they cannot drive.

NOTES

[1]Ernst Mayr, "The Joy of Birds," *Natural History,* Sept. 1983, inside front cover.

[2]Masakazu Konishi, "Night Owls Are Good Listeners," *Natural History,* Sept. 1983, p. 57.

[3]Richard L. Williams, "Science Tries to Break New Ground in Predicting Great Earthquakes," *Smithsonian,* July 1983, p. 42.

[4]Seymour M. Hersh, "The Pardon," *Atlantic,* Aug. 1983, p. 55.

[5]"Sunscreens," *Consumer Reports,* 48 (1983), 275.

[6]David S. Wilcove and Robert F. Whitcomb, "Gone with the Trees," *Natural History,* Sept. 1983, p. 82.

[7]Kenneth P. Able, "A Migratory Bird's Baedeker," *Natural History,* Sept. 1983, p. 22.

[8]Jeanne McDermott, "The Solid-State Parrot," *Science 83,* June 1983, p. 59.

[9]Adapted from Williams, p. 42.

[10]Adapted from Donald Dale Jackson, "Close Encounters with the Creatures of Another World," *Smithsonian,* Nov. 1982, p. 77.

[11]Adapted from "Government to Consider Simpler Nutrition Labels," *Consumer Reports,* 48 (1983), 108.

[12]Adapted from Allen A. Boraiko, "The Indomitable Cockroach," *National Geographic,* 159 (1981), 130, 132, 134, 138, 140, 141.

[13]"Too Much Sugar?" *Consumer Reports,* 43 (1978), 139.

[14]Adapted from Saul Krugman, "The Conquest of Measles and Rubella," *Natural History,* Jan. 1983, p. 16.

[15]"Alcohol in Perspective," *Consumer Reports,* 48 (1983), 353.

[16]"Alcohol in Perspective," p. 352.

[17]"Tuna vs. Porpoises: The Survival of an Endangered Species," *Consumer Reports,* 44 (1979), 11.

[18]Adapted from Krugman, "The Conquest of Measles and Rubella," pp. 16, 18, and 19.

[19]Adapted from Williams, pp. 42–44, 46.

[20]Adapted from Nigel Smith, "Enchanted Forest," *Natural History,* Aug. 1983, pp. 14, 18.

[21]Adapted from Richard D. Lyons, "Drugs: New Method Proves Effective," *New York Times,* 19 July 1983, Section C, p. 1.

[22]Lewis Simons, "New Jersey Shows a Different Face in this Bewitching Province of Pines," *Smithsonian,* July 1983, p. 80.

[23]Adapted from Catherine Caulfield, "Dam the Amazon, Full Steam Ahead," *Natural History,* July 1983, p. 60.

[24]Adapted from Williams, p. 42.

[25]Adapted from Boraiko, p. 140.

[26]Adapted from John Bartlett, *Familiar Quotations* (Boston: Little, Brown, 1955), pp. 679, 501, 1005, 986, 954, 963.

[27]Adapted from "Alcohol in Perspective," p. 353.

[28]Adapted from Caulfield, pp. 60, 62.

[29]Helen F. James and Storrs L. Olson, "Flightless Birds," *Natural History,* Sept. 1983, p. 31.

[30] Adapted from Boraiko, p. 132.

[31] Adapted from Caulfield, p. 62.

[32] Williams, p. 43.

[33] Adapted from Geoffrey B. Sharman, "They're a Marvelous Mob: Those Kangaroos!" *National Geographic,* 155 (1979), 192, 197, 200–201, 207, 209.

PARAGRAPH REVISION

WHAT IS A PARAGRAPH?

- Utterly pure water—H$_2$O molecules and nothing else—probably does not exist anywhere. Water can form solutions with thousands of substances, and what does not dissolve in water often remains suspended in it. Water everywhere is a chemical brew as ancient as the seas or as new as today's chlorinated tap water.[1]

What is the sample paragraph about? *Pure water.* What point does the paragraph make about pure water? *Utterly pure water probably does not exist anywhere.* These two questions—*What is it about?* and *What point does it make?*—can be asked in regard to any paragraph of explanation or argument.

The answer to *What point does the paragraph make?* tells us its main idea, and this main idea we will call the **theme.** The theme of the paragraph above is stated in its first sentence: *Utterly pure water probably does not exist anywhere.* In the following paragraphs, too, the first sentence is the theme sentence:

theme sentence { • A. *To most of us, plants appear passive in the face of attack by herbivores.* Near my home in New Hampshire, some black cherry trees are totally defoliated by the eastern tent caterpillar almost yearly. They seem destined to lose their entire crop of leaves each June and to replace their canopies with a new crop each July, after the tentmakers are gone. On a larger scale, a summer of gypsy moth defoliation in the extensive oak forests of the northeastern United States can resemble a winter with no snow. Oak trees, too, must replace their lost canopies with a second crop of leaves.[2]

theme sentence { • B. *We found that tigers moved around their territories frequently and were rarely found in the same place on two consecutive days unless they had made a large kill.* They moved an average of six to twelve miles per night, with males moving significantly farther on a day-to-day basis. The tigers visited most parts of their home ranges every two to three weeks, and although these movements were related to finding and killing prey, it became obvious that they were also intricately linked to the maintenance of rights to an area. The maxim seemed to be "use it or lose it," as on two occasions tigers had their home ranges appropriated by others when they failed to use all portions of their territory.[3]

In paragraph A, the first sentence states the theme that plants seem to us to be passive when attacked by herbivores. The rest of the paragraph explains the theme by giving examples that cause us to think of the plants as passive. Paragraph B also begins with its main point: the researchers' discovery that the tigers they studied moved frequently around their (the tigers') territory unless they had made a large kill. The rest of the paragraph develops as an explanation of this theme.

Developing or leading to the main idea is the job, so to speak, of any paragraph in which the writer intends to explain something or to present an argument. In order to do this well, all the sentences must work together. None of the following passages qualifies as an effective paragraph.

x A. Like a bandit, the first boll weevil arrived from south of the border back in the heyday of Billy the Kid. We haven't zapped the boll weevil yet. Hatched from an egg left inside a cotton boll, the weevil grub eats the heart out of its home. In Texas children swarmed over fields hand-picking weevils. There's a famous song about the boll weevil. Some people, thinking only God could remove the weevil, held prayer meetings to ask for deliverance. Cheap cigars were called boll weevils.[4]

Passage A has no central focus. It only apparently passes the test posed by the question *What is the paragraph about?* Even though all the sentences in A are about the boll weevil, they are so unrelated that they cannot work together.

x B. Why do Americans wear designer jeans? Many people spend three or four times more than they have to. Do consumers know that they do not get more for their money? *You get what you pay for* is not true in this case; in fact, you pay for a lot more than you get. So why is it that people buy designer jeans?

The sentences of B seem unable to get started on the job of addressing the opening question. This passage depends on repetition. It does not develop or lead to an idea and therefore cannot make a point.

x C.   The result of the poll may come as a surprise to teachers and administrators, but the fact is that two-thirds of the student body consider cheating acceptable under certain circumstances. Though their position is not morally defensible, many students say that cheating at school is different from and less serious than cheating in the outside world—for example, at a job. And more than half think that "since everyone does it," cheating cannot be a serious violation of their ethical codes. It seems clear that most students do not find cheating in school acceptable.*

The sentences in passage C appear to be working together until the very end. The last sentence, however—*It seems clear that most students do not find cheating in school acceptable*—contradicts the point that the paragraph was making, that for most students cheating is rather easy to justify. This paragraph could be effective if the writer acknowledged and used the contradiction. The point could be *Although according to the poll two-thirds of the student body consider cheating acceptable, in fact most students do not.* The writer could then offer evidence to invalidate the poll or to make us evaluate its information in a new way. As it stands, the paragraph is ineffective because the last sentence merely contradicts the preceding sentences. The writer gives the reader no indication that the contradiction will or can be resolved.

SUMMARY

Argumentative and explanatory paragraphs make a point about something. All the sentences should work together to make this point. They must focus on one topic, develop or lead to a point about the topic, and deal with rather than ignore any contradictions that arise. The main point of a paragraph is its theme.

---

*Passages excerpted from student writing are marked with an asterisk (*).

Exercise 6—1

NAME _____

In the space provided after each of the paragraphs below, indicate the theme of each.

1. At midday, the scene is quiet. Nothing stirs under the baking sun except perhaps a vulture, soaring on hot air currents. The desert creatures have not gone—they are in the shade of bushes or underground. Even some of the plants are "taking a siesta," having folded their leaves or closed their leaf pores.[5]

   _____

2. Many North American birds change their behavior entirely each year in order to survive in the tropics. Some become aggressively territorial, others that were solitary join flocks, while certain sedentary species become long-distance wanderers. A few birds even make abrupt switches from aggressive individualism to mild-mannered flock participation.[6]

   _____

Exercise 6—2

In the space provided after each passage, indicate whether it is an effective paragraph. If it is not, indicate whether its difficulty arises from (1) lack of focus, (2) repetition, or (3) contradiction.

Example: Many city dwellers live in such a rush that they do not eat a good breakfast. They see nothing wrong with having breakfast while running down the street to catch the bus. People who live on the run do not have time for healthy breakfasts. In fact, eat and run is all they have time to do. A nourishing breakfast has become an impossibility or a thing of the past for many people who live in cities. Nourishment has been sacrificed to rushing.

_____ *repetition* _____

1. A description of an interaction between an individual and a television poses a serious problem: what exactly occurred? Instead of addressing this question, we might first ask: what did not happen? After turning the television on, the viewer did not move for an hour; he did not say three consecutive sentences during that hour. He undoubtedly did not think during that hour.

What occurred during that hour was nothing. The interaction was no inter-action at all. But we cannot really say, and perhaps the viewer would report it quite differently.*

---

2. The loss of hair is a trying experience. A headful of thick hair is a blessing, but its loss is painful. Both men and women find the experience difficult and not at all pleasant. If there's anything people do not look forward to, it is the loss of hair. Hair loss can be very upsetting. An ordinary yet difficult experi-ence, losing one's hair can be a source of great anxiety.

---

3. Wherever we go in any part of the world except in the arid deserts or on the high seas, we are likely to find ferns. They are found sparingly in the Arctic and Antarctic Circles and in quantities in tropical jungles. They are found on the tops of mountains and in low swamps; in dimly lit, moist cave-like crevices and in sunny open fields; on high, dry, and windswept cliffs and in and on still waters or ponds or lakes. Since some ferns are evergreen, these species can be observed in the wild even in winter. And many ferns take kindly to pots and terrariums, where they can be studied and appreciated indoors.[7]

---

4. We usually forget our dreams as soon as we wake up. Is it really possible to rid yourself of your own bad dreams? Counting to five during a dream takes as long as counting to five while awake. People sometimes recognize that they are dreaming while they are dreaming. There is an interesting article on dreaming in the *Smithsonian*. The physical characteristics of dreaming sleep have only begun to be understood in the past 50 years. Countless ex-amples exist of scientists who made great breakthroughs during dreams and awoke with the solution to their problems.[8]

Exercise 6—3

NAME _____

Find a paragraph in your own writing—or write a new one—that states the theme in the first sentence. Write the paragraph below and underline the theme sentence.

_____

_____

_____

_____

_____

_____

Exercise 6—4

Write three sentences of your own that could be the theme sentences of three separate paragraphs. Begin with one of these and write a paragraph.

_____

_____

_____

_____

_____

_____

_____

_____

_____

_____

_____

_____

_____

PARAGRAPH DEVELOPMENT

Adding and Subtracting Sentences

- A. 1. Early to bed, early to rise makes a man healthy, wealthy, and wise. 2. Such a lifestyle, since it would encourage work and limit play, might well contribute to a person's wealth.
- B. 1. Early to bed, early to rise makes a man healthy, wealthy, and wise. 2. It does not, however, allow one a very active social life.

A sentence often adds to or strengthens another sentence. In example A above, sentence 2 gives a reason that sentence 1 could be true. Sometimes, on the other hand, a sentence subtracts from or weakens the statement made by a preceding sentence. In example B above, sentence 2 does not deny the possible truth of 1, but it subtracts from it by suggesting that as desirable as being healthy, wealthy, and wise is, acquiring such a condition may have a drawback: having no social life.

Another example of the adding or strengthening relationship can be seen in the following sentences:

- 1. In order to prepare students to live in today's world, colleges should require courses in both computer programming and fiction writing. 2. These courses would provide practical training and engage students' imaginations.

The second sentence tells readers why they should agree with the first. Using sentence 1 again, we can supply a sentence that, instead of adding to it, pulls away or subtracts from it:

- 1. In order to prepare students to live in today's world, colleges should require courses in both computer programming and fiction writing. 2. However reasonable such a proposal may sound, it is altogether unrealistic.

In this case, the second sentence disagrees firmly with the first, making us dismiss the first even though it seems reasonable.

Both kinds of sentences are useful in developing paragraphs. "Adding" sentences strengthen by giving us further reason to believe or by allowing us more thoroughly to understand a previous sentence. "Subtracting" sentences make us reconsider or see the limitations of preceding sentences. In a paragraph, this function of adding or subtracting is important in relation to the theme sentence. Sentences that add to the theme *support* it, while sentences that subtract from the theme show us its *limitations*.

Exercise 6—5

NAME _____

Indicate whether the second sentence in each set adds to or subtracts from the preceding sentence.

Example: Baseball and football strikes are unfair to the fans. Both sides seem to lose sight of the faithful spectators, taking for granted that loyalty will bring spectators back to stadiums whenever players and owners can arrange to agree. _____*adding*_____

1. My roommate and I have only one serious disagreement. She insists on sleeping with her night light on, while I can't sleep except in total darkness. _____

2. My roommate and I have only one serious disagreement. That one, however, outweighs all our areas of agreement. _____

3. Students who need to put their problems aside will find relief in daytime television soap operas. In order to take advantage of this temporary escape, though, one must be willing to tolerate a certain amount of ribbing. _____

4. Students who want to put their problems aside will find relief in daytime television soap operas. It might be wiser, however, to find relief in good physical exercise. _____

5. An income-related National Health Insurance (NHI) plan would work very simply. When people earning $30,000 per year incurred medical expenses totaling $3000, they would pay a $400 deductible and 25 percent of the remaining $2600, or $650. _____

6. Lighting a cigarette on a smoking regulated vehicle these days will almost certainly arouse the hostility of nonsmokers. Smokers will find numerous dirty looks, coughs, grunts, protests, and curses directed at them. _____

7. Littering is nasty, filthy, and selfish. Therefore don't do it. _____

8. Cats can add real pleasure to apartment living. The smell of the catbox, however, overpowers the pleasure. _____

9. If we are not prepared to discuss total disarmament, we have two major alternatives to the present all-volunteer army. The first is a draft with no exemptions except in extreme hardship cases. _____

In item 10, indicate whether the *third* sentence adds to or subtracts from the first.

10. If we are not prepared to discuss total disarmament, we have two major alternatives to the present all-volunteer army. The first is a draft with no exemptions except in extreme hardship cases. The second is an army so attractive in terms of salaries, benefits, education and cultural opportunities, and vacations as to be competitive with civilian professions. _____

Exercise 6—6

NAME _____

Write a sentence that could follow each of the following five sentences. Your sentences should be adding or subtracting as indicated.

Example: Painting my apartment this week was hard work, no fun, and an unbelievable mess.

Adding: _Going through it again would be worse than moving to another place._

Subtracting: _But now that it is finished, I know it was worth doing._

1. Americans' desire to be physically fit has created a huge market for running gear.

Adding: _____

_____

2. Television may be harmful to your health.

Adding: _____

_____

3. It is to the advantage of college students to have a legal drinking age of twenty-one.

Subtracting: _____

_____

4. Working while going to school is itself an education.

Subtracting: _____

_____

5. Having to produce papers by an inflexible due date often causes students to sacrifice excellence in their work.

Adding or subtracting: _____

_____

Exercise 6–7

NAME _____

Write two sentences to follow each of the sentences below. One should add to and the other should subtract from the first sentence.

Example: Domestic car manufacturers should refuse to cater to the minority's demand for luxury vehicles.

Adding: _Then they would be able to concentrate on competing with foreign car makers._

Subtracting: _These luxury vehicles, however, are here to stay._

1. It has become necessary to ask whether a liberal arts education is worth the cost.

Adding: _____

_____

Subtracting: _____

_____

2. Learning a foreign language can be difficult for many reasons.

Adding: _____

_____

Subtracting: _____

_____

3. A study week immediately preceding final exams gives students a chance to review the course material thoroughly.

Adding: _____

_____

Subtracting: _____

_____

4. Pets can be a real nuisance.

Adding: _____

_____

Subtracting: _____

_____

5. Money earned from a job is different from money received as a gift.

Adding: _____

_____

Subtracting: _____

_____

Direct, Pivoting, and Suspended Patterns of Development

theme sentence { • *Millions of people, despite the affection they feel for their pets, do not appear to mind discarding them when the animals become old, bothersome, or inconvenient.* Many people simply abandon them. A quick look around a summer resort after Labor Day will reveal any number of dogs and cats waiting on the doorsteps of boarded-up cottages. Visit any college in June and count the hungry, left-behind pets roaming around the campus. And perhaps worse off than those abandoned outside are those left locked in vacated apartments when their owners move.[9]

theme sentence { • People tend to think of black bears as those cute roadside beggars in our national parks. *But black bears are not a bit cuddly.* The average adult male weighs about 300 pounds. Both male and female can climb a tree with the agility of a cat and have been clocked on the ground at 30 miles per hour. Naturally shy but also amazingly strong, a black bear is nothing to fool with if injured or menaced.[10]

Some paragraphs start in one direction and keep going, while others start in one direction and then make a turn. In the first paragraph above, the theme sentence is first, and all the sentences that follow support it by adding evidence that it is true. This paragraph—theme plus supporting sentences—develops just as we might have predicted after reading the first sentence. This pattern of development can be called the **direct pattern**.

The second paragraph begins by stating a popular belief, and we might expect it to continue by giving examples of people who appear to think black bears are cute. Instead, however, the second sentence reverses the direction of the paragraph by telling us just how untrue the popular belief is. The second sentence subtracts or pulls away from the first: *But black bears are not a bit cuddly* takes over the paragraph. It—rather than the sentence with which the paragraph set out—is the theme sentence. The rest of the sentences support the theme by adding evidence of the uncuddly nature of black bears. The development of this paragraph can be called **pivoting**, since it surprises us by pivoting away from the direction in which it set out. The clue that it will pivot is the word *but. However, though,* and sometimes *of course* also function as pivoting words.

The direct pattern of development is quite common. A direct paragraph may be as simple as the one on abandoned pets (theme plus supporting sentences), or it may be somewhat more complex. For example, in the following paragraph, the theme sentence is preceded by two introductory sentences:

introductory sentences { • But that's not all by half. While lifesaving is basic to the Coast Guard's existence, it is only one of so many missions that even the
theme sentence { service's chiefs have trouble explaining them to the public. *The world's largest search-and-rescue outfit is also the world's largest marine police force.*

| | Boarding parties leave cutters almost every day to search for illegal |
| support | catches or equipment aboard Communist-bloc processing ships in Alaskan waters or Japanese long-liners off Cape Cod. Or they stop shrimpers, sloops and coastal freighters to look for marijuana, cocaine, Quaaludes, and other forms of illicit trade.[11] |

In still another case, a direct paragraph may state its theme, then admit a sentence showing a limitation of the theme, and then return (often restating the theme) to proceed in the original direction.

theme	• *Doctors are worried about the surge of competitive athletics among chil-*
limitation	*dren between five and fourteen.* Orthopedists do not, of course, suggest that all sports activity is detrimental (the physical and social benefits are obvious). But they do warn against thinking of children simply as
support	small adults. Children are far more vulnerable, because their bones are still growing. Growth areas are made of cartilage, which is two to five times weaker than regular bone and does not harden completely until a child is well into the teens. Intensive training in one sport, marathon training before the mid-teens, and early participation in collision sports can cause what are called stress and avulsion fractures. And such a fracture in a growth area can be serious: one limb can grow longer than the other, and bones can grow crooked or stop growing altogether.[12]

The paragraph states its theme (*doctors are worried*) and supports it (by telling us *why* doctors are worried), but in the course of its development the paragraph includes a sentence that limits the theme. That doctors are not worried about all participation in all sports limits the doctors' position and assures us that they are being reasonable.

The pivoting paragraph often states its theme in the second or third sentence but not always. The theme can even be last:

> • Black representation on sports honor rolls has been even more disproportionate. For example, the past nine Heisman trophies, awarded each year to the "best" collegiate football player in the land, have gone to blacks. In the final rushing statistics of the 1982 NFL season, thirty-six of the top forty running backs were black. In 1982, not a single white athlete was named to the first team of a major Division I All-American basketball roster. Similarly, twenty-one of the twenty-four athletes selected for the 1982 NBA All-Star game were black. Since 1955, whites have won the NBA's "most valuable player" award only five times, as opposed to twenty-three times for blacks. And, of course, boxing championships in the heavier weight divisions have

theme sentence — been dominated by black athletes since the 1960s. *But a judicious interpretation of these and related figures points toward conclusions quite different from what one might expect.*[13]

The first seven sentences of this paragraph tell us about black representation on sports honor rolls. Sentences 2–7 support the statement in sentence 1 that blacks are disproportionately represented. Then, in the last sentence, the paragraph turns and suggests that the likely interpretation of these facts is wrong, that a judicious interpretation is different from what we might expect. The last sentence is effective because it dramatically opposes the case that the paragraph appears to have been building (that black representation on sports honor rolls is easy to interpret). The surprise value of a delayed pivoting sentence increases its effectiveness.

Many paragraphs in English are direct, quite a few are pivoting, and some are what can be called **suspended**. A suspended paragraph keeps the reader in suspense by withholding the theme sentence until the end.

- A Spanish lieutenant of Naples in the seventeenth century wore them daringly in public. Some English gentleman about 1805 wore only one and called it a "quizzer." The first person to be painted wearing them was a monk in the thirteenth century. Orientals loved them but found they wouldn't stay on. And one of the first to sell them in Philadelphia, in 1783, advertised "a bushel basketfull." *The objects in question are eyeglasses, reading glasses, that common everyday boon to millions whose arms have grown too short or whose light bulbs too dim for them to make out fine print.*[14] (theme sentence)

Speaking of sentences that add to or subtract from the theme is not very useful in the case of the suspended paragraph. It is better to think of it as a narrative, discussion, or collection of details leading up to a theme.

Some paragraphs have implied rather than stated theme sentences. They often develop according to narrative or descriptive order. In the following example, the writer appears only to be describing "last night's dinner," but he is also making a point:

> I passed the salad bowl to my little brother and then turned back to my plate. I used my fork to twirl up a single strand of spaghetti. It was longer than the one I had just eaten. Satisfied at my discovery, I ate this one, too. There were a lot of strands of spaghetti on my plate, and I knew that I could never compare them all, so I resigned myself to just eating them. I looked over at my glass of milk. It seemed to be about half full. Then I reconsidered; perhaps it was more like two-thirds full. I resolved this dilemma by emptying the glass of however much there was in it. There was no question now that the glass was completely empty—if, that is, you ignored the few drops still sitting at the bottom. I decided not to look at my salad plate for fear that I would think about it.*

The paragraph is about food and appears to say "Last night's dinner was like this," but its more important purpose is to reveal a mind and how it works. The writer makes an almost compulsively analytic attention to ordinary details seem amusing rather than distressing.

SUMMARY

All paragraphs develop. The three main patterns of paragraph development are the direct, pivoting, and suspended patterns. A direct paragraph states its theme early and ends with sentences that support the theme. When a direct paragraph includes sentences that oppose the theme, those opposing or limiting sentences are placed between the theme and the supporting sentences. A pivoting paragraph starts in one direction and then turns and develops in a different direction. It may or may not have supporting sentences after the theme. A suspended paragraph keeps the reader in suspense by withholding its theme until the end (or nearly the end) of the paragraph.

Exercise 6—8

NAME _____

In the space provided after each paragraph, indicate the pattern of development. Underline the theme sentence. One paragraph has an implied theme sentence; instead of describing its development, state the theme it implies.

> *Example:* <u>Paying bills by telephone certainly seems quick and easy.</u> Just pick up your phone, tell the bank to pay your utility bill, insurance premium, credit card bills, and the like. No checks, no envelopes, no stamps. Your account is debited and the companies' accounts are credited. It all happens electronically in a computer.[15]
>
> _____*Direct*_____

1. An average training session for college wrestling takes place in a room heated to 90°F. and lasts approximately three hours. Calisthenics, for example, 60 push-ups and 20 pull-ups, open the work-out. "Cals" are followed by drilling holds and moves. Most of the practice centers around live competition in small groups. Wind sprints conclude the activities. In addition, during some other part of the work-out day, as well as on the "day off," wrestlers lift weights for at least thirty minutes, and running is recommended for every other day. There is an unwritten law which states that one can never be too well conditioned: Adversary X is always working five minutes more.[*]

_____

2. "Olga wept . . ." could serve as the refrain in any account of the spread of women's gymnastics across America in the last two decades. It was Olga Korbut's dramatic flub at the 1972 Olympic Games in Munich that showcased the strengths and vulnerabilities of girl gymnasts and turned their routines into dramas of temperament, minefields of daring. Television made the showcase worldwide. When seventeen-year-old Olga blew her uneven-bars routine and was awarded a dismal 7.50, she wept—poignantly—and the television cameras made her distress seem intimate, heroic. The next day for the finals the TV coverage was even more intense, and "the elf from Grodno" (as some insisted on calling her) came through with a 9.80 on the uneven bars, a 9.90 on beam, and a 9.90 for floor exercises, scores that netted her two gold medals and a silver. Although Olga did not rack up the highest all-around score, she emerged as the true star of the Munich Olympics, and

little girls the world over were passionately smitten. When Olga Korbut came to America a year later, Chicago's Mayor Daley proclaimed March 26 "Olga Korbut Day," President Nixon invited her to the White House, and she performed to a raucous house at Madison Square Garden. Olgamania proved to be not a fleeting rage. In 1972, the Year of Olga, there were approximately 15,000 gymnasts practicing in private clubs in America; ten years later there were 150,000 gymnasts, many of them Olga-inspired.[16]

---

3. *Don Quixote* is the story of a man's self-deception. Quixote, an aging bachelor with patronizing friends and family and nothing to do except read romances, leaves his dreary existence and enters the world of knights, sorcery, and idealism by succumbing to his "madness." He is transformed by his delusion, gaining a set of rules to live by, heroes to imitate, and plenty of ways to prove himself. Ridiculous and pathetic as his "adventures" may seem, they exhilarate Don Quixote. And who could ask for anything more than to live in a world where you gain as much glory from defeats as you do from victory? A world in which you are invincible unless your enemies use sorcery, which is evil and "against the rules" and therefore cannot damage your prestige?*

---

4. The climate of the Earth has varied considerably over time. One hundred million years ago, ichthyosaurs were frolicking in the warm, shallow seas of what is now Kansas. And Ohio was once a frozen tundra where huge woolly mammoths trod. Yet what puzzles many scientists is not that the climate varies but that it has remained as stable as it has.[17]

---

5. A rectangular yellow tray sat neatly on the formica top of a table for two. The chair opposite me was empty. "This is college life?" I asked myself. "Yes," I responded instantly, "no doubt about it: this is college food." The appetizers for tonight's dinner consisted of similar-sized bowls of macaroni and fruit salad. After finishing the last bright red artificially colored cherry, I turned to the main course. Tonight the spotlight was on a "savory" beef concoction. Portions of rice and leaf spinach flanked the variegated slices of meat. A mild gravy masked the whole array of foods and set the inoffensive

tone of the meal. I gulped down two cups of tasteless lemonade and pushed myself away from the table. It was over. No harm done.*

---

6. If a cough lasts longer than a week following a cold, a doctor's help should be sought. A persistent cough can be a sign of pneumonia, bronchitis, or other illness, and it warrants medical examination. Specific therapy may be essential to treat the underlying disease or infection. For chronic coughs, self-medication with cough remedies is usually inappropriate, and most doctors discourage their use.[18]

---

7. Last night, facing a blank page, I began to think about the last thing I had written on my typewriter. I had destroyed it with great care that morning, because I did not want to die in the subway and have people find it when they cleaned out my apartment for the next tenant. It occurred to me suddenly that every word of it was intact on the ribbon, which is carbon, not cloth, and designed so that it cannot be typed over. Even though the paper was destroyed, anyone who wanted to could sneak into my room, steal the ribbon, run it through a print-out, and recover every torn-up secret. It is unlikely that anyone would bother, but the thought of it was enough to begin a story about paranoia. A plot came from looking at a blank page.*

Exercise 6—9

NAME _____

Beginning with one of the following sentences or with a sentence of your own, write a paragraph with direct development.

   A. Taking a train is a leisurely way to travel.
   B. Politeness often prevents conversation.
   C. Many people think that taking supplemental vitamins is essential for good health.

_____

_____

_____

_____

_____

_____

Beginning with the same sentence you used in the previous paragraph, write a paragraph with pivoting development.

_____

_____

_____

_____

_____

Exercise 6—10

Write a paragraph leading up to one of the following sentences or to a sentence of your own.

   A. Grades should be abolished.
   B. I have learned my lesson.
   C. Living away from home has more problems than I expected.

_____

_____

_____

_____

_____

_____

Complete one of the following sentences and write a paragraph with direct, pivoting, or suspended development. Indicate the pattern you have used.

1. My room looked as if . . .
2. In a library, one does not expect . . .
3. Money . . .
4. Family reunions . . .
5. Compared with . . .
6. People who jog every day . . .

_____

_____

_____

_____

_____

_____

_____

_____

x While lifesaving is basic to the Coast Guard's existence, it is only one of so many missions that even the service's chiefs have trouble explaining them to the public. The world's largest search-and-rescue outfit is also the world's largest marine police force. Boarding parties leave cutters almost every day to search for illegal catches or equipment aboard Communist-bloc processing ships in Alaskan waters or Japanese long-liners off Cape Cod. Or they stop shrimpers, sloops, and coastal freighters to look for marijuana, cocaine, Quaaludes and

digression { other items of illicit trade. *Contraband drugs may now rank second in value behind oil among our imports.*[19]

In a unified paragraph all sentences work together. The sentences of explanatory and argumentative passages work together to develop or lead to one idea —the theme. The paragraph above has been adapted to illustrate paragraph disunity. The last sentence digresses from the theme. As you can see, the digressing sentence is connected to the previous sentence, since both are about drugs. But a sentence about drugs does not automatically belong in a paragraph about the Coast Guard's policing duties, even if those duties include arresting drug smugglers.

The following paragraph illustrates another kind of disunity—contradiction of theme:

x While different plants require different amounts of light and water, they can all use the same fertilizer. The "same" does not mean "just any" however. Shop owners should carefully choose the product

contradiction { they recommend. *The customer, too, has a responsibility and should not*
(and { *blame generally reliable shopkeepers if they sometimes make a mistake in*
digression) { *their recommendation of a fertilizer.* To determine a fertilizer's worth, store owners should look for a label displaying three numbers, always posted in the same order. These three numbers represent the three active ingredients—nitrogen (N), phosphorus (P), and potassium (K)—and indicate the percentage of each element in the mixture. Hence, when the label reads "16–8–8," the bag contains sixteen parts nitrogen, eight parts phosphorus, and eight parts potassium in every 100 parts material. Each of these elements plays an important role in plant life: nitrogen makes plants greener while potassium and phosphorus help their root and vascular systems. Thus fertilizer marked "15–0–0" may make a plant greener but will do little to foster healthy growth, while one marked "35–15–20" will help produce a heartier plant—and a happier customer.*

This paragraph is about the necessity for plant shop managers to know their business and be able to give the best possible advice about plant fertilizer to customers. But the writer temporarily leaves the theme to insist that a customer should be satisfied if a shopkeeper makes an occasional mistake. This opinion is inconsistent with the point of view expressed in the rest of the paragraph and leaves the reader wondering if the writer has forgotten the paragraph's point.

Another kind of disunity occurs when a writer states a limitation to the theme in the last sentence. Then the reader does not know how to evaluate the theme or the limitation, as you can see after reading the following paragraph.

x Tricking two different but related crop pests into a fatal courtship may one day lead to a novel form of insect control. The method involves manipulating the sexual fancies of male cotton bollworms and female tobacco budworms with a lab-made chemical that duplicates a substance secreted by female budworms. By saturating the air with the chemical, scientists have enticed the two species to mate with each other rather than with their own kind. Because the insects are physically incompatible, they lock together permanently. Within hours, the mismatched lovers die. *However, this method will never get rid of all the bollworms and budworms—enough of each will find proper mates and reproduce normally.*[20]

(*limitation of theme* — bracket annotation beside the italicized final sentence)

The last sentence opposes the main point of the paragraph (tricking these pests may one day lead to a novel form of insect control). That this method will not get rid of all bollworms and budworms does not make the paragraph's main idea less novel and interesting, but introducing the limitation of the method at the end weakens the paragraph by creating a sense of uncertainty for the reader. This last sentence should be incorporated into the paragraph earlier (perhaps with a concession: *although this method will not get rid of all the bollworms . . .*), or it should be dealt with in a different paragraph altogether.

To ensure paragraph unity, follow these guidelines:

1. Include only material that is closely connected to your theme. In other words, include only material that helps in getting the paragraph's job done. A noncontributing sentence is a digression.
2. Do not include material that contradicts your theme. If you see a valid objection to your theme, deal with it, but do not leave it as an unacknowledged contradiction in your paragraph.
3. If there are exceptions to the point you make, acknowledge them early and go on to make your point. Do not end the paragraph with a sentence that states the limitations of your theme.

One way of checking that your paragraph is unified is to see whether all the sentences are subordinated either to the theme sentence or to another sentence that is already subordinated to the theme sentence. In the following paragraph, for example, two sentences (A and B) explain what plant shop managers must be able to teach their customers. The other four sentences give examples of A and B:

theme sentence	Plantshop managers must be able to instruct their customers in the care of any houseplant in the shop.
subordinated to theme sentence	A. They must know the various lighting requirements of each plant genus.
subordinated to A	1. *Impatiens,* for instance, grow best at a light intensity of about half that needed to grow quality *nephthitis.*
also subordinated to A	2. Some plants, such as *ficus benjamina,* may receive severe shock if they are moved from one angle of sun exposure to another.
subordinated to theme sentence	B. Watering also varies depending on the plant genus.
subordinated to B, which is already subordinated to theme sentence	1. Contrary to what their rich color and texture would suggest, for example, begonias and succulents such as donkey tail and string of pearls should be watered only when the soil is completely dry—once a week at most.
also subordinated to B	2. Plants like moondrops, on the other hand, often need water twice a day.*

SUMMARY

Paragraph unity is created and maintained by making all the sentences in a paragraph work together. In an explanatory or argumentative paragraph, all the sentences work together to develop or lead to the theme. Disunity is created by including irrelevant points (digressing), by contradicting the theme, and by placing exceptions or limitations to the theme at the end of the paragraph.

Exercise 6—11

NAME _____

In the space provided after each paragraph, indicate whether each is unified or not. If not, explain the cause of disunity—digression, contradiction, or limitation of theme at the end—and circle the material that creates disunity.

> *Example:*   An important technique employed by Defoe in *Robinson Crusoe* is the distortion of time. Time—and keeping a record of it—are very important to Crusoe from the moment he realizes he has survived the shipwreck alone. He keeps a journal, recording each day meticulously, and when his ink supply runs out, he finds another means. He creates a makeshift calendar by driving a post into the ground and marking each passing day with a notch. Periodic reference to this calendar and the seasons provides the reader with the idea that time is progressing but fails to convey the actual passage of time. Crusoe also plants a garden each year, which takes a great deal of time but which is essential to his survival. Crusoe's stay on the island is calculated exactly—28 years, 2 months, and 9 days— yet his stay actually seems timeless. Each day is the same as any other day and is marked by Crusoe's following his established schedule. His labors are endless; hacking away shelves from logs for days, constructing fences and walls for months, and the perpetual designing and redesigning of his "castle" cannot be measured by conventional time.*
>
> _____ *Digression*

1. Vampires, the outlaws of the bat world, got their frightening name when the explorer Cortes and his troops returned to Europe from Mexico with tales of a bloodsucking night-stalker. Vampire bats walk up to their sleeping victims —most often horses, cattle, and other livestock—and slice the skin with surgical precision, lapping up the resultant blood so quietly and efficiently that the unwilling donor seldom arouses. The bats' saliva contains a chemical which prevents the blood from clotting, while its flattened nose facilitates an unimpeded strike with its sharp upper teeth. The reputation of most bats is really undeserved.[21]

2. London is sinking. And while Britain's capital descends a foot per century into its bed of clay, the entire island made up of England, Scotland, and Wales is tilting into the sea, the southeast corner where London is situated leading the way. This rising of the water level is compounded not only by sinking and tilting but by something else—the current melting of the polar icecaps. All three factors combined have caused a full two-and-a-half-foot rise in high tides at London Bridge during the past hundred years.[22]

3. A century ago the boll weevil was an obscure insect living a tenuous existence on scattered wild plants in Mexico. It was barely known to science when, in the 1880s, it began gobbling up cotton fields so quickly that the growing of cotton soon had to be abandoned in central Mexico. American biologists had to write to France to find the boll weevil's scientific name, *Anthonomus grandis*. Only three specimens were available in all the world's insect collections. Hatched from an egg left inside a cotton boll, a weevil grub eats the heart out of his home.[23]

4. Sara and I share a very small and extremely crowded studio apartment on the west side of campus. Before she moved in, I had the apartment to myself, and the only "company" was the telephone. Now I sometimes wonder if I have too much company; the two of us often bump into each other, bruise our shins on the furniture, and knock noisy pots and pans around our cluttered kitchen. But our accidents are usually borne humorously, and since they are shared, they add some life to an otherwise gloomy and desolate living quarters.*

5. In this vast melting pot of ours that has never completely melted, some nationality group is celebrating with heartfelt nostalgia virtually every day. The Italians of New York have their Feast of San Gennaro on Mulberry Street; the Irish in cities like Boston and the Poles in Chicago never let you forget where they come from. But nobody is as stubborn and fervent about it all as the Scots. Because I admire stubbornness, I may enroll in one of their clans.[24]

6. A rectangular yellow tray sat neatly on the formica top of a table for two. The chair opposite me was empty. "This is college life?" I asked myself. "Yes," I responded instantly, "no doubt about it: this is college food." The appetizers for tonight's dinner consisted of similar-sized bowls of macaroni and fruit salad. After finishing the last bright red artificially colored cherry, I turned to the main course. Tonight, the spotlight was on a savory beef concoction. As I had so often done in the past, I questioned the dining service's use of adjectives. A dash of salt reminded me how delicious the last roast beef dinner I had at home was. Portions of rice and leaf spinach flanked the variegated slices of meat. A mild gravy masked the whole array of foods and set the inoffensive tone of the meal. I gulped down two cups of tasteless lemonade and pushed myself away from the table. It was over. No harm done.*

Exercise 6–12

NAME _____

If there is a paragraph in your own writing that is not unified, revise it and write your revision in the space provided below.

_____

_____

_____

_____

_____

_____

PARAGRAPH CONTINUITY

Although he may have been evil, the serpent who persuaded Eve to eat of the fruit of the tree of knowledge was doing Adam and Eve a favor. If _____ had not eaten the forbidden _____, _____ would have remained mere ornaments in God's model world. The _____ was starting _____ on _____ journey toward godliness by giving _____ knowledge. By having _____ eyes opened, _____ came to be in partial control of _____ destinies. _____, _____ knowledge of good and evil made _____ obedience to God (when _____ did _____) more noteworthy, because _____ were capable of _____, not just blind servitude.

If your paragraphs maintain *continuity,* they *continue* from sentence to sentence in a clear, logical way. A paragraph's clear progress from sentence to sentence is ensured by *signs of continuity.* In the paragraph above, some of these signs have been omitted. Compare the version above with that which follows, in which the missing words have been replaced:

Although he may have been evil, the serpent who persuaded Eve to eat of the fruit of the tree of knowledge was doing Adam and Eve a favor. If <u>they</u> had not eaten the forbidden <u>fruit</u>, <u>they</u> would have remained mere ornaments in God's model world. The <u>serpent</u> was starting <u>them</u> on <u>their</u> journey toward godliness by giving <u>them</u> knowledge. By having <u>their</u> eyes opened, <u>they</u> came to be in partial control of <u>their</u> destinies. <u>Furthermore,</u> <u>their</u> knowledge of good and evil made <u>their</u> obedience to God (when <u>they</u> did <u>obey</u>) more noteworthy, because <u>they</u> were capable of <u>disobedience,</u> not just blind servitude.*

Words or phrases such as *for example, however, therefore,* and *furthermore* are transitional signals that show how one sentence carries on or continues from the preceding sentence(s). These signals tell us that the previous statement will be expanded, supported, or qualified in some way. In the paragraph above, *furthermore* introduces a sentence that expands on the advantage gained by Adam's and Eve's having eaten the forbidden fruit. Using such words accurately is essential if your paragraphs are to make sense.

The following list indicates the kinds of transition and some examples of each kind:

CONSEQUENCE:
• therefore, then, thus, hence, accordingly, as a result

LIKENESS:
• likewise, similarly

CONTRAST:
- but, however, nevertheless, on the contrary, on the other hand, yet

AMPLIFICATION:
- and, again, in addition, further, furthermore, moreover, also, too

EXAMPLE:
- for instance, for example

CONCESSION:
- to be sure, granted, of course, it is true

INSISTENCE:
- indeed, in fact, yes, no

SEQUENCE:
- first, second, finally

RESTATEMENT:
- that is, in other words, in simpler terms, to put it differently

RECAPITULATION:
- in conclusion, all in all, to summarize, altogether

TIME OR PLACE:
- afterward, later, earlier, formerly, elsewhere, here, there, hitherto, subsequently, at the same time, simultaneously, above, below, farther on, this time, so far, until now

Another kind of signal allows writers to make clear that they are continuing to discuss the same idea, person, or item introduced earlier. Common signals of this kind, as you can see from the Adam/Eve/serpent paragraph, are pronouns and repeated words. Others are demonstrative adjectives and repeated sentence patterns.

PRONOUNS:
- The serpent was doing Adam and Eve a favor. If *they* had not eaten the forbidden fruit, *they* would have remained mere ornaments in God's model world.

REPEATED WORDS:
- Their knowledge of good and evil made their *obedience* to God (when they did *obey*) more noteworthy, because they were capable of *disobedience*.
- In October 1976, a *fire* that took the lives of 25 people broke out in a Bronx social club. Tragic as it was, the *fire* became the backdrop for a bureaucratic farce.

346

- "If men are to be drafted, women should be too." *This* opinion is shared by people who disagree with each other adamantly on other points.

- *It is true that* higher education should not be limited to privileged social classes. *It is as true that* a college curriculum must be planned on the assumption that students have mastered the tools of elementary literacy and communication.
- *When archaeologists dig into the soil of* Italy or Greece or any other region of the ancient world, *they resurrect* pottery, metals, masonry; *when they dig into the sands of* Egypt, *they resurrect* not only hard materials but the normally perishable contents of dump heaps—wood, baskets, cloth and discarded papers.[25]

SUMMARY

Paragraphs should *continue* clearly and logically from sentence to sentence. Two kinds of signals help to ensure continuity: (1) words like *however, therefore,* and *for example* indicate the logical relationship of a sentence with the one or several that precede it; (2) pronouns, repeated words, etc. tell the reader the same subject continues to be discussed.

Exercise 6—13

NAME _____

Write sentences using the following kinds of transition signals. You will need to write at least two sentences in each case. Underline the signal of transition.

Example: Sequence: The shopkeepers must provide, and be able to advise their customers concerning, various soil mixtures for propagating and maintaining their plants.

<u>Finally</u>, successful plant shop owners must know some basic facts about plant pathology.

1. Consequence: _____

_____

_____

_____

2. Likeness: _____

_____

_____

_____

3. Contrast: _____

_____

_____

_____

4. Example: _____

_____

_____

_____

5. Sequence: _____

_____

_____

_____

Exercise 6–14

NAME _____

In the space provided below, explain how each underlined word or phrase helps us to understand the writer's meaning easily. (If you have difficulty wording your explanations, look back to pp. 391–392 and review the lists of continuity signals.)

Example: Early to bed, early to rise makes a man healthy, wealthy, and wise. This <u>adage</u> remains largely uncontested by being largely untested.

> *This adage tells us that the writer is continuing to discuss the previous statement.*

While different plants require different amounts of light and water, they can all use the same fertilizer. The (1) <u>"same"</u> does not mean "just any," (2) <u>however</u>. Shopkeepers should carefully choose the product (3) <u>they</u> recommend. To determine a (4) <u>fertilizer's</u> worth, they should look for a label displaying three numbers, always posted in the same order. (5) <u>These</u> three numbers represent the three active ingredients—nitrogen (N), phosphorus (P), and potassium (K)—and indicate the percentage of each element in the mixture. (6) <u>Hence</u>, when the label reads "16–8–8," the bag contains sixteen parts nitrogen, eight parts phosphorus, and eight parts potassium in every 100 parts of material. Each of (7) <u>these</u> elements plays an important role in plant life. (8) <u>Nitrogen</u> makes plants greener while potassium and phosphorus help their root and vascular systems. (9) <u>Thus</u> fertilizer marked "15–0–0" may make a plant greener but will do little to foster healthy growth, while one marked "35–15–20" will help produce a heartier plant —and a happier customer.*

1. *same:* _____

_____

2. *however:* _____

_____

3. *they:* _____

_____

4. *fertilizer:* _____

_____

5. *these:* _____

_____

6. *hence:* _____

_____

7. *these:* _____

_____

8. *nitrogen:* _____

_____

9. *thus:* _____

_____

Exercise 6—15

NAME _____

Write two different sentences that could follow each of the sentences below. Circle the signals of continuity.

    Example: Sentence 1. Learning to speak a foreign language requires a special kind of attitude.

                Sentence 2. (First), it is necessary to be willing to make many mistakes.

                Sentence 2. (That attitude) is difficult for adults to acquire.

1. Sentence 1. Living for the future or in the past causes us to lose the present.

    Sentence 2. _____

    Sentence 2. _____

2. Sentence 1. Most people will not stand up for what they believe.

    Sentence 2. _____

    Sentence 2. _____

3. Sentence 1. High school students do many things partly or even mainly so that they can tell people about them afterward.

    Sentence 2. _____

    Sentence 2. _____

4. Sentence 1. Summer jobs can be disastrous.

    Sentence 2. _____

    Sentence 2. _____

5. Sentence 1. Zoos and museums are alike in many ways.

    Sentence 2. _____

    Sentence 2. _____

Exercise 6–16[26]

NAME _____

Two sentences have been omitted from the following paragraph and printed immediately below it. Decide where they should be inserted and indicate by writing the numbers of the sentences in their proper sequence.

1. The garter snakes emerge from hibernation in late April and early May. 2. The females leave the communal den soon after, emerging singly or in small groups over a period of several weeks. 3. Garter snakes are unable to shiver to warm themselves and generate little heat from their bodily processes, so they must rely on their surroundings for the heat necessary to fuel their bodily functions. 4. Garter snakes seek the environment with the highest temperature and emerge from hibernation when the temperature above ground is higher than the temperature in the den.

5. Large numbers of males appear first. 6. It is this dependence on an external heat source that initiates emergence from hibernation.

Proper sentence order: _____ _____ _____ _____ _____ _____

Exercise 6–17[27]

The sentences of the following paragraph have been printed out of their proper order. Relying on the meaning of the sentences and the signs of continuity, decide what the proper order is and indicate it in the space provided by writing the numbers of the sentences in their proper sequence.

1. We have paid in fragility. 2. And so, I've always felt just a bit sad that mammals—in contrast to most so-called lower creatures—have lost virtually all power to regenerate lost parts. 3. But nature gives nothing without exacting a price in return. 4. Warmth, intelligence, and a full head of hair have their advantages after all. 5. We can heal some prodigious wounds, but we cannot re-form a lost finger or limb. 6. On the whole, I've always been delighted to be a mammal.

Proper sentence order: _____ _____ _____ _____ _____ _____

Exercise 6–18

In the space provided, write a paragraph about sports, a traffic accident, the draft, how to handle money, the counseling service, or a subject of your own choosing. Circle the signals of continuity.

PARAGRAPH REVISION

x A. 1. When drugstore and supermarket chains began selling large numbers of houseplants at extremely low prices, small plant shops had to start competing fiercely with these big businesses for the same segment of the plant market. 2. As one might expect, the chain stores won a majority of the battles, and many small retailers opened with a flourish in March only to liquidate what they had left six months later. 3. *Yet in spite of these failures, a good deal of hope for success remains for small plant dealers if they understand their product.* 4. *In the past, as the assistant manager at a wholesale greenhouse nursery, I noticed that* most of the difficulties that victimize shopkeepers stem from this very lack of sufficient scientific knowledge about the plants they sell. 5. The owners often think of their plant shops as a type of card and gift shop. 6. Consequently, they forfeit the one major advantage they have over large stores: the opportunity to help their customers grow lush, healthy plants. 7. In other words, if houseplant shop owners want respect, steady customers, and a chance to make sizable profits, they must learn some basic horticultural facts.*

• B. When drugstore and supermarket chains began selling large numbers of houseplants at extremely low prices, small plant shops, unable to compete, started going out of business at a rapid rate. Many small retailers opened with a flourish in March only to liquidate what they had left six months later. But price tells only a part of the story: the shopkeepers themselves were often to blame for the failures. Many of them thought of their businesses as a type of card and gift shop and failed to acquire sufficient scientific information about the plants they sold. Consequently, they forfeited the one major advantage they had over the large stores: the opportunity to help their customers grow lush, healthy plants. If small shopkeepers want respect, steady customers, and a chance to make sizable profits, they must learn some basic horticultural facts.*

A and B are the rough draft and revised versions of the introductory paragraph of an essay on what small plant shop owners can do to stay in business. A has two clear problems:

1. Unity: part of sentence 4 is a digression.
2. Continuity: sentence 3 throws the development of the paragraph off.

Unity: In the past, as the assistant manager at a wholesale greenhouse nursery, I noticed that shifts our attention away from the main idea (the cause of houseplant shops' going out of business) and focuses our attention instead on the writer himself. Although it gives him the authority necessary to write his essay, the writer's experience is irrelevant *in this paragraph*. If he wanted to show that he knows the problem firsthand, he could very nicely introduce his essay by describing an encounter with a small retailer at the wholesale nursery.

Continuity: As the paragraph stands, there is a distinct break between sentence 3 and sentence 4. Sentence 4 does not continue from sentence 3. At first, we are likely to think that the writer simply needs to start a new paragraph with sentence 4. However, sentences 4 and 5 continue to describe the problem introduced by sentences 1 and 2, and sentence 3 is actually a premature statement of sentence 7 (*there is hope for success for the small dealer* is similar to *if houseplant shop owners want steady customers and a chance to make sizable profits,* and *if he understands his product* is similar to they must *learn some basic horticultural facts*). The writer was so eager to tell us the solution that he told it to us before he had finished describing the problem. Therefore he has reached approximately the same conclusion twice, and his paragraph develops twice instead of once.

Strategy for revision: Combine the sentences dealing with the problem that cannot be solved, and then move to the more significant problem that can be solved. The paragraph can then end with a statement of the solution—a statement that serves as the thesis of the whole essay.

REVIEW AND REVISION EXERCISES

Exercise 6—19

NAME _____

Read the following paragraph and answer the questions about it below.

1. People do not gather in front of television sets just to watch programs. 2. They also go there to show off their knowledge and wit to other people watching T.V. 3. This situation can be observed in any T.V. lounge on campus. 4. No matter what program is being watched, the viewers will comment on it. 5. Sometimes the comments will be made because the speaker has a strong feeling about the subject. 6. Far more often the speaker is only trying to demonstrate his expertise to the rest of the people in the room.*

1. What is the theme sentence of this paragraph?_____

2. What is its pattern of development? _____

3. Why is sentence 5 out of place? _____

_____

Where would you put sentence 5 if you were revising the paragraph?

_____

4. Condense this paragraph as much as you can without losing any essential elements of meaning.

_____

_____

_____

_____

_____

_____

Exercise 6—20

Write a paragraph about people's behavior at dorm meetings, during exams, in line at the post office or bank, or on the first day of classes. Underline your theme sentence and indicate the pattern of development.

_____

_____

_____

_____

_____

_____

_____

_____

Exercise 6—21

NAME _____

Read the following paragraph and answer the questions below.

1. Football games in Philadelphia are big events and the NFC championship game was an even bigger one. 2. Weather doesn't bother Eagles fans, and they continue their ritual of throwing tailgate parties before the game regardless of the elements. 3. Each minute of the day is filled with emotion. 4. Even as the herds of people funnel slowly through the gate, they use the time to exchange tips on how to keep warm or how to smuggle their canned and bottled drinks past the ticket-taker. 5. For the ticket-takers, too, it is a ritualistic day. 6. They stand by the gate in the bitter cold for hours and never see a game and never stay warm. 7. They rarely smile as you pass through the gate.*

1. What is the theme sentence of the paragraph? _____

2. What is its pattern of development? _____

3. What kind of advice would you give to help the writer revise this paragraph? In the space provided below, write a paragraph first describing the strengths of this piece and then recommending changes.

_____

_____

_____

_____

_____

_____

_____

Exercise 6—22

NAME _____

Choose a paragraph from your own writing that you think is a strong one. Write a paragraph briefly explaining why it is effective. If the paragraph is part of a longer paper, you may well want to explain how it functions in the whole piece.

_____

_____

_____

_____

_____

_____

_____

_____

Exercise 6—23

Choose a paragraph from your own writing that needs to be revised. In a paragraph or in several sentences, explain first its strengths and then the revisions it requires. If the paragraph is part of a longer paper, you may well want to explain both the strengths and the necessary revisions in terms of the paragraph's function in the whole piece.

_____

_____

_____

_____

_____

_____

_____

Revise the paragraph and write your revision in the space below. Underline the theme sentence and indicate the pattern of development.

_____

_____

_____

_____

_____

_____

_____

_____

Exercise 6—24

NAME _____

Write a paragraph on one of the following subjects using a direct pattern of development.

1. nuclear waste
2. acid rain
3. computer games
4. your probable career choice
5. a part-time job you have had

_____

_____

_____

_____

_____

_____

_____

_____

Underline the theme sentence and circle the signs of continuity.

Exercise 6—25

NAME _____

Using the same subject that you chose for Exercise 6-24, write a paragraph with pivoting development. If you wish, you may use some of the sentences from the previous paragraph in this one.

_____

_____

_____

_____

_____

_____

_____

_____

_____

Underline the theme sentence and circle the signs of continuity.

Exercise 6—26

Use a subject of your own choosing or one of those listed in Exercise 6-24 to write a paragraph with suspended development.

_____

_____

_____

_____

_____

_____

_____

_____

_____

NOTES

1"Water Filters," *Consumer Reports*, 48 (1983), 68.

2Jack C. Schultz, "Tree Tactics," *Natural History*, May 1983, p. 12.

3Mel and Fiona Sunquist, "The Tiger Singles Scene," *Natural History*, Jan. 1983, p. 47.

4Adapted from Noel D. Vietmeyer, "Our 90-Year War with the Boll Weevil Isn't Over," *Smithsonian*, Aug. 1982, pp. 60–63.

5Napier Shelton, "The Rhythms of Nature," *Saguaro National Monument* (Washington, D.C.: U.S. Department of the Interior, 1972), p. 79.

6Roger F. Pasquier and Eugene S. Morton, "For Avian Migrants a Tropical Vacation Is Not a Bed of Roses," *Smithsonian*, Oct. 1982, p. 170.

7Broughton Cobb, "Forward," *A Fielding Guide to the Ferns and Their Related Families* (Boston: Houghton Mifflin, 1963), p. xv.

8Adapted from Ruth Mehrtens Galvin, "Control of Dreams May Be Possible for a Resolute Few," *Smithsonian*, Aug. 1982, pp. 101–102.

9Adapted from Patricia Curtis, "Animal Shelters Struggle to Keep Up with Millions of Abandoned Pets," *Smithsonian*, Sept. 1982, p. 45.

10Adapted from Adele Conover, "Getting to Know Black Bears—Right on Their Own Home Ground," *Smithsonian*, Apr. 1983, p. 87.

11Adapted from William H. MacLeish, "The United States Coast Guard: Poor, but Proud and Looking Ahead," *Smithsonian*, July 1982, pp. 33–34.

12Adapted from Elizabeth Stark, "Growing Pains," *Science 83*, Aug. 1983, pp. 88–89.

13Harry Edwards, "Educating Black Athletes," *Atlantic*, Aug. 1983, p. 31.

14Adapted from Dora Jane Hamblin, "What a Spectacle! Eyeglasses, and How They Evolved," *Smithsonian*, Mar. 1983, p. 100.

15"Paying Your Bills By Phone? We Have a Surprise for You," *Consumer Reports*, 48 (1983), 57.

16Adapted from James Wolcott, "The Neat Stuff," *Harper's*, July 1983, p. 44.

17M. Mitchell Waldrop, "Why Is the Earth Neither Too Hot Nor Too Cold?" *Science 83*, Aug. 1983, p. 100.

18"Cough Remedies: Which Ones Work Best?" *Consumer Reports*, 48 (1983), 60.

19Adapted from MacLeish, pp. 33–34.

20Adapted from "Update," *Science Digest*, June 1983, p. 22.

21Adapted from Donald Dale Jackson, "Close Encounters with the Creatures of Another World," *Smithsonian*, Nov. 1982, p. 78.

22Jane Wholey, "Saving London from an Impending Threat of Flood," *Smithsonian*, Aug. 1982, p. 78.

23Adapted from Vietmeyer, p. 60.

24Adapted from Richard L. Williams, "Their Hearts Are in the Highlands—of North Carolina," *Smithsonian*, July 1982, p. 116.

25Lionel Casson, "'It Would Be Very Nice If You Sent Me 200 Drachmas,'" *Smithsonian*, Apr. 1983, p. 117.

26Adapted from Wayne Lynch, "Great Balls of Snakes," *Natural History*, Apr. 1983, p. 65.

27Adapted from Stephen Jay Gould, "A Life and Death Tail," *Natural History*, June 1983, p. 12.

PRINCIPAL PARTS OF COMMONLY USED VERBS

INFINITIVE	PRESENT	PAST	PAST PARTICIPLE
to be	am, are, is	was, were	been
to beat	beat	beat	beaten, beat
to begin	begin	began	begun
to bend	bend	bent	bent
to bind	bind	bound	bound
to bite	bite	bit	bitten
to blow	blow	blew	blown
to bring	bring	brought	brought
to build	build	built	built
to burn	burn	burned, burnt	burned, burnt
to burst	burst	burst	burst
to buy	buy	bought	bought
to cast	cast	cast	cast
to catch	catch	caught	caught
to choose	choose	chose	chosen
to cost	cost	cost	cost
to cut	cut	cut	cut
to deal	deal	dealt	dealt
to do	do	did	done
to drink	drink	drank	drunk, drunken
to eat	eat	ate	eaten
to fall	fall	fell	fallen
to feel	feel	felt	felt
to fight	fight	fought	fought
to fly	fly	flew	flown
to forget	forget	forgot	forgotten, forgot
to freeze	freeze	froze	frozen
to give	give	gave	given
to grow	grow	grew	grown
to hang (execute)	hang	hanged	hanged
to hang (suspend)	hang	hung	hung
to have	have, has	had	had
to hear	hear	heard	heard
to hide	hide	hid	hidden, hid